SUSSEX CHURCHES & CHAPELS

DAVID BEEVERS

RICHARD MARKS

JOHN ROLES

THE ROYAL PAVILION, ART GALLERY & MUSEUMS, BRIGHTON

SPONSOR'S PREFACE

This book has generously been sponsored by Sotheby's, Sussex. It has been written to accompany the exhibition 'Treasures from Sussex Churches', held at Brighton Museum and Art Gallery between 2 September and 26 November, 1989.

SOTHEBY'S
FOUNDED 1744

Brighton Museum and Art Gallery would also like to acknowledge the financial support of Blackwall Securities plc and Cox and Barnard (Hove) Limited in mounting the exhibition.

ISBN 0 948723 11 4

CONTENTS

FOREWORD
BY THE BISHOP OF CHICHESTER

The aim of this book and the accompanying exhibition is to put the Churches and Chapels of Sussex into a national and local context and at the same time to look in detail at the history of the Church in Sussex from Saxon times until the end of the nineteenth century. It is hoped that by reading the essays in this book and examining the photographs, many of which have not been previously published, the church visitor will gain an insight into the work of the Church in the community and appreciate its rôle as the greatest patron of the arts in the Middle Ages and again in the nineteenth century. The book takes a deliberately ecumenical stance; churches and chapels of different denominations all testify to the faith of previous generations. With care and understanding, as well as money, the precious heritage of the past can be handed on to future generations. If this book encourages visitors' awareness of the diversity of the places of worship in Sussex and attracts support for their preservation, it will have succeeded in its aim.

† ERIC CICESTER

ACKNOWLEDGEMENTS

The Royal Pavilion, Art Gallery and Museums would like to thank the following individuals and institutions who have contributed in many different ways in the preparation of this book: Michael Archer, Geoffrey Brandwood, Trevor Brighton, Brighton Polytechnic Library, Brighton Reference Library, Sarah Brown, Marion Campbell, Neil Caplan, Sarah Carthew, Anthony Wells-Cole, Barbara O'Connor, Peter Cormack, Stephen Croad, Joyce Crow, Jonathan Cryer, Catherine Cullis, Nigel Cunningham, East Sussex Record Office, Helen Faulkner, John Filkin, Mimi Fiteni, Martin Hayes, Kenneth Hoskins, Hamish MacGillivray, Fiona Marsden, Timothy McCann, David Park, Canon Geoffrey Parkes, Jane Rick, Leonard Roles, Janet Seeley, Maureen Simmonds, Nicholas Sinclair, Christopher Stell, Neil Stratford, Sussex Archaeological Society, Shelley Tobin, Leslie Weller, West Sussex Record Office, Stephen Wildman, Victoria Williams, Fred Woodley, Lucy Wyld.

John Betjeman's *Hymn* is quoted by courtesy of John Murray (Publishers), Ltd.

PHOTOGRAPHIC ACKNOWLEDGEMENTS

The authors would like to thank the following for granting permission to reproduce copyright photographs or for making photographs available. The colour plates of Coombes and Hardham are reproduced by courtesy of the Royal Commission on the Historical Monuments of England; the remaining colour plates are by Nicholas Sinclair. The interior of Warminghurst, reproduced on the cover, was photographed by John Roles. Photographs not individually credited are the copyright of the Royal Pavilion, Art Gallery and Museums; most were specially taken by Fred Woodley.

British Architectural Library/R.I.B.A. p. 65
The British Library Board pp. 68, 90, 93, 130
Chichester Cathedral Treasury, by courtesy of Canon Geoffrey Parkes p. 125
Chichester Diocesan Board of Finance, Archdeacon Hare Collection pp. 3, 35, 63, 72, 75, 138, 142, 144
Conway Library, Courtald Institute of Art p. 95
Mary Farnell p. 123
Hastings Museum and Art Gallery pp. 59, 106, 119, 135
Richard Marks p. 90
National Museum of Wales, Cardiff p. 95
The Reeves Collection, reproduced by courtesy of the *Sunday Times* and the Sussex Archaeological Society pp. 17, 48, 77, 133
John Roles pp. 33, 38, 51, 115
Royal Commission on the Historical Monuments of England pp. 3, 5, 6, 8, 9, 11, 14, 21, 24, 30, 33, 42, 45, 46, 53, 56, 57, 60, 65, 88, 93, 97–103, 107, 109, 111, 113, 115, 120, 152, 155, 157–159
The Sussex Archaeological Society pp. 71, 119, 128, 132
The Board of Trustees of the Victoria and Albert Museum, London p. 24
Thc Worshipful Company of Goldsmiths pp. 118, 122

One

MEDIEVAL CHURCHES IN SUSSEX

FOR the dedicated and casual church visitor alike, a tour of medieval places of worship in Sussex can be a rewarding and enjoyable experience, even if the area does not immediately spring to mind when 'church' counties are discussed. There is no easily identifiable local style and most of the parish churches built before the middle of the sixteenth century are of modest size. The reasons for this are partly economic – Sussex in the later Middle Ages did not share in the prosperity enjoyed by East Anglia and the West Country which resulted in rebuilding of churches on a grandiose scale. Of the three largest churches only the diocesan cathedral of Chichester survives. The great Cluniac priory church of St. Pancras at Lewes and the Benedictine abbey founded at Battle by William the Conqueror to commemorate his victory in 1066 were both destroyed during the Dissolution of the Monasteries under Henry VIII. The stylistic affiliations of all three lie outside Sussex and their architectural impact locally was on the whole peripheral. Some of the parish churches serving south coast ports, which date variously from the late Saxon period to the fifteenth century, were built on an impressive scale, and most of the other grander places of worship are former monastic churches and collegiate foundations like Boxgrove (W), Arundel (W) and Etchingham (E). Sussex churches have also suffered from the heavy hands of Victorian restorers (see pp. 67–78). The drawings made before the mid-nineteenth century by Grimm, the Lamberts and Henry Petrie reveal the havoc caused by clumsy restoration; all too often the feeling of optimism raised by an intact exterior such as Udimore (E) gives way to disappointment when the interior turns out to have been ruthlessly scraped and the original uneven stone paving replaced by mass-producted tiles or wooden blocks.

There are some unrestored gems, notably Burton, Didling and Warminghurst (W). Moreover, if the later medieval churches are few in number and relatively unimportant, the fact that after the early thirteenth century Sussex became a back-water in architectural terms has its positive side in that churches of the late eleventh to the early thirteenth centuries survive in considerable numbers. Most are simple and unpretentious, but many benefit from very attractive locations, notably some of the Downland churches which are often isolated from their scattered communities and have picturesque settings against the dramatic backcloth formed by the Downs. Didling and Coombes (W) are good examples, the latter indistinguishable at a distance from a flint barn. Ford (W) stands on its own in flat fields near the coast. Others like Greatham, Shermanbury, Wiston (W) and Penhurst (E) nestle close to the

WORTH (E): Exterior from the south-west, early 11th century

local great house, underlining the historically intimate relationship between parson and squire as patron of the living. The lasting impression of a typical Sussex church is of a modest structure dating principally from between the eleventh and early thirteenth centuries and comprising a square-ended chancel, unaisled nave, and lit by small round-headed or lancet windows, perhaps with a small timber porch, and a bell-tower capped by a shingled oak spire.

Flint is a building material associated with churches of the Downland and coastal area between Chichester and Eastbourne, but it was not the only material used for churches in medieval Sussex. In the Weald sandstone was employed, with varying hues according to the particular quarry. Some of the churches (including Bosham and Sidlesham) on the coast south of Chichester make use of local rubble stone. Good stone was transported considerable distances. Sandstone quarried at Eastbourne was taken to Arlington church in 1462–4 (*Sussex Arch. Colls.*, vol. LIV) and the excellent ashlar limestone of Climping, Chichester Cathedral and New Shoreham (W) was shipped from Quarr on the Isle of Wight and the famous quarries at Caen in Normandy. Brick is found in later medieval churches at Herstmonceux (probably from the same kilns as the castle), East Guldeford and Twineham (E) and the free-standing domestic chapel at Stansted (W). The medieval church serving the remote woodland community at Plaistow (W), north of Petworth, was entirely half-timbered and porches were chiefly constructed of oak, as at West Chiltington, West Grinstead (W) and elsewhere. The internal structures of roofs are almost entirely timber, with only a handful of stone vaults. Stone spires are equally rare – Chichester Cathedral and, in East Sussex, Chiddingly, Dallington and Northiam. Oak shingles or tiles are used for the unpretentious broach spires seen throughout Sussex. The cutting and laying of these tiles was a specialist craft, and shinglers are referred to in fifteenth and sixteenth-century churchwardens' accounts at Arlington and Lindfield (*Sussex Arch. Colls.*, vols. XIX, LIV). In the coastal and Downland areas the roofs of churches were probably originally shingled, thatched or tiled and split slabs of sandstone known as Horsham slates are a common roofing material particularly in the northen part of Sussex. In flint churches plaster was used to cover external walls as well as interior surfaces, as can still be seen at Hardham (W) and Udimore (E).

Christianity was present in Sussex in Roman times, but was only adopted quite late by the Saxons. Aethelwalh, King of the South Saxons, was baptised in the early 670s under the influence of his overlord King Wulfhere of Mercia, but the impetus behind the establishment of the Christian faith seems to have come from the north in the person of St. Wilfrid, Bishop of York. He preached the faith in Sussex between 680 and 685/6 and established a bishopric at Selsey (W). A number of Sussex churches incorporate Saxon work, but the only major survival is Worth (E). The building, which recently was damaged by fire, probably dates from the first half of the

SOMPTING (W): Tower from the west, 11th century and later

NEWHAVEN (E): G. de Paris watercolour dated 1883 of the apse and tower, late 11th–early 12th century (Hare Coll., Church House, Brighton)

eleventh century and has a round apse and tall nave with a lower porticus projecting from its north and south faces. The porticus, a subsidiary space used for Masses, burials or private prayer, is a feature of Saxon churches and another exists at Bishopstone (E), converted into the south porch in the twelfth century. Bishopstone has been dated as early as the eighth century, although the tenth is more likely. Excavations at Bargham near Angmering (W) have revealed a late Saxon church with a ground plan similar to Worth (*Sussex Arch. Colls.*, vol. XCIX). Worth exhibits the *repertoire* of late Saxon architectural features: long-and-short quoins at the angles, pilaster strips on external walls, half columns, squat and rather rough window shafts. Several other Sussex churches incorporate some of these features, including Coombes, Old Shoreham, Woolbeding, the lower stage of the tower at Sompting (W) and Arlington, in addition to Bishopstone. The tower of Jevington (E) has typically late Saxon turned baluster shafts in the bell openings and the lower part of the tower at Bosham (W) also probably dates from before the Norman conquest. Bosham was an important church in late Saxon times and it is portrayed in idealised fashion in the Bayeux Tapestry. However, the tall and elaborately moulded chancel arch almost certainly dates from after 1066. The same applies to a considerable number of village churches in Sussex which belong to the so-called Saxo-Norman overlap. In areas like Sussex which lacked good free-stone Anglo-Saxon building techniques such as long-and-short work continued after the Norman conquest and in many instances there can have been little to distinguish an early eleventh from an early twelfth-century village church. One indication of a post-Conquest date is the presence of Romanesque architectural features like semi-circular shafts, attached half-columns on the reveals of arch jambs, roll mouldings (particularly on soffits of chancel arches) and carved capitals which permit a visual transition from square upper structure to column or half-column. All these features originated on the Continent during the second quarter of the eleventh century and represent a more sophisticated technique of construction than had existed since Roman times. The presence of such features has led to the re-dating of certain structures. For example, Bosham chancel arch, Clayton and the upper sections of Sompting tower and its ground-storey arch can be placed in the late eleventh or even early twelfth centuries rather than the pre-1066 period (R. Gem in *Anglo-Norman Studies Proc. Battle Conference,* vols. IV, V). This is also the date of an extensive group of more modest churches in Sussex, usually with a square-ended chancel and unaisled nave, e.g. Buncton, Chithurst and Coates (W); sometimes, as at Greatham (W), there is no division between nave and chancel. North Marden (W), Keymer and Newhaven (E) have apses and some churches have west towers; those at St. Michael's in Lewes, Piddinghoe and Southease (E) are round, a type more commonly associated with East Anglia.

That so many Sussex churches have been little altered since Norman times is due to the small size of some parishes, sparse population and lack of prosperity in later medieval times. The basic parish system was probably in existence by the Norman conquest and in the Middle Ages Sussex (or more accurately the diocese of Chichester) comprised more than 280 parishes. In 1377 the population aged over fourteen averaged only 20–30 per square mile compared with 30–40 for the neighbouring county of Kent (E. Kemp in *Studies in Sussex Church History,* ed. M. J. Kitch).

Not all of the medieval churches in Sussex were parish churches, i.e. churches serving the community of a geographical area and to which tithes and other payments in money and kind were due for weddings, funerals and other clerical functions.

SHIPLEY (W): Exterior from the south, *c.* 1135–40

Chapels also existed to serve outlying areas, like Buncton, or monastic estates, as at Otteham near Polegate and Langney at Eastbourne (E). St. Nicholas' church at Bramber (W) was originally the chapel for the castle and dates from very soon after the conquest. The chancel capitals, with rather crudely carved heads and animals, are derived from capitals at Bernay Abbey and the monastery of La Trinité in Caen, both in Normandy. Viewed from the east Newhaven with its apse and square tower is also more typical of Normandy than England, but as Saxon apses occur at Worth (and the destroyed churches at Bargham and St. Nicholas at Angmering) this feature may not be a direct Norman importation. It is also debatable whether the capitals and other Romanesque features found in Sussex village churches were derived directly from the Continent or were related to the great churches of Chichester Cathedral, begun after Ralph de Luffa became bishop in 1091, Battle Abbey founded in *c.* 1070, and Lewes Priory, the principal Cluniac house in England which was established in *c.* 1078. Chichester has lost its original east end and the elevation was altered after a great fire in 1187. Chichester, Battle and Lewes all originally had east ends in the form of an ambulatory with radiating chapels; that at Battle may be contemporary with the east end at St. Augustine's Abbey, Canterbury, in which case it shares with it the distinction of being the first building in England to adopt this particular plan. The ground plan of the eastern part of Lewes Priory consisted of two pairs of transepts as well as an ambulatory with radiating chapels. This seems to have been the second church on the site, begun soon after 1096 and dedicated between 1142 and 1147 (J. T. Smith in *Sussex Arch. Colls.*, vol. CII). The plan is based on the third abbey church at Cluny in Burgundy. The elevations of Lewes and Battle are unknown but the austere three-storey bay design of Chichester Cathedral, which appears to derive either from Archbishop Lanfranc's cathedral at Canterbury of the 1070s or from the monastic church of Saint-Etienne in Caen, is not reflected in any Sussex parish

TORTINGTON (W): Detail of beakhead decoration on chancel arch, *c.* 1140–50

churches. Some richly carved capitals of *c.* 1120 from Lewes indicate that the priory had access to pictorial sources and it may be more than coincidental that St. Nicholas at Brighton was in the possession of Lewes and has an elaborately carved font of *c.* 1150–75. At least one Sussex church seems to have found its inspiration from the Continent. The upper stages of the tower at Sompting, which appear to date from the late eleventh century, end in four gables capped by a low spire known as a 'Rhenish helm' from its similarity to a type of Romanesque spire common in the Rhineland; the present spire dates from the early fourteenth century (F. G. Aldsworth and R. Harris in *Sussex Arch. Colls.,* vol. CXXVI).

Anglo-Saxon sculptural traditions long survived the Norman conquest. The impressive relief of Christ at Jevington (E) still retains Scandinavian interlace and some capitals at Steyning (W) incorporate foliage designs based on pre-Conquest manuscript illuminations. Steyning also has lions executed in very shallow relief and acting as surface decoration rather than forming part of the structure of the capital. These features seem to indicate the handywork of Anglo-Saxon carvers. The same may also be true of the chancel arch capitals at Selham (W), which are more three-dimensional and therefore probably of slightly later date. The church at Shipley (W) has grotesque-animal corbels to the west tower arch, but the general stark simplicity of this building is far removed from the monster-inhabited world evoked by the Steyning and Selham capitals. Shipley, which originally consisted of a long unaisled nave, central tower and rectangular chancel, is constructed on an unusually large scale for a parish church in this period. This and the absence of ornamental details can be explained by the fact that it was built by the Knights Templars in the late 1130s to serve as a preceptory (R. Gem in *Anglo-Norman Studies Proc. Battle Conference,* vol. VI).

Some other Sussex churches also date from the second quarter of the twelfth century. Only fragments remain of the naves of Boxgrove Priory and New Shoreham (W), but the latter retains its transepts and lower stage of the tower which were constructed in this period. At Old Shoreham (W), two doorways, the tower and its arches and the transepts date from *c.* 1140, which is probably the date of the nave of Amberley and Tortington (W). These churches all show an increase in decorative embellishment compared with the late eleventh and early twelfth centuries. Chevron or zig-zag and billet ornament enframes doorways, arches and windows, notably at Old Shoreham and Amberley; beakhead occurs on a doorway at New Shoreham and the chancel arch at Tortington.

Around 1160–70, as elsewhere in England, this taste for decoration broke loose into a riot of sculptural enrichment, notably in the lower storey of the tower at Climping, at Broadwater and the nave of Steyning. These buildings stand at the beginning of a fifty-year period in which medieval church architecture in Sussex can lay claim for inclusion in any national survey of the subject. To these years belong the retrochoir and embellishments to the earlier work at Chichester Cathedral, the chancel of Boxgrove Priory (closely dependent on the Chichester retrochoir), Bayham Abbey (E) and a series of parish churches distinguished by their grand scale including the choir of New Shoreham. The largest have nave aisles (e.g. Rye and Eastbourne in East Sussex, Bosham, Sidlesham, Climping, Broadwater, Steyning in West Sussex) and some also possess clerestories, as at Steyning and Rye. The half-century between *c.* 1170 and 1220 also saw the transition from the exuberant decoration of late Romanesque to the more austere Early Gothic style. Chevron and beakhead disappeared, rounded arches and windows were replaced by pointed, capitals and corbels moved from either figural or scalloped to stylised upright leaves, then water leaf and finally to the trefoil-shaped design known as stiff-leaf; round and octagonal piers and chamfered rather than wall-moulded arches are other characteristic features of the early thirteenth century. The more elaborate buildings have pointed rib-vaults, as in the cathedral and in the Bishop's Chapel at Chichester, Boxgrove, New Shoreham and the smaller but elegant chancel at Burpham (W). Windows are sometimes enframed by shafts, e.g. Chichester (also the main piers here), Boxgrove, Climping, Steyning, Appledram, Bosham (W) and Hellingly (E). The east ends of this period are square, lit by harmonious groupings of lancet windows. These vary in number from two, Coates and Barlavington (W), to five, as at Bosham and (a very late example) the Franciscan church at Chichester. Three is the usual total, sometimes set somewhat apart from each other (Amberley, Climping (W), Hellingly, Udimore (E)), in other places grouped closely (Boxgrove, North Stoke and Up Marden (W)). Udimore, North Stoke and Up Marden are all modest buildings but the early English Gothic style is just as noble there as in the more grandiose churches.

Late medieval churches come as an anti-climax after the glories of the period *c.* 1170–1220. The pace of change, as usual, was for the most part dictated by the non-parochial buildings. Towards the end of the thirteenth century single and grouped lancets were replaced by bar traceried windows of various designs, which mark the beginning of a movement towards the reduction of wall surfaces in favour of glazing. Bar tracery began in France and the first use of it on a major scale in this country is in Henry III's Westminster Abbey. Its first appearance in Sussex is in the cloister and west wall of the refectory at Battle, a monastery with close royal links (the east end of the abbey church was even rebuilt in the early fourteenth century in imitation of Westminster). Bar tracery in its most simple geometric form is also present in the fine chapel of Petworth House (W), in the chancel side windows of the Franciscan church at Chichester, built after 1269 and probably finished by 1282, and four nave bays of *c.* 1270 in the cathedral.

Little building of distinction took place during the first half of the fourteenth century. The Lady Chapel of Chichester Cathedral was reconstructed and enlarged around 1300, which is approximately the date of the interesting chapel of St. Mary's Hospital in the same city. Several parish churches possess Decorated tracery windows, as at Trotton, Sutton and Ifield (W), West Firle, Ripe and Winchelsea (E), but only the last building is of significance and even this is incomplete. The principal remains are of the chancel with its side chapels of *c.* 1290–1310, constructed on an impressive scale with splendid traceried windows, tall shafted piers and sedilia, piscina and monuments all with elaborately carved crocketed and cusped gables, some with ogee arches. The church was conceived as the crowning glory of the new town established by Edward I, which explains its architectural sophistication. Winchelsea also possesses the more modest ruins of the chancel of the Franciscan church, probably constructed in the following decade.

Two of the largest churches in Sussex erected in the period *c.* 1350–1540 were primarily collegiate establishments (churches served by a community of secular priests to pray for the soul of the founder) and hence greater prominence is given to the chancel. Etchingham (E) was rebuilt by Sir William de Echyngham (d. 1389). It was under construction in 1366 and a contract dated 1369 for part of the work exists. The window tracery here is still entirely Decorated, but at Arundel (W), founded by the Earl of Arundel and dating from after 1380, the Early Perpendicular style appears in the window design and the profile of the piers. Several parish churches were

NEW SHOREHAM (W): Choir south arcade, early 13th century

BOSHAM (W): Chancel arch and chancel interior looking east

WINCHELSEA (E): Interior from north aisle *c.* 1290–1310

rebuilt towards the end of the fourteenth century on quite a large scale. Alfriston (E) is a cruciform building with chancel, transepts and aisled nave. It dates from *c.* 1370 and in the window design the last stages of the Decorated style rub shoulders with the new Perpendicular tracery. Poynings (E), constructed by a bequest of Michael, Lord Poynings (d. 1369), is also cruciform and here the windows are all Perpendicular; the surviving medieval glass indicates a date of *c.* 1390–1400. In West Sussex Westbourne and the chancel of West Tarring also date from the late fourteenth century. The fifteenth and early sixteenth centuries produced nothing remarkable in Sussex. The two surviving medieval parish churches of Hastings (E) were reconstructed over a long period following the French sack of the town in 1377. Mayfield (E) was rebuilt after a fire in 1389 and Pulborough (W) and Penhurst (E) were erected in the fifteenth century. The early sixteenth century saw the building of Twineham and East Guldeford (E), the latter consecrated in 1505. Both are modest structures and their chief interest lies in the use of brick as the building material. For the most part Perpendicular work in Sussex churches consists of the addition of a few chapels, towers and windows to the existing fabric. The chancel at Herstmonceux (E) was remodelled in brick in *c.* 1440 and a new north chapel added; the Oxenbridge family paid for the re-building of the chancel of Brede (E) at the end of the fifteenth century and, in the early sixteenth century, the construction of the south chapel. The naves of Westbourne and Bayham Abbey were rebuilt in this period and Westham (E) and the parish church of Battle received new windows. Several towers were built. The costs of the new tower at Bolney (E) are recorded in the churchwardens' accounts for 1536–8 and the tower of Angmering (W) is dated 1507. The Pelham family evidently paid for a number of towers in East Sussex as its buckle badge appears on the stonework. The badge occurs at Ashburnham, Chiddingly, Crowhurst, Dallington, East Hoathly, Laughton, Ripe and Wartling.

Internal furnishings of churches were as subject to change as much as architectural tastes and styles in wall-painting and stained glass. The separation of clergy from the laity was strengthened from about *c.* 1300 by the introduction of wooden screens between the chancel and the nave, and a number survive in Sussex (see below, p. 97). Almost a century later wooden benches for the congregation began to be installed in the nave; until then what little seating there was consisted of a few benches against the walls for the old and the infirm. The introduction of seats is probably connected with the increasing emphasis on sermons as part of late medieval worship, which also accounts for the presence of pulpits in a few churches such as the fine stone examples at Arundel and Climping (W) and the oak pulpit at Rye (E). In general, however, few medieval fittings and furnishings in Sussex churches survived the upheavals of the sixteenth and seventeenth centuries and subsequent neglect. In order to glean an impression of how a village church appeared and functioned towards the end of the Middle Ages we have to fall back on documentary evidence. The churchwardens' accounts of Arlington (E), a typical coastal area flint church with architectural features dating from the late Saxon period to the fourteenth century, are particularly instructive. The accounts which are now in the British Library (MS. Add. 33192) cover the period 1455–1479 and have been published in *Sussex Arch. Colls.*, vol. LIV. They reveal that the church contained numerous images, probably in the form of wooden, alabaster or stone statuettes, before which lights or candles burned. In a chapel in the churchyard stood an image of the Virgin and other images included those of St. Pancras (to whom the church is dedicated), St. Catherine, St. Margaret, St. Michael and St. Nicholas. Lights also burned before the great beam over the chancel screen on which stood the Rood, or figure of Christ on the Cross flanked by the Virgin and St. John the Evangelist. In addition to the stone or marble high altar with its incised consecration crosses placed at the east end of the chancel, there was an altar of St. Catherine and St. Pancras. The altars would be dressed with textiles and ornamented with a cross and candlesticks. The Holy Sacrament (consecrated bread) was kept in a box known as the pyx suspended above the high altar and covered by a canopy. In 1458–60 a new pyx cost 5d.; in the same period 6d. was spent on silk lace for the canopy. Vestments included a cope, a chasuble, two surplices and a rochet (an abbreviated form of surplice). The plate must have included a chalice and paten for Mass, and a censer was repaired in 1460–62. The taking of wine during Mass was reserved for the clergy, with only the bread administered to the congregation. Even then most lay-folk only made their communion once or twice a year, chiefly at Easter. During the Middle Ages the Mass was seen as a mysterious sacrifice offered for the congregation rather than a ceremony in which it participated actively.

The most solemn and dramatic rituals in the Church's calendar were the Passion ceremonies at Lent and Easter, indirect reference to which is made in the Arlington accounts. In 1456–57 a total of 5s.6d. was spent on the white Lenten veil which was hung in front of the high altar. Veils concealed the Rood and images during Easter and in the churchwardens' accounts for the destroyed church of St. Andrew at Lewes in 1531–2 there is a payment for the line to pull up the Rood veil on Palm Sunday (*Sussex Arch. Colls.*, vol. XLV). A large taper known as the Paschal candle was

ARUNDEL (W): Interior of Fitzalan Chapel, end of 14th century

blessed on Holy Saturday and kept burning on the Easter Sepulchre until Holy Trinity; at Arlington the cost of making this candle varied between 3d. and 4d. The eastern of the two early fourteenth-century arches between the chancel and the north chapel was probably the location of the Easter Sepulchre which contained the Blessed Sacrament. Quite often these were elaborate and permanent structures which also served as tombs for well-to-do individuals. A number of recessed altar-tombs dating from the first half of the sixteenth century had this dual function, including the Dacre monument at Herstmonceux (E) (see below, p. 106). Reference is made in the St. Andrew, Lewes, accounts for 1523–4 to the vigil that was kept over the Sacrament in the Easter Sepulchre between Good Friday and Easter Day. An important part of the Easter ceremonies was the Adoration of the Cross, which took place on Good Friday and during the course of which offerings were made. This was known as 'creeping to the cross' and it is mentioned in the West Tarring churchwardens' accounts for 1556 (Dallaway, *Parochial Topography of the Rape of Bramber,* vol. 2, pt. ii). The Arlington accounts do not include an inventory of the church goods. Being a country church it was probably not as well-supplied as was St. Andrew's at Lewes. In 1540 the latter possessed four silver chalices, a silver pyx, two silver cruets (for wine and water during Mass), a copper pax (for the kiss of peace), a silver censer, three crosses, two iron, two pewter and twenty brass candlesticks. Vestments numbered five copes, six surplices, five rochets, and twelve other robes, two of which were of silk embroidered with a cross and other devices. There were several altar cloths and a canopy cloth which hung over the high altar,

altar curtains, three banners and veils to cover the Rood and the images during Lent. The service books included four missals, four antiphoners (music for the canonical hours), two manuals (a book of occasional services) and three processionals. This is an impressive list, even for a town church, and together with the Arlington accounts serve to show just how richly-endowed the churches of Sussex were on the eve of the Reformation.

R.M.

Two

SUSSEX CHURCHES AND THE REFORMATION

TODAY most medieval churches in Sussex are far removed from the richly painted, multi-imaged interiors evoked by the churchwardens' accounts of Arlington and St. Andrew's, Lewes (see above, pp. 10–12) and still faintly reflected at Hardham and West Chiltington (W). The reasons for the loss of almost all medieval furnishings and fittings lie in the religious upheavals which began in the early 1530s and continued into the second half of the sixteenth century. The break with Rome which took place in the 1530s was led by Henry VIII and engineered by his able minister Thomas Cromwell for reasons connected with the king's desire to divorce Catherine of Aragon and marry Anne Boleyn; however, they and their successors would not have been able to impose their will with so little opposition had there not been a groundswell of dissatisfaction in England with the wealth and privileges of the Church, especially of the higher clergy and the great cathedral and monastic corporations. Amongst the more reformist elements there was concern with the low educational standards of many parish priests. The king harnessed this resentment to his quarrel with the Pope and although the final result was a Protestant national church which went far beyond the king's intentions, even without the issue of the Royal divorce some major conflicts between England and the papacy were unavoidable.

There is little evidence of religious dissent in Sussex prior to the 1530s, although Lollards were present in the first half of the fifteenth century, one of whom was burnt in 1432. Ironically Reginald Pecock, Bishop of Chichester, one of the greatest opponents of John Wycliffe's followers, was himself charged with heresy in 1457 and compelled to resign his see; the attack on Pecock, however, seems to have been largely inspired for personal and political reasons. The late medieval parish clergy in Sussex probably were much like their colleagues elsewhere in England and clerical incomes here were about the same as in most dioceses. However, Sussex had comparatively few rich benefices, which meant that it was not easy to attract well-educated parish priests; in Henry VIII's reign only one-third of the parish clergy in Sussex were university graduates. There is little reliable indication as to the moral health of the seventeen Sussex religious houses in the early sixteenth century, apart from Boxgrove Priory (W) where a visitation in 1518 revealed considerable laxity. The chief contact lay people had with them was as landlords and here the religious acted no differently from their secular counterparts. Lewes Priory owned 20,000 acres in the county and drew income from nineteen church livings (Lewes was the twenty-fourth richest monastery in England). Although the Sussex friaries continued

CHICHESTER CATHEDRAL (W): Painting on wood by Lambert Barnard depicting Henry VIII offering his protection to the Cathedral; below are busts of English kings, *c.* 1535–6

to be recipients of bequests in wills up to the Reformation the houses of the regular orders had long ceased to attract major benefactions. The Dissolution of the Monasteries in 1536–40 seems to have passed without open dissent in Sussex. Their inmates were pensioned off, their rich plate and valuables confiscated by the Crown which also appropriated their lands, and their buildings demolished or converted. The loss to the artistic heritage of Sussex was immense, particularly the great monastic churches at Lewes and Battle. The former in 1538 was granted to Thomas Cromwell, who gave it to his son Gregory as a residence. Almost immediately an Italian gangmaster named Portinari and twenty-five labourers set to work. Portinari wrote to Cromwell hoping he would 'be much satisfied with what we do' and soon the vast and venerable church was 'pulled down to the ground'. Conservatism in religious belief did not inhibit some individuals from profiting from the Dissolution. Sir Anthony Browne, Master of the King's Horse, was to prove a staunch supporter of the

Catholic faith, but in 1539 he was the grateful recipient of the buildings of Battle Abbey and proceeded to erect himself a suitable residence. Once again, like Lewes, the church was demolished at once. The only former monastic churches remaining today to any extent are the choir of Boxgrove, the over-restored church of the Augustine Canonesses at Easebourne (W), the chancels of the Franciscan churches at Chichester and Winchelsea (E) and the chapel of the Austin Friars at Rye (E), in addition to the ruins of Bayham Abbey which had been suppressed by Cardinal Wolsey in 1525.

The Henrician dissolutions seem to have had little direct effect on the laity of Sussex; for those who rented the former monastic lands it was merely a matter of exchanging one landlord for another. Other government measures impinged more directly as they concerned the manner and nature of worship in churches. Cromwell's chief purpose was to reform certain abuses and enhance lay education and involvement in religion. In 1536 parish clergy were ordered to teach the Paternoster, Creed and Ten Commandments to their congregations and two years later bishops were urged to set a date by which every incumbent had to obtain an English Bible for public reading in his church and instructions were issued that sermons were to be given every quarter by licensed preachers. At the same time the great shrines with their miracle-working relics were destroyed and their lavish fittings and offerings confiscated by the Crown; also all those images whose use was abused (an ambiguous term) were to be taken out of churches. Thomas Becket was particularly singled out and in November 1538 his image was ordered to be removed from churches and his name erased from the calendar of saints. In the same year parishes were ordered to keep proper records of marriages, births and deaths.

What impact did these measures have in Sussex? St. Richard of Chichester still attracted devotion in Sussex and there are small payments to his shrine in the cathedral recorded in the churchwardens' accounts for the destroyed church of St. Andrew at Lewes between 1526/27 and 1531/32. The destruction of the shrine in 1538 is therefore unlikely to have been welcomed in every quarter. The parish church at Wisborough Green (W) possessed an impressive list of relics which were proscribed at this time, including a crucifix containing some of the Virgin's milk and relics of Thomas Becket, SS Edmund, Giles, Silvester, Sebastian and several of the apostles. The canons of Chichester seem to have been inclined to conservatism, for in September 1535 one of Cromwell's agents wrote that they were 'somewhat papastical with privy surrurations'. Two of them were executed for their opposition to the changes and Bishops Sherborne (resigned 1536) and Day (1543–1551, 1554–6) were both traditionalists. The rich and powerful Sherborne was sufficiently prudent to renounce papal jurisdiction in England and accept the king's supremacy over the Church. Lambert Barnard's well-known panel painting in Chichester Cathedral depicting Henry VIII confirming to Sherborne his protection of the cathedral may have been commissioned by the bishop in 1535–6 as a pictorial expression of his trust in the king's goodwill towards the see and of his acceptance of the Royal Supremacy (E. Croft-Murray in *Archaeological Journal,* vol. CXIII). In 1535 it was reported that on the whole the king's orders were being obeyed in Sussex, although there was some laxity in removing the Pope's and Becket's names from service books. The incumbents of Brede, Eastbourne and Ticehurst (E) were also opposed to the changes. There is a lack of information on the attitudes of the parish clergy in the county during the last ten years of Henry VIII's rule; no journal survives for Sussex such as that kept by the conservative Yorkshire priest Robert Parkyn in which he recorded his revulsion against the changes introduced during the Reformation (edited by A. G. Dickens in *English Historical Review,* vol. LXII). An analysis of wills from East Sussex indicates resistance to the use of Protestant formulae as opposed to traditional invocations amongst the laity, although often the style of the preamble would have been determined by the parish priest who drew up the will. Only three entirely Protestant wills exist from Henry VIII's reign, in 1542, 1543 and 1546, two of which are from Rye and Winchelsea which lie close to the boundary with the more radical county of Kent, where wills show a shift away from traditional wording as early as 1538 (G. J. Mayhew in *Southern History,* vol. V). Another indication of change is the purchase in 1538–40 by the churchwardens of St. Andrew at Lewes of a Bible in conformity with Cromwell's injunctions.

Under Edward VI (1547–1553) the Church of England emerged as a Protestant church with its own vernacular liturgy and separated from Rome. Inevitably these dramatic changes, initiated by Thomas Cranmer, Archbishop of Canterbury, and the successive Protectors, Somerset and Northumberland, had a strong impact in Sussex. The conservative Bishop Day was deprived of his see in 1551 and replaced by the much more radical John Scory who had been Cranmer's chaplain. A number of the clergy evidently took advantage of the dispensation to marry, but many of the upper clergy and gentry seem to have shared Day's outlook. A letter from Thomas, Lord de la Warr, one of the commissioners appointed in 1553 to confiscate plate from churches in Sussex, reveals evidence either of special pleading by the commissioners themselves or of concealment by the parishes:

> '. . . and although the said money, plate and ornaments received for the Kings commoditie useth not to such a vallue as I wold wyshe it did, yet I assure you I and the rest of the commissioners have done the best we cold do for the Kings Majestie's advantage. Surely there be many poore parishes and their ornaments are very old broken or very little worthye for of long time there was none given to the church, and as for chalices they are very slender, and thereof or any other plate, there is small store within this Rape [of Bramber]' (J. E. Couchman in *Sussex Arch. Colls.,* vol. LIII).

The churchwardens' accounts for the churches of St. Andrew and St. Michael in Lewes chronicle the destruction wreaked on the fabric and furnishings of Sussex churches in conformity with government policy during Edward VI's reign (*Sussex Arch. Colls.,* vol. XLV). During 1546 the parish of St. Andrew in Lewes was united to St. Michael's and shortly afterwards the former church was demolished. In 1547–8 three alabaster altars were sold to 'the frenche men'; these were almost certainly Nottingham alabaster altarpieces carved with the Passion and other scenes, many of which found their way into churches on the Continent at this time. In the following year three altars were removed. One Myles made the communion table which replaced them at a cost of 15d., and three yards of carpet were purchased to cover the table. Some broken church silver was sold and the wife of the parish clerk made an ancient cope into a carpet. Disposal and destruction of images is recorded. In 1548 'ye popes hed' was sold and in 1548–9 John Harmon the glasier was paid 2s.6d. 'for defacying off ii windows' which must have depicted idolatrous subject-matter. A copy of Erasmus' *Paraphrases* was purchased in conformity with Cranmer's injunctions. The *Paraphrases, Book of Homilies* and the Bible were obtained by the church-wardens at West Tarring (W) at about the same time (Dallaway, *Parochial Topography of the Rape of Bramber,* vol. 2, pt. ii).

By the end of the reign in 1553, the effects of the Reformation were clearly

The execution of Richard Woodman and nine other Protestants at Lewes in 1557. 19th-century engraving

apparent in the landscape as well as in worship in Sussex. The monasteries had gone and the chantries and collegiate foundations dissolved. The parish churches had lost their best plate, many of their images in sculpture, stained glass and murals had been destroyed or defaced, altarpieces had been replaced by tables and books and services in the vernacular were in use instead of Latin. The pace of change may not have been as swift in the more remote country parishes as in urban areas like Lewes, but change there had been. The reactions of the vast majority of Sussex folk to these events are unrecorded, but probably they were neither strongly Protestant nor fervently Catholic, as was the country as a whole. Lord Paget summed up the situation in a letter to Protector Somerset. 'I fear at home is neither [religion]. The use of the old religion is forbidden, the use of the new is not yet printed in the stomachs of eleven of twelve parts of the realm' (quoted in A. G. Dickens, *The English Reformation*). On the other hand there is an increased use of Protestant formula in the wording of Edwardian wills in the Wealden, coastland and marshland parishes, which were particularly susceptible to reformist ideas emanating from Kent (G. J. Mayhew in *Southern History,* vol. V). Moreover, it is evident from the persecutions of Queen Mary's reign (1553–1558) that the reformed religion had taken root in Sussex. The Marian reaction had the opposite to the desired effect in ensuring that the new religion would be imprinted indelibly on the country at large. The restoration of the Catholic faith in Sussex was accomplished with particular severity. Scory was ejected from the see, to be replaced once more by the more pliant Day, and some fifty-seven parish priests were also deprived, presumably for the most part because they had married. Much more tragic was the large number of burnings for heresy in Sussex under Mary's rule. Totals for the Sussex executions vary between twenty-three and forty-one, but whichever is the correct figure the county saw more deaths than anywhere else except London (67), Kent (58) and possibly Essex (39). The majority of victims were husbandmen and craftsmen from the eastern part of the county and the severity of the persecution here was probably due to the zeal of leading local Catholic gentry, especially the Gage family at West Firle. Efforts were made to repair some of the damage caused to church fittings during Edward VI's reign as well as restore some of the trappings of Catholic worship. At St. Michael's in Lewes a new Rood was set up and painted, stone altars replaced the communion table, an Easter Sepulchre constructed and a defaced picture of the patron saint made good (*Sussex Arch. Colls.*, vol. XLV). The churchwardens' accounts for West Tarring include payments for making the figures of St. Mary and John (presumably from the Rood loft), the purchase of a missal and other service books and receipts from the restored tradition of creeping to the cross (Dallaway, *Parochial Topography of the Rape of Bramber,* vol. 2, pt. ii). A parishioner of Westfield (E) returned to the church half the proceeds from the vestments and ornaments which he had bought from the church and resold; another layman from Ovingdean paid for an image of St. Wulfran. No attempt was made to restore any of the Sussex religious houses, although Sir Anthony Browne established new chantries at Battle and Midhurst.

Almost immediately after she came to the throne in 1558 Elizabeth I once more and finally cut the ties with Rome and re-established the Church of England. However, notwithstanding the strength of Protestantism in Sussex as evidenced by the Marian heresy trials and executions the new religious settlement proved difficult to impose in the county. The principle of 'cuius regio eius religio' which applied officially in parts of contemporary Europe also operated in practice at parish level in early Elizabethan Sussex. The majority of the ruling classes and office-bearers

SELSEY (W) OLD CHURCH: Wall-monument to John and Agatha Lewis of *c.* 1537 with the central religious imagery (probably a Trinity or *Pieta*) completely defaced. Engraving by T. King, in Dallaway, *History of Sussex,* Vol. I, 1815

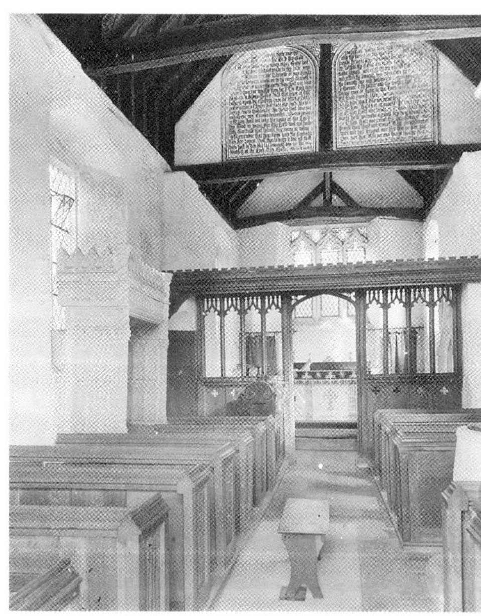

BURTON (W): Interior looking east with the wall-monument of Sir William Goring on the left and texts painted on the walls and above the screen

retained their allegiance to the Catholic faith and therefore impeded the progress of the Reformation. There were also problems at the head of the Chichester diocese. Bishop Day had died in 1556, his successor Christopherson immediately fell foul of Elizabeth and died in 1559. The vacancy was filled by William Barlow, who was in sympathy with the Elizabethan settlement, but he was unable to exert his authority in the diocese until the early 1560s. His difficulties were compounded by the hostility of the cathedral clergy, who were the most highly educated members of the priesthood. Of the thirty-nine benefices associated with the cathedral, four were resigned by their incumbents and seven were vacant through death before Parker assumed control; it became necessary to remove the incumbents from no fewer than nineteen benefices, chiefly between 1559 and 1564. Only eight of the cathedral clergy fully accepted the new settlement. There were also a large number of deprivations amongst the parish clergy in the period 1559–64. In the country as a whole about 300 clergy were removed from their livings in these years, of whom a total of approximately sixty came from the Chichester diocese. Other livings were vacant through resignation of the incumbent and at least some of those who took this action did so for reasons of conscience. The Catholic sympathies of some of those deprived of their parishes are evident both from wills and their subsequent careers. David Michell, for example, a former monk of Lewes Priory, was deprived as rector of Horsted Keynes (E) and after 1560 lived at Firle Place, the seat of the staunchly Catholic Gage family. Not all of the parish clergy who inclined to the old faith were rooted out. A number remained in their livings, supported and protected by the local gentry and resisting stubbornly if not always actively the government's attempts to impose the new order. The authorities' problems were compounded by the large number of vacant livings caused by the death of the incumbent: between 1558 and 1567 at least seventy-four out of the more than 270 parishes in the diocese of Chichester lost their priest through death. In 1563 a survey of the state of the diocese revealed that no fewer than forty-nine churches and one chapel had no priest, including such important establishments as Boxgrove (W), New Shoreham (W), and Winchelsea (E). Even Rye (E) only had one curate (*Sussex Arch. Colls.*, vol. LXI).

In these circumstances it is not surprising that many parishes only reluctantly and slowly dispensed with the trappings of Catholic worship and introduced the new Protestant furnishings. Progress was faster in some parishes, particularly in the towns. At St. Michael's in Lewes the altars were removed and the Latin service books sold as soon as Elizabeth succeeded to the throne; by 1561 West Tarring had a communion table but still retained a missal and two antiphoners amongst other Catholic service books, which were not replaced by the Book of Common Prayer until 1569. Significantly, the Latin books from West Tarring were taken to Patching (W) at about the same time as this parish was singled out in the report of a visitation of the Chichester diocese carried out by the commissioners of Archbishop Parker. Their findings reveal the strength of traditional beliefs and customs in the Sussex parishes and are worth quoting at some length:

> 'In the church of Arundel certain altars do stand yet still to the offence of the godly . . . They have yet in this diocese in many places images hidden up and other popish ornaments, ready to be sett up for mass again within 24 hours' warning; as in the town of Battell and in the parish of Lindfield where they be yet very blind and superstitious . . . There be schoolmasters who teach without licence and be not of sound and good religion, as the schoolmaster in the town of Battell, the vicar of Findon, and the schoolmaster that teacheth in the lodge of Stansted who teacheth

Mr. Stoughton's children, being comptroller of my lord of Arundel's house. In the town of Battell, when a preacher doth come and speak anything against the pope's doctrine they will not abide but get them out of church . . . It is the most popish town in all Sussex . . . In some places because the rood was taken away they painted there in that place a cross with chalk, and because that was washed away with painting and the number of crosses standing at graves in the churchyard taken also away, they have since made crosses on the church walls within and without, and upon the pulpit and Communion Table in despite of the preacher. This was done of very late in Patching since I preached there. And in the churches they have put crosses upon their stalls whom they favour, and upon my farmers stall they have chalked a gibbet

In many places they keep yet their chalices, looking for to have mass again, when as they were commanded to turn them into Communion cups after one fashion, keeping still weight for weight that the parish might not be charged with buying of one altogether new; and yet they have so charged their parishes, to keep their chalices, hoping for a day for the use of the same; and some parishes say that their chalices were stolen away, and therefore they ministered in glasses and prophane goblets. In many places the people cannot yet say the Commandments, and some not the articles of their belief, when they be examined before they come to the Communion, and yet they be of the age of forty and fifty years. The ministers there are for the most part very simple.

In the cathedral church very few preachers are resident; only four out of thirty-one prebendaries – the dean, schoolmaster, lecturer, and one other – of the others some are laymen, some no preachers, and others far distant. In the city of Chichester few of the aldermen are of good religion.

Many gentlemen at Easter receive Communion at home in their chapels, and choose priests from a distance, as Sir Thomas Palmer, Sir Edward Gage, and James Gage. They use in many places ringing between morning prayers and the litany, and all the night following All Saints' Day as before in time of blind ignorance and superstition taught by the pope's clergy. The collection for the poor is not made in many places according to the statute.

Certain parishes keep Dr. Sander's book called *The Rock of the Church,* wherein he doth not account the bishops now to be any bishops-as Sir David Spencer, parson of Clapham, and Mr. Kinge, parson of Stanmer. Except it be about Lewes and a little in Chichester, the whole diocese is very blind and superstitious for want of teaching: except Mr. Coxe, and one more, few go out of their own churches to preach. There is one Father Moses, sometime a friar in Chichester, and he runneth about from one gentleman's house to another with news and letters, being much suspected in religion, and bearing a popish Latin primer with him "with dirge and the Letanye praying to Saints", and in certain houses he maintained the popish doctrine of purgatory and the praying to dead saints. Many bring to church the old popish Latin primers, and use to pray upon them all the time when the lessons are being read in the time of the litany. In some places the rood lofts still stand, and those taken down still lie in the churches ready to be put up again. Some old folks and women used to have beads in the churches, but those I took away from them, but they have some yet at home in their houses.'

Some Elizabethan sepulchral monuments have inscriptions still invoking prayers for the soul of the deceased. One example is a small brass to James Smyth, a former chaplain of the Savoy Hospital in London, who died in December 1565 and was buried at Stoughton (W). Here and there pre-Reformation stone or marble altar-slabs survive with their incised consecration crosses, as at Aldingbourne, Broadwater and West Chiltington (W). A few churches retain some unaltered medieval plate, the best

CLIFFE (Lewes E): Painted plaster board bearing the Royal arms and supporters, letters ER (for Elizabetha Regina) and the date 1598

being the paten belonging to Donnington (W). The comment made by Parker's commissioners regarding retention of Rood-lofts with their Roods is borne out by the churchwardens' accounts for Lindfield (W). The commissioners described the parish as 'very blind and superstitious' and it obviously persisted in being so as it was not until 1583 that efforts were made to remove the Rood-loft (*Sussex Arch. Colls.*, vol. XIX).

By the time the Lindfield loft came down the tide had began to turn in Sussex. Bishop Curteys (1570–82) filled vacant livings with Cambridge-educated preachers who could be trusted, although this policy also sowed the seeds of the strong Puritan clerical movement which emerged in Sussex in the 1580s and 1590s. The Catholic gentry were increasingly excluded from office and gradually the practices of the old faith were eradicated from the parishes and those who adhered to it were reduced to a small minority worshipping in secret. Some recalcitrant individuals were still capable of public dissent towards the end of the century. Between 1585 and 1588 one Walter Cushman of Buxted (E) not only 'mayntayned divers popish errors' he also 'led his horse up and down the Church and about the Communion Table in the Chancel'; he subsequently renounced his Catholic views (W. E. Tate, *The Parish Chest*).

The tumultuous events of the reigns of Henry VIII and his three children left their mark on the fabric and furnishings of many Sussex churches. Few retain any pre-Reformation fittings apart from fonts, benches and some screens. The only traces of Roods are some beams, as at Old Shoreham and Poling, and the loft over the screen at Burton (W). Medieval wall-paintings have only survived through being concealed under whitewash and plaster, little stained glass exists and no images and no vestments. A survey of East Sussex churches in 1568–7 revealed many to be in a poor state of repair, often due to neglect of the chancels by the lay rectors. Pevensey was particularly ruinous: 'verye mutche in decaye for lacke of stone timber lead shingle and glasse'. Rye was in little better shape: 'Or chancell is in decaie for that it doth raine into the same and hath done a long tyme by reason it is open in the rouffe thereof' (*Sussex Arch. Colls.*, vol. LIII). The survey frequently notes that churches were not whitewashed and 'beautified wth sentences of scripture'. Traces of the Word in the form of Biblical texts enclosed in cartouches survive in several Sussex churches including Coombes (W), Arlington and Southease (E), sometimes painted over the pictorial imagery of medieval murals which were so disliked by the reformers. A well-preserved series of texts can be seen at Burton (W), the interior of which provides the best impression of a medieval Sussex church after the reformers of the late sixteenth and early seventeenth centuries had accomplished their tasks. Burton retains some medieval seating, together with the chancel screen and loft which still have traces of colour. The altar has gone, replaced by a communion table and rails (apparently dating from a restoration in 1636) and instead of the Rood there is a plaster board painted with the Ten Commandments. Apart from the remains of a late medieval mural of a female saint on a window splay religious imagery is absent. The windows contain clear glass and the walls are whitewashed, enlivened only by Biblical texts and, over the blocked south doorway, the Royal Arms and the date 1636. Royal Arms were set up in prominent positions in churches from the later years of Henry VIII's reign after the ties with Rome had been cut and to emphasise the monarch's authority as Supreme Head of the Church. Many churches in Sussex still preserve panels bearing the Royal Arms, the earliest example of which is in Cliffe church, Lewes (E), and is dated 1598. Returning to Burton, there are two recessed marble wall-tombs of the standard late medieval design, both for members of the Goring family. That of Sir William Goring (d. 1553) and his wife lacks the usual image of the Holy Trinity or *Pietà* and the brass inscriptions bear Protestant invocations in accordance with their wills (*Sussex Rec. Soc.*, vol. XLI).

Another pair of sepulchral monuments provide a suitably symbolic conclusion to this essay. In the retrochoir of Chichester Cathedral are the last resting places of Bishops Day and Barlow. Of opposing religious views, they now lie side-by-side in plain rectangular tomb-chests which are almost indistinguishable from each other.

R.M.

Three

ROMAN CATHOLICISM IN SUSSEX

THE Reformation did not change England overnight from a Catholic to a Protestant country. Throughout the religious changes of successive monarchs there were those who clung to the old ways and opposed the alterations to centuries of accepted practice and belief. It would be naïve to expect these to be swept away and there is plenty of evidence to suggest that many of the changes were only grudgingly accepted. The authorities were well aware of this, Bishop Barlow reported in 1564 that although the county 'is free from all violent attemptes eyther to afflicte the godlye or to distourbe the stablisshed good orders of this Realme. Not withstandinge I doubte of secrett practises which perhappes myghte breake oute into open violence, were yt not for feare of your Lordshippes vigilante Aucthorite'.

The speed with which the new ideas were accepted depended heavily upon the local landowner's religious beliefs. He was in a position to pressurise his tenants and, if he controlled the advowson (i.e. the right to appoint the incumbent) he could install a favourable priest. Thus Sir William Goring, a protestant, could present Christopher Elderfield to the living of Burton (W) in 1633. Three years later the importance of gentry patronage and social hierarchy was writ large over the newly painted Royal Arms on the south wall of Burton: 'Obey them that have the rule over you'.

Until 1570 occasional attendance at the parish church, whilst avoiding communion and baptism services, was accepted practice. In 1568 it was stated that 'many Gentlemen at Easter receive Communion at home in their chapels and choose priests from a distance'. Sir Thomas Palmer of Parham had a Marian priest (that is a clergyman appointed under Mary and subsequently expelled) as his chaplain and only took communion at home. In the 1579 Archdeaconry Visitation it was reported that he and his wife 'received [communion] but once last yere and that [was] at eastar'. Once the Pope had excommunicated the Queen and following the revolt of the Northern Earls and the Ridolfi Plot, those with Catholic sympathies were more clearly identified as a threat and stronger measures were taken against them.

There were two main periods of active persecution of Catholics, the first extending up to the beginning of the seventeenth century and then a revival of tension in the middle of the same century. The proximity of Sussex to the Continent and the relative strength of Catholic influence meant there was strategic concern over the loyalty of the area in times of crisis. The first arrests of Sussex Catholics took place in August 1580 when John Gage was placed in the Fleet Prison and Richard Shelley of Warminghurst and Edward Shelley of Bentley were sent to the Marshalsea. The only executions occurred during the Armada crisis eight years later. In August 1588 Edward Shelley was one of six men executed at Tyburn and the following month two priests went to their deaths in Chichester (two others recanted and were reprieved). The last were trained in Continental seminaries which from 1574 sent priests to England, making their way up the Arun where they were then hidden amongst the network of inter-linked Catholic estates along the Sussex–Hampshire border. This is the era of secret hiding places in Catholic households, the priests' holes of popular mythology. After 1585 it became a capital offence to harbour a Catholic priest in a private house. In 1592 it was believed that there were three priests staying in Edward Gage's house at Bentley and another in the Shelley household at Mitchelgrove. In 1594 Nicholas Beard stated that Thomas Leedes kept a priest named Norton at his house called Wappingthorne. It was said of Wappingthorne and of Washington House that 'these houses are receptacles for priests, and have great convenience for hiding them; in Wolfe's house in a little gallery there is a place for an altar, and the massing stuff and a cover of boards over a great cupboard which can be taken off'. The latent hostility to Catholicism only really raised its head in times of political crisis; for much of the time gentry families lived peacefully side by side in Sussex. The Toleration Act did not apply to Catholics and so they remained liable to substantial penalties even after 1689.

Non-attenders at church (known as Recusants from the Latin verb to refuse) who did not receive communion or attend mattins were supposed to be reported by the churchwardens to the diocesan authorities and magistrates where they faced fines and other penalties. In practice many wardens were unlikely to present their

EASEBOURNE (W): Monument to the First Viscount Montague (d. 1592) by Richard Stevens of Southwark

ARUNDEL, St. PHILIP NERI R.C. CATHEDRAL (W): From the *Building News*, 1873

social superiors and landlords. There was much fudging as when William Coldham was reported in 1625: 'He hath not received the sacrament for five years whether a recusant or not I refer it to your judgement'.

The Catholic religion survived in the households of a small number of important gentry families who progressively isolated themselves from the surrounding communities and were thus able to maintain islands of the old religion by creating coherent and largely self-sufficient Catholic households. This isolation can be seen at Slindon in 1640 where the churchwardens presented the Lewkenors and their household 'whoes names we know noth neither can wee learne'. A number of well-known Catholic gentry avoided persecution and even retained public office for many years like Sir Henry Compton of Brambletye who managed to remain a magistrate and Deputy Lieutenant of the County despite his religious beliefs.

In the larger gentry households masses, fasts and festivals that were the essence of the old religion could be practised discreetly. The association between Catholic gentry and Catholic community is clearly seen in the succession of seventeenth and eighteenth-century records detailing the numbers of recusants. In 1676 the Compton Religious Census lists 385 recusants in forty-seven parishes; in reality the distribution was far more limited, ten parishes alone contributing 290 recusants. The link between the remaining Catholic gentry and these parishes is clear. Easebourne and Midhurst, the site of the Cowdray estate of the Montagues, lists ninety-six Catholics, the Caryll household at Benton probably accounts for the forty listed under Shipley parish and similarly with the Gages at Firle and so on. The registers of the early Catholic missions reveal that the congregation was drawn from areas where the Catholic gentry held property. The Burton registers show worshippers came from Duncton, Woolavington, Graffham, Sutton, Watersfield, Petworth, Byworth, Fittleworth and as far afield as Wisborough Green and Billingshurst. In other words, these estates were providing a focus of Catholic belief for a dispersed Catholic population.

The major Catholic estates were to be found in West Sussex: the Brownes at Cowdray Park, the Carylls of West Grinstead and Harting, the Kempes of Slindon, the Shelleys at Clapham and the Howards at Arundel. These were wealthy families. It was claimed that John Caryll (1583–1654) could travel from Sompting via Findon, Ashington, West Grinstead and Horsham to Rogate and Harting without ever leaving his own land. The major Catholic houses had chapels within them, as at Slindon, Lady Holt, Burton and Cowdray.

By 1580 there were some fifteen greater gentry families who were firm recusants. The numbers of Catholics after initially declining seem to have stabilised at something under one per cent of the county's population. Legislation increasingly excluded them from public office; facing heavy fines and financial penalties they were forced to turn in on themselves for personal security. Marriage was only possible within the small network of loyal Catholic families and inevitably social and economic isolation took its toll. The family links became increasingly complex. The mother of Sir Garrett Kempe of Slindon was a daughter of Edward Gage of Firle while Kempe himself married Elizabeth Caryll. The first wife of Sir Thomas Palmer of Parham was a daughter of John Caryll of Warnham, his sister married John Caryll and his daughter married John Leedes of Wappingthorne in Steyning. All were Catholic families.

Obviously many found these pressures too much and lapsed from the faith. Others tried to retain their estates by occasionally conforming and attending the parish church, like John Newland, of whom a former servant claimed that it was thought 'by most that he did goe to church to save his lands'. Newland was discharged from sequestration in 1650 'not appearing to be a Papist'. Maintaining religious convictions was obviously more difficult for those Catholic families who found themselves isolated and in hostile territory. Often the only answer was to move, like the Threeles who left their estate near to the Protestant hot-bed of Rye and moved to Rotherfield.

Keeping children in the faith was another problem. They could be sent abroad or educated by a private tutor employed within the household. Later the Catholic missions might include a school. At West Grinstead in 1727 the rector presented 'Mrs. Hay (as they call her) School m(istres)s to the Popish children'.

Recusants continued to be presented as at Midhurst in 1625 where a Mr. Oxenbridge was 'thought to be a priest' or George Fortescue three years later 'whome wee suppose a priest'. But the physical danger to the fugitive priest had largely passed by the second decade of the seventeenth century. This did not, however, prevent the annual presentment of a long list of Catholic recusants from Midhurst for 'We have many popish recusants that impingue the King's Supremacy in causes ecclesiasticall . . .'.

Catholic they may have been but many of these families still erected sizeable monuments in their parish churches. The leading Elizabethan Catholic was Anthony Browne, 1st Viscount Montague, whose Battle estate was a Catholic outpost in Protestant-dominated East Sussex. In 1559 he had spoken against the Elizabethan religious settlement in the House of Lords and under Queen Mary he created new chantries in Battle and Midhurst churches, replacing those dissolved under Edward VI. Yet he was also very much an accepted member of the ruling elite. He had made major financial gains from the Dissolution of the Monasteries and was accepted by Elizabeth as a loyal subject. Indeed she stayed at Cowdray in 1591 and later visited Browne on his death bed. His splendid memorial of painted and gilded marble and alabaster originally stood in Midhurst parish church (W) but in 1851 it was moved to a side aisle in Easebourne church and had to be cut down from its original design. At Midhurst the effigies of his two wives had lain on either side of his central kneeling figure, which was dressed in ruff and mantle and collar of the Order of the Garter, while four obelisks rose from the corners of the monument. At Easebourne the obelisks could not be fitted in and the two female effigies are now forced to lie side by side and much of the original grandeur of the monument is lost as a result. A more typical monument can be seen in Shipley church (W) to Sir Thomas Caryll (d. 1616). Edward Gage of Bentley, Framfield and Isfield was forced abroad in 1606 and when he died his memorial in Framfield church (E) made clear his religious sympathies by quoting from the Roman breviary.

As McCann has demonstrated, the crucial factor in the survival of Catholicism therefore remained the rôle of the landowner. The presence of the Gages at West Firle probably explain why the preambles to wills from this parish during the Reformation period remain so staunchly traditional. Similarly, West Grinstead provides no evidence of any Catholic presence until after the Carylls acquired the estate in 1638. No single recusant from this parish was presented between 1559 and 1597, 174 males from West Grinstead signed the 1642 Protestation against the Catholic religion and in 1676 the churchwardens could report 'We have no dissenters in our parish, we have none that refuse to receive communion'. In 1671 John Caryll made provision for a priest to serve West Grinstead as well as two travelling missionaries in the Sussex/Hampshire border area. Consequently by 1685 sixteen

BRIGHTON, St. JOHN R.C. CHURCH (E): Watercolour by W. A. Delamotte, 1853

recusants are listed, in 1724 fourteen families out of 106 in the parish were Catholic and by 1749 there were 140 Catholics. Similarly, under Lady Montague's influence, Battle was a Catholic centre in the 1590s. It declined after her death and by 1626 only six are reported.

By the early eighteenth century the cumulative effects of punitive legislation was placing an increasing financial burden on Catholic families. The suspension of the penal laws in 1689 had not applied to Catholics and in 1713 taxes on Catholic-owned land were doubled; by 1721 severe limitations existed on the purchase and sale of lands by Catholics. In December 1749 John Baptist Caryll sold off his remaining estate to the Protestant Merrick Burrell and moved abroad. Surprisingly, the Catholic presence in West Grinstead survived this blow as the Catholic Mission itself remained, administered by the Franciscans until 1814 and by secular clergy up to the present day. The community built a church in 1875 and under the guidance of Mgr. Jean-Marie Denis further nineteenth-century developments included a priory, an orphanage administered by the Dominican sisters and the shrine of Our Lady of Consolation (*Sussex Arch. Colls.*, vol. CXXIV).

It was only in 1791 that the building of Catholic chapels for public worship was legalised provided that they had no bell or steeple. Such places of worship still had to be registered at the Quarter Sessions. The Roman Catholic Emancipation Act in 1829 provided political freedom. This helped to make Catholic worship more readily available as private and institutional chapels were now available for public use. Only one new Catholic church was built in Sussex in the decade after 1829 – the church of St. John the Baptist in Brighton, built in 1835 to replace the smaller structure which had stood in the High Street since 1806. This earlier structure had been a response to the influx of French Catholics fleeing the French Revolution. Catholics remained a very small proportion of the county's population, less than half a per cent in 1851. One-third of these twelve hundred people lived in Brighton. The institution of the Roman Catholic hierarchy in 1850 might have been expected to provide another spur to church building but by 1860 Elleray lists only five new Catholic churches built since 1800. Indeed by 1900 the total is only forty-four. By contrast Elleray quotes 210 Anglican and 256 Non-Conformist buildings constructed in the same period. The bulk of new Catholic churches were built in the urban centres and coastal resorts, such as St. Mary Magdalene, built in 1862 to the designs of Gilbert Blount and St. Mary Star of the Sea, Hastings built in 1882 to the design of Basil Champneys. Of later nineteenth-century Catholic churches easily the most spectacular is St. Philip Neri, Arundel, erected between 1870–1873 to the designs of John Aloysius Hansom and Son, the former better known as the inventor of the Safety Cab – the Hansom Cab. It towers over Arundel like a French Gothic cathedral, dwarfing the ancient Anglican church of St. Nicholas. Although its scale is impressive, the setting promises rather more than the building actually delivers on closer inspection. Otherwise nineteenth-century Catholic church architecture in Sussex is not outstanding, although two buildings dating from the end of the century, the church of the Sacred Heart in Petworth (W), designed by F. A. Walters in 1896, and that of St. Thomas of Canterbury in St. Leonards (E), by C. A. Buckler in 1889, are worthy of note.

J.R.

Four

THE CHURCH AND THE COMMUNITY FROM THE MEDIEVAL PERIOD TO THE EIGHTEENTH CENTURY

PARISH churches are traditionally studied through their architecture whilst their contents have been regarded as art objects and it is all too easy in this secular age to forget the important religious, social and economic rôle they played within their local community. The medieval church provided a focus for community life through the numerous holy days which marked the passing of the seasons. But the church was more than this, it provided a source of recreation and entertainment and acted as a venue for virtually all communal activity. A variety of sources of evidence can be used to provide an outline of the changing rôle of the church in the community. These include documents like the series of annual accounts rendered by the churchwardens and overseers of the poor and there are records of the ecclesiastical courts and of probate records. The registration of marriages, births and deaths was introduced in 1538 and by the seventeenth and eighteenth centuries a myriad of printed forms existed including bastardy bonds, apprenticeship indentures and settlement certificates. A major source of information is, of course, the fabric and furnishings of the parish church itself.

The churches we see today are the accumulation of centuries of alterations, additions and rebuildings and the surviving fabric provides evidence of its community's economic well-being. The results of a stagnating local economy and a falling population are illustrated by a lost aisle at Ovingdean (E), a lost chancel and aisles at Southease (E), a chancel at Alciston (E) shortened in the thirteenth century, at Botolph's (W) a blocked arcade of the same date, whilst at Lullington (E) all that remains is the chancel. Nowhere is this more graphically seen than in the huge chancel at Winchelsea (E), where the quality of the surviving work illustrates both the wealth and importance the town once held, just as the lack of a nave underlines its subsequent decline. Similarly the small isolated Norman two-cell structures found so often on the Sussex Downland, as at Up and North Marden, Buncton, Hardham or Chithurst (W), are also evidence of economic stagnation. These churches survive largely intact because the parish could not afford to rebuild in the latest architectural fashion and there was no population pressure requiring a new or enlarged structure. An isolated church may indicate the existence of a lost settlement; at sites like

Berwick (E) and Botolphs (W), amongst others, there is evidence of house platforms near the church. Examples of post-medieval emparking, that is the physical removal of a settlement away from the parkland estate of the local gentry, leaving an isolated church, are to be found at Buxted (E) and Parham (W).

The remaining fragments of sculpture, stained glass and above all wall paintings reveal the medieval community's real belief in demons and the intercessory powers of saints, the fires of hell and the rewards of salvation. The terrors of Judgement Day are graphically represented by the glass fragments at Ticehurst (E) or the Doom over the chancel arch at Clayton (E). This concern manifested itself in quite lavish bequests providing fittings and ornaments to decorate the church. Under the terms of the will of William Saunders in 1512, Wadhurst church (E) was to gain from the sale of certain lands. From the proceeds a variety of vestments were to be bought and 'a cote of rede satyn frynged wit silk for the rode standinge above the churche of Wadeherst which I will to hange there contynually'; also 'a like cote for Saint Mighell' and money was provided for the same statue to be gilded. In an interesting example of local parochial rivalry, an additional purchase was to be made of 'a goodly censor of silver parcell gilt biggar than it at Tysherst'.

The concern for the soul of the departed manifested itself in the requests for Masses, although few were as specific as William Grenehyll, the parson of Twineham

BREDE (E): Poor box inscribed with the date 1687 and the initials of the responsible churchwardens

AMBERLEY (W): Seventeenth or eighteenth century hour-glass supported by winged cherub heads

(E), who in 1542 specified ten Masses for his burial, these to include Masses of the Nativity, the Resurrection, the Ascension, the Holy Ghost, the Five Wounds, the Assumption, the Passion and All Saints, as well as the Mass of the Day and of the Requiem. More typical was John at Mare of Wivelsfield (E), who required twenty priests to sing dirges and masses for his soul, each to received sixpence for their trouble, or William Jefferay of Chiddingly (E) who willed himself buried 'in the myddyll passe before the roode at my father's fett' and provided for wax tapers to burn before the sepulchre for seven years in his memory. The wealthy endowed a priest and chantry chapel, the less well-off joined with others to form a guild to serve the same purpose. The guilds, many of which are only known through bequests, were similar to the Fraternity of the Blessed Virgin of Comfort, founded at West Tarring (W) in 1528 with one of its prime objectives being to support a priest to assist the parish priest. The chantries and guilds were dissolved in 1547. So despite the relative paucity of documentary evidence the vast amount of material wealth expended on the upkeep and beautification of the county's churches makes clear the central rôle that the church occupied in the lives of Sussex men and women. The parish church was the physical expression of the community's faith.

Medieval life was very insecure and uncertain, harvest failure or disease could strike at any time and with them, the threat of the Last Judgement must have seemed very real. In 1348–9 the Black Death may have carried off one third of the population but this was only the most well-known of a succession of medieval epidemics. The church offered reassurance in the form of a regular performance of an elaborate ritual in a familiar setting.

The pre-Reformation churches were well appointed with vestments, service books and plate as a glance at the inventories for Rotherfield (E) or St. Andrew's, Lewes (E), shows. These items played an important part in the rich cycle of ceremonial and ritual which was swept away by the Reformation. Graham Mayhew has recreated the ceremonial year in Rye where the calendar was punctuated by a series of communal feast days and holy days marking the changing seasons and important civic events. At the end of August on the feast of St. Bartholomews, the Mayor was chosen by the commons assembled in the churchyard, a week later most of the town officers changed, with the new churchwardens being sworn in at Michaelmas. The beginning of winter was marked by the Feast of All Saints at the end of November. Christmas Night saw a special midnight service, with the church bells 'ryngyng the berthe off Jesu Chryste our blessed savyor'. The cycle continued through Twelfth Night, Epiphany and Lent to the peak of the Christian year at Easter.

Easter week began with the traditional procession celebrating Christ's entry into Jerusalem on Palm Sunday and the Rye churchwardens' accounts refer to repairs to four silk streamers and banners. Other indirect evidence for processions comes from the West Tarring accounts where the 'makynge of the Kanape' refers to the canopy which protected the reserved Sacrament during the processions. The Wednesday before Easter saw the evening service of Tenebrae at which the 51st Psalm was sung by the choir when the church was in darkness. Holy Thursday provided another procession while Good Friday saw the start of the re-enactment of the disciples' vigil outside Christ's tomb in the ritual of the Easter Sepulchre. In this ceremony the reserved Sacrament was placed on the sepulchre on Good Friday and watched night and day until Easter Sunday when it was returned to the altar. A number of churchwardens' accounts provide for the provision of bread and drink to the sepulchre watchers and bequests often include the provision of wax tapers and candles to burn before the sepulchre. John Hamond in 1484–5 bequeathed 'towards the making of the sepulture in the seid church of Tyseherst 20s. so that it be made on thes side [this side of] the Fest of Estre . . .'. Spring was heralded by the festivities of May Day and the ceremonial year continued with Ascension Day, Whit Sunday, Trinity Sunday and Corpus Christi.

There were also a variety of other holy days associated with saints and feasts in the Christian calendar. In Protestant Rye the curate, William Inold met with opposition when in 1537 he was still trying to celebrate these 'idell holydays' which were greeted 'with solemn ringing, singing, procession and decking the church . . . as though they had been the highest days of the year'. The collection and decoration of the church with foliage to celebrate a variety of Christian festivals was a long-established tradition rejected by the Protestant reformers. At Wivelsfield in 1634 Elizabeth Goodman pulled down 'the May boughs, in a rude and scornful manner, which were brought into the church to adorn it'. Rye also had its own mystery play performed annually at Easter; the accounts for 1522–3 include payment for the stage and 12d. was 'payd for a coote made when the Resurreccion was playde for hym that in playing represented the part of almighty god'. From other churchwardens' accounts it seems similar plays took place at West Tarring, Steyning and St. Andrews, Lewes. The loss of this rich ceremonial tradition left not only a spiritual hiatus, as familiar and comforting ceremonial was swept away, but a social void. Records of the town of Rye between 1485 and 1560 reveal payments made to groups of players from over thirty neighbouring towns and villages, many of whom appeared on several occasions. Such groups performed in or about the church as in the case of 'the players of Romeney, the which played in the chirche' or 'the pleyers of Wynchilsea, the whiche pleyed in the churche yarde uppone the days of the Purification of our Ladye'.

Evidence can be found of archery, football, bowls and even cricket taking place in Sussex churchyards. It was only in the seventeenth century that the yards began to fill with headstones; prior to this they acted as an enclosed communal space used for a variety of secular purposes as well as burial. Archery butts are referred to in the West Tarring churchwardens' accounts for 1544 when 3s.2d. is 'ghethered for the target' (i.e. the butts). In 1622 several boys are accused of playing cricket in the churchyard at Boxgrove in time of divine service and there was a Hailsham man who 'fell down dead as he was playing a match of football upon the Sabbath day'. Other traditional recreations were threatened as the religious climate changed. The Horsham burial register on 21st May, 1582, records 'John Rowe als. Sparrowe killed with ye fall of a Maypole, as it was asettinge up'. Forty years later the congregation at Eastergate are trying to use a 'peece of timber which formerly had bene a maypole' as a ladder. These references perhaps suggest that such celebrations were falling into disfavour. Even the traditional rogationtide perambulation of the parish boundaries which had survived the Reformation fulfilled an important social function and there was ill-feeling if the day was not crowned with 'cakebread and drinking'.

It was customary for the upkeep of the churchyard fence to be the concern of individual farms and landowners. The sections for which they were responsible were clearly marked with their initials and these 'church-marks' survive from several parishes including Cowfold, where 81 tenants shared the obligation, Lindfield (dated 1636) and Chiddingly (dated 1771) where the custom seems to have survived into the present century. The importance of maintaining the fence is made clear in the case of the four Sutton men presented 'for not making up the church wall, which lies down to the ground, and the bodyes of the dead are dayly ready to be digged up of hogges'.

The church was the place where the community gathered together to witness the individual parishioner's rites of passage through baptism, marriage and funeral service. The often quoted passage from Chaucer where the Wife of Bath says 'Husbandes at chirche dore have I had five' illustrates the fact that the marriage contract took place in the porch before the couple proceeded inside for the Nuptial Mass. Baptism began in the porch where the priest first received the child and administered purifying salt before moving inside to the font. The funeral service commenced inside the church. Mothers came to church to give thanks in the Churching of Women service for their safe delivery. The women were met at the porch as were penitents receiving absolution. The porch was also used to seal business transactions as in 1662 when John Miller asked for payment to be made 'at or in the south church-porch of Chitingly'; the will of the Rector of Maresfield (E) specified that a sum of money bequeathed for educational purposes was to be paid over at 12 o'clock in the church porch.

The principal parish officers were the two churchwardens who were appointed annually, usually at the Easter Vestry meeting, where they might be selected by all or the decision might lie with a more select group of parishioners. The origins for this office are uncertain but there is evidence of their existence by the fourteenth century. At a later stage it was common for one churchwarden to be the incumbent's candidate, with his colleague chosen by the parish. In larger parishes assistants or sidemen might be appointed. The churchwardens were responsible for the maintenance of the church fabric, the security of its contents and the provision of the necessary service books, vestments and fittings necessary for the proper conduct of the services. They were expected to oversee and report upon the conduct of the laity

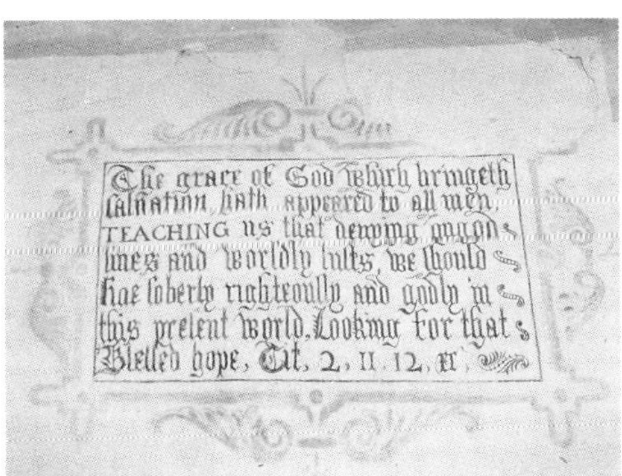

BURTON (W): Seventeenth century religious text painted on plaster

HASTINGS, St. CLEMENT (E): Painted benefaction board dated 1721 recording the gifts of Archibald Hutcheson

and the clergy, to maintain proper accounts and from 1538 maintain with the incumbent the registration of all those baptised, married or buried.

The other parish officers could include overseers of the poor, the constable, the beadle and the parish clerk. The latter was usually appointed by the incumbent to arrange baptisms and communions and he came to lead the responses in the service. The constable had a wide range of law and order and licensing duties. Parish beadles could fulfill a variety of rôles including, in some parishes, the rôle of constable. Whatever title they were given, these officers were often provided with a staff of office such as still survive at Fletching (E) and Buxted (E).

Fund-raising was an important element of the churchwardens' duties. Income was received from a variety of sources including bequests and gifts; substantial fees were charged for burial within the church and payment had to be made if the church bells were to ring out at marriages and funerals. One of the most regular features of fund raising was the church ales, at which the churchwardens provided a plentiful supply of food and drink. These functions involved the whole community and were intended to raise considerable sums of money. Originally the ale may have taken place in the nave of the church, uncluttered as it then was by congregational seating, but by the fifteenth century many parishes had built 'church houses' as venues for such activities. At West Tarring the first reference to such a building occurs in 1524 and in 1541–2 St. Andrew's, Lewes, purchased a new key and lock for their 'cherche house'. The century following the Reformation brought considerable opposition to the use of church property for such activities, largely because of the excessive drinking and sexual licentiousness that was all too often the result. In 1604 formal opposition was expressed in the 88th canon: 'the churchwardens or questmen and their assistants shall suffer no plays, feasts, banquets, suppers, church ales, drinkings . . . or any other profane usage to be kept in the church, chapel or church yard'. It may be inferred that such activities were not easily suppressed since the following question appeared in Bishop Montague's 1630 visitation of the Diocese of Chichester: 'Have there been kept in the church, chapel or churchyard any plays, feasts, suppers, church ales, temporal courts or leet day juries, ministers or meetings for rates and taxations, especially at the Communion Table?'. Gradually these occasions disappeared from churchwardens' accounts. The last reference to them at West Tarring being in 1589, although in the 1640s the Sussex magistrates still had to ban church ales for desecrating the Sabbath.

Other sources of income were required and increasingly the Church turned to church rates and to pew renting. Until the late fourteenth century churches had been free of any form of congregational seating except for the aged and the infirm and the introduction of benches was probably related to the growing importance of sermons. Early examples of such benches can still be found in a number of Sussex churches including Loxwood (W), Didling (W) and Tortington (W). The practice of charging rents for occupying pews spread rapidly during the sixteenth and seventeenth centuries.

The social hierachy was maintained in the seating plans of churches. The squire's family pew was a prominent feature at Parham (W), where easy chairs and a fireplace were provided for comfort; at Warbleton (E) the Roberts' family pew dates from 1722 and towers over the nave on stilts. The rights to a particular pew were frequently referred to in property leases and there are many examples of disputes taking place over ownership of a specific pew. At Woodmancote (W) in the 1670s the rector and members of the West family came into conflict when the former destroyed the great pew 'in which the family of the Wests had nested themselves, by the

RYE (E): Lithograph

permission of former parsons, so long that they would now have it to be their owne'. The rector's precipitate action led to Jacob West coming to church with a chair to occupy the bare ground where 'his' pew had formerly stood.

Churchwardens' accounts frequently contain references to congregational seating. At Rotherfield (E) in 1532 there is payment for the carriage of timber from Framfield from which 'pewes and setys [were] made in the chirch on the XIX day May'. At Horsham in 1628 seats are purchased in the newly erected gallery and twenty years later the Bolney churchwardens allow Elias Blunt and Edmund Harper to 'build each of them a seate in the said church nere unto the North doore'. Plans of pew allocations survive for a number of Sussex churches including Ticehurst. The authorities were concerned over the haphazard nature of such development which lead to pews of varying heights blocking the view of the congregation. Action was taken against Sir Edward Bishop of Parham (W) to ensure the reduction in height of his servants' pew which stood near the communion table. During the 1630s attempts by the Laudian hierarchy to achieve a more uniform height for pewing were resented by many churchwardens who argued, like those of Warnham (W) and Horsham, that they formed no hindrance to the services. The popularity of box pews in the seventeenth and eighteenth centuries made the appropriation of private pews easier. With lockable doors, high wooden sides and with seats often facing inwards so that many found themselves with their backs to the preacher box pews must have encouraged inattention to the sermon. They were a complete anathema to nineteenth-century restorers who ripped them out at the first opportunity. Nevertheless they survive in Sussex, most notably at Warminghurst (W) although they can also be found at Shermanbury (W), East Guldeford (E) and Chiddingly (E) amongst others.

Particular seats were often associated with a specific farm or family and at West Grinstead (W) and Shermanbury (W) the names of the farms are recorded on the reverse of the benches in early nineteenth-century lettering. It was common for male and female seating to be segregated hence references like that at Rotherfield in 1620 where a newly installed pew was appropriated for use as 'women's seats'. This differentiation of seating could also apply to social and economic status, so that when in 1818 the Church Building Society was formed it insisted when giving grants for church extensions that a proportion of the resulting seating had to be free. Many churches provided separate entrances and seating arrangements, for rich and poor, male and female. At St. John's, Chichester, built in 1813, the galleries have separate entrances to the main doors which lead into the body of the church.

One of the most obvious ways that the Church impinged on the life of the individual was in the imposition of tithes. The clergyman's benefices would usually include a portion of land assigned to him known as the glebe. The Church also levied a tithe, normally of one-tenth of agricultural produce to support the incumbent of the parish. Complications arose because in the Middle Ages the rector often appropriated the major part of the tithe (on corn, hay and wood) and left an appointed vicar with the Small Tithe on the less valuable and more troublesome items to collect such as milk, cheese, fish and wild fowl. After the Reformation the monastic lands and rights fell into secular hands, leaving many parishes with a lay rector who had appropriated the tithe, leaving the vicar impoverished.

The Tudor period witnessed a major shift in the duties of both incumbents and particularly churchwardens who were no longer restricted to ecclesiastical and moral duties. The minister was now expected actively to encourage his flock to contribute towards poor relief and his presence was required when physical punishment was to be inflicted on vagabonds. The churchwardens found themselves becoming an arm of local government with new responsibilities for the care of the poor, highway and bridge maintenance, the assessment and collection of church rates, the destruction of vermin, the organisation of parish musters and the care of parish weaponry.

The continuing concern of the churchwardens for the moral welfare of their communities and their resulting presentments to the ecclesiastical courts provide vivid glimpses of seventeenth-century church services. The impression is one of a noisy gathering with much talking and laughing and even swearing although it was still apparently possible for Thomas Brett 'to slepe in the sermon tyme' at Cuckfield (E). In 1585 John Baker of Folkington (E) is accused 'for playing cardes in service tyme' and violence was not unheard of. In 1601 Richard Woods of Slaugham (E) was charged with 'breaking Thomas Mutton's head in the churche' while Thomas Danche, who on St. Stephen's Day 'being druncke he came into the [Iden] church, and in tyme of divine service spued there'. At Kingston boys and servants were found 'striving and jostling and pricking one another'. Fines for drunkenness and swearing were common; in the Horsham churchwardens' accounts for 1646 the normal rate appears to be 5s. for drunkenness and 12d. for swearing. The problem of unruly dogs in church, desecrating the sanctuary or simply causing a nuisance, could lead to the appointment of a dog warden to control them. James Long received 10d. in 1643–4 for keeping the dogs out of Horsham church.

Church attendance was compulsory from the Reformation into the seventeenth century, although illness and infirmity were taken into account as at Binsted (W) in 1624 where 'all our parrishioners have receaved except the wife of Thomas Page; shee is lame; and John Browman's wife lyeth in and Richard Mittnes is sicke; the next

Communion they will receave'. Working on the Sabbath and the opening of shops and alehouses during time of divine service were other frequent reasons for prosecution. Some of the actions seem harsh as at Findon (W) in 1622 when four men having attended the service then set out to bring in the harvest; an Arundel barber, William Mansell, was presented in 1621 'for trymmyng' on the Sabbath. Elizabeth Collins of Chalvington (E) was accused of washing clothes on Easter Day and Lambert Combert of Slaugham 'for beating his wife on the 29 June last, being sabbath day, in time of divine service'. The Wisborough Green (E) churchwardens acted against John Hales in 1622 because of his alehouse 'where many have prophaned the Sabbath day by unlawfull games and drinking, in tyme of common prayer'. From the diary of an East Hoathly (E) shopkeeper, Thomas Turner, we find that he and his fellow churchwarden, Jeremiah French, set out on Sunday, 25 April 1756, to check the local alehouses. The prime concern in these causes may well have been financial; the alehouses were frequented by the poor with the result of 'the wastinge of their strength, time and mony untill such time as they become a parish charge'.

The church building itself can provide evidence of contemporary attitudes and illustrate parish life. By the seventeenth and eighteenth centuries the church interior was much altered since the Reformation. The whitewashed walls were often adorned with scriptural texts and in a prominent position an ornate pulpit with a large sounding board and hour-glass was placed; these illustrated the important rôle of the sermon. Mid seventeenth-century painted texts can still be seen at Burton (W), whilst at Kingston Buci (W) and Southease (E) the texts are supported by cherubs. Text boards can still be found at Penhurst (E). Amberley, Ferring, Houghton and Warnham (W) still preserve the iron stand adjacent to the pulpit where the hour-glass formerly stood. Unfortunately thieves have stolen the hour-glasses themselves including the most notable Sussex example at Amberley in which the glass was supported by winged cherubs. Contemporary attitudes to social hierarchy are revealed in some of the examples of Royal Arms which were ordered to be hung in churches after the break with Rome. They could be painted on wood or canvas, made of plaster (St. Thomas Becket, Cliffe, Lewes, E), cast from iron or made from Coade stoneware (Petworth 1812, W). At Burton (W) the arms of Charles I are painted directly onto the wall below the exhortation to 'Obey them that have the rule over you'. At Udimore (E) the churchwardens proudly displayed their names with the encouragement to 'Fear God, Honour the King'. Many were painted by local artists and display great exuberance and naïvity in execution.

More than a third of the Canons (ecclesiastical laws) issued in 1604 are concerned with the workings of the church courts. They were particularly worried about sexual morality, incest and marriage between close relatives. A table showing the prohibited degrees of affinity between close relatives was published and it was reproduced in the Book of Common Prayer. Every church should have possessed and displayed a copy, although at Pulborough in 1625 the churchwardens stated that 'wee cannot finde any table of the degrees of affinity'. Examples of sexual licence were frowned upon. In Racton (W) in 1625 John Bargis faced prosecution 'for saying he had had carnall knowledge of the body of Jellyan Browne' and a couple in Felpham (W) were presented in 1622 'for fornicacion out of matrimony'. Punishments for such offences might well include public penance, involving an appearance in church and possibly at other locations like the market cross, dressed in a white sheet confessing their sin, expressing their sorrow and requesting forgiveness. After assurances in respect of future behaviour the offender would be re-admitted to the church. This

ALDINGBOURNE (W): Royal arms of William III, painted on board

was a considerable ordeal involving public humiliation in front of fellow-parishioners and efforts at avoiding undergoing public penance through the payment of a substantial fine were common. Lesser offences such as non-attendance, poor behaviour during the service or tippling on the Sabbath were liable to a fine and a confession of error in front of the minister and churchwardens rather than the whole congregation.

These public cermonies should be seen not only as punishment and a deterrent, but also as a way of maintaining the unity of the community. Serving public penance acted as a public notice that the offender had rejoined the flock. Social pressure by the community was a powerful force and penalties often involved public ridicule. The ducking stool was employed in Rye in 1589 when a married woman was discovered to be still associating with a sailor despite a previous action ordering her to desist. In places like Rye the town authorities took the lead in such matters as the ecclesiastical courts proved ineffective. By the early seventeenth century many parishes were looking to the magistrates to act in their stead. Public humiliation was at the root of the Rye authorities' 'Decree against Whoredom' which in 1581 ordered that all unmarried women 'gotten with childe, or found to offend that waye, shall have a partlet made of yellow and grene clothe . . . to ware about their neckes uppermost upon their garment . . .'. Other punishments included whipping, either while walking behind a cart as in Rye or at a whipping post. The latter, like the stocks, were often found in or adjacent to churchyards. At Harting (W) the stocks still remain *in situ* and at Warnham (W) they are preserved inside the church. In 1675 Sir John Trevor paid tax on the stocks and whipping post at Glynde (E).

The concern over sexual behaviour had a practical as well as a moral justification. Any children resulting from an illicit liaison were liable to become a future charge on the parish, hence the strenuous efforts of the wardens to find a father (not necessarily the real father) who would support the child. This explains the action taken against Elizabeth Streater in Itchingfield (W) in 1625 'for being unlawfully bigotten with child and having a bastard by James Kemsall, both of them remaining in her mother's house'. Such occurrences were made the more likely since sexual intercourse was expected once a couple were engaged and there are a number of examples of females jilted once male ardour had cooled. Many refused to reveal the real father, blaming it on a soldier, a vagrant or other untraceable outsider, but later confessions as to the real father were common during labour. Mary Barber claimed that one Richard Browne had agreed to support her child but then she confessed during labour 'that Pont lay first and last with her and Richard Browne once, and that all was done within one weeke'.

Serving as a parish officer required a considerable commitment of time and effort. In February 1757 a great deal of time was spent by Thomas Turner, an overseer from East Hoathly, in trying to arrange the marriage of Ann Durrant, a pregnant East Hoathly parishioner living in nearby Laughton, to George Hyland, a parishioner of Laughton. He was successful, but the parish had to pay the bridegroom £6.10s. and five stone of beef as well as paying for the wedding licenses and dinner and a ring for the bride. On a similar case later in the same year Turner rushed to Ringmer to arrest the man and travelled to Lewes to obtain the marriage licence. The marriage occurred in East Hoathly and the couple travelled to Uckfield to be sworn before the magistrates, only then could husband and wife be dispatched to their new abode in Hellingly. All this activity occupied Turner from two in the morning until nine at night. In return officers received only the expenses listed in the churchwardens' accounts (D. Vaisey (ed.), *The Diary of Thomas Turner*).

The pressure to keep families together and therefore not burden the rates was intense and there are many examples of presentments of husband and wife for living apart. Adultery theoretically carried the death penalty, but in reality offenders like Peter Soane of Henfield (W) who was seen with another man's wife 'in time of divine service upon Sondaies in a scandalous and suspicious manner', were unlikely to face the ultimate penalty.

The Church licensed teachers and so effectively controlled educational provision. At Bexhill (E) in 1597 the rector, Thomas Pye, 'repayred the chantry Chappel and turned it into a Schole House'. At Lurgashall (W) a school met regularly in the sixteenth-century timber gallery on the south side of the nave.

The Elizabethan Poor Law formalised the existing tradition of charitable alms giving. The wealthy had always given alms for the poor particularly during Christian festivals like Christmas. Wills often included the provision of funeral doles to the poor. After the Reformation the congregation were actively encouraged to give alms to the poor. As the offertory was sung and the communicants moved from the nave into the chancel the Book of Common Prayer allowed them to place their offerings in the poor box. A number of poor boxes survive most notably at Poling (W) and Brede (E). At the former the pedestal alms box is set on the wall below a stone inscribed 'Remeber the Poore' which echoes the words of Bishop Ridley's 1550 visitation of the

Diocese of London 'the minister at the time of the Communion, immediately after the offatory shall monish the communicants saying these words or such like: Now is the time if it please you to remember the poor man's chest with your charitable alms'. At Brede the box is inscribed with a series of initials and the date *1687*. Testators were actively encouraged to remember the poor in their bequests. In 1558 Rafe Swanne of Brighthelmstone gave 12d. to the poor box and in 1548 Richard Nicholl gave 5s. 'to goddes chest there for poore people' in Rye church.

It was only in the sixteenth century that compulsion was applied to the provision of alms for relieving poverty. With the loss of the charitable functions of the monasteries at the Reformation the parish was made responsible for the care of the impotent poor. After 1563 alms collectors could be appointed and in 1572 the office of Overseer of the Poor was created. Initially they merely supervised endowments and charities but later they came to assess the inhabitants for a poor rate. The provision of a parish poor rate was allowed in 1597, local houses of correction were built after 1610 and workhouses appeared in the eighteenth century. Paupers were to be supported by the parish of their birth. The level of local rates varied according to the prevalent economic and social conditions. The Weald had a large, mobile population and faced heavier expenditure than the smaller Downland parishes which were often dominated by a single landowner who acted to limit the size of the dependent population.

A less attractive aspect of attitudes to the poor was the practice of forcing them to wear badges. This was introduced in Edward VI's time, was revived at the end of the seventeenth century and was not repealed until 1810. Such badges survive from Fletching parish (E); these are similar to those introduced at Horsham in 1665 for those in receipt of poor relief who 'shall wear on the right arm in open view as a badge of their poverty, two letters, H P in colours yellow and blue'. The letters were to be at least four inches high. The deserving poor were increasingly reliant upon charity. Most parishes in the seventeenth and eighteenth century had a wide range of local charities which provided money, food or clothing. The existence is recorded on numerous surviving bequest boards. Dole cupboards intended to receive food, bread and clothing given for the benefit of the poor can still be seen at West Chiltington (W), Nuthurst (E) and Salehurst (E).

The powers of the parish were denuded by nineteenth-century legislation. The 1834 Poor Law created elected Boards of Guardians of the Poor who largely superseded the rôle of the Overseers although the office was not formally abolished until 1925. The creation of parish councils and Rural and Urban District Councils in 1894 saw the removal of civil functions from the parish vestries.

J.R.

Five

SUSSEX NON-CONFORMITY

THE contrast between the wealthy established parish church with its centuries of tradition and the small impoverished dissenting chapel can be clearly seen in many towns and villages in Sussex. At Billingshurst (W) the main street is overlooked by the parish church of St. Mary, whilst quietly hidden on the opposite side of the road, set back behind iron railings and a hedge and approached up a slippery flagstone path, lies the Free Christian Unitarian Church. A small squat building described by Nairn and Pevsner as like a 'demure Georgian Cottage' it is situated in a small burial ground where its founder and first preacher, William Evershed, is buried. Erected in 1754 and later enlarged with the provision of a baptistry and vestries, its site has been adversely affected by the encroachment of surrounding development.

Few passers-by cast a second glance at this or any of the other many Non-Conformist chapels in Sussex. Certainly many seem drab, if not a little forbidding; they are private places hidden away and usually locked, open only to the faithful. Often they have strange sounding names like Zion, Ebenezer, Zoar or Jireh which seem to symbolise their place apart from the world. Yet most of these names have biblical origins like the delightful former chapel at Pell Green, Wadhurst (E), named 'Rehobeth' from the Hebrew word for 'room' or the Zoar Chapel at Wisborough Green (W) meaning 'place of refuge'. Never easy to find, the dissenting chapel does not advertise its presence with a spire or tower. The Calvinistic Independent Providence Chapel, Chichester (W), lies in a small side street away from the cathedral. The building is set back from the street, originally almost completely masked by a high brick wall, whilst the hooks of the original shutters are clear reminders of the strength of ill-feeling that Non-Conformists could face even as late as 1809 when Providence was built. Similarly, the Wesleyan Methodist Chapel at Winchelsea (E), built in 1785, discreetly merges into the surrounding street scene.

When you walk into a Non-Conformist chapel you are entering a functional building. Plain woodwork and bare plastered walls, with no stained glass, no sculpture, in fact no adornment of any kind. This is a building designed for prayer and for singing, not for complex liturgical ritual. The spoken word is at the heart of all branches of Non-Conformity and the internal lay-out of the chapels reflect this. Upon entering, the eye is immediately drawn to the pulpit centrally sited facing the entrance as at Providence Chapel, Chichester, where the mahogany pulpit is entered from above. The minister literally descended into the pulpit from his first floor vestry. Below it the clerk's reading desk is surrounded by a four-sided railed enclosure where the deacons and elders took their place on fitted seats, whilst the congregation is provided with rather less comfortable open-backed pews. These were benches designed for seated worship, since prayer took place either sitting or standing, never kneeling as in the Anglican Church, hence the absence of hassocks. At Providence the pulpit and twin reading desk are lit by double gas lamps, but often the pulpit is flanked by two windows stretching from floor to ceiling in order to maximise the amount of daylight; this arrangement can still be seen in the Wesleyan Chapel in Winchelsea. Facing the pulpit over the entrance doorway is a clock, prominently positioned, not for the convenience of the congregation but for that of the minister. On the surrounding walls are rows of chapel hat pegs and the overall impression is of an interior filled to overflowing with congregational seating separated not by the wide processional aisles common in Anglican and Roman Catholic churches but by narrow functional passage-ways for access.

When the Lord's Supper was celebrated, perhaps monthly, the ceremony was conducted using vessels made of pewter, contrasting with the richness of Anglican silver communion plate. At Providence baptisms were undertaken using a small porcelain bowl, whereas the Baptist denomination's belief in complete immersion required the erection of a baptistry such as was added to the General Baptist chapel at Horsham (W) in 1722. A number of chapels, like Ditchling or Providence, have a minister's house attached to the main building which in the latter case consists simply of a sitting room, kitchen, bedroom and a minister's vestry complete with a discreet window overlooking the chapel interior, allowing the minister to time his entry. Providence could seat some 250 people. Who were these people who composed the congregations of the numerous small chapels in Sussex?

All the denominations comprising English Non-Conformity placed their emphasis on an individual's relationship with God; it was a question of personal faith rather than a religion based on established complex ritual. Although strictly speaking Non-

LEWES, JIREH CHAPEL (E): The pulpit dominates the galleried interior. Note the railed communion area, box pews and rows of hat pegs

Conformity only occurred after 1662 when Anglican ministers who refused to conform were ejected from their livings and therefore became Non-Conformist, its origins lay with the English Reformation and the introduction of the vernacular bible. As Thomas Hobbes wrote: 'Every man, nay every boy and wench that could read English thought they spoke with God Almighty and understood what he said', but until 1662 radical Protestants were largely contained within the body of the Established Anglican Church.

Following the compromise Elizabethan religious settlement the Puritan element in the Church, which was gaining in strength, continued to press for further more radical reform. The Puritans have been described as simply the 'hotter sort of protestants' and they were influential in the coastal towns and the Wealden parishes of East Sussex. The Weald had a long tradition of independent thought; it was here that the medieval heresy of Lollardy had flourished and most of the Protestant martyrs executed during Queen Mary's reign originated in the eastern division of the county. The strength of Puritan feeling can be seen in the late sixteenth-century baptismal registers of these parishes, where names like Repent to Perform thy Vows, Fight the Good Fight of Faith White of Ewhurst and Search the Scriptures Moreton of Salehurst were common. In Warbleton during the incumbency of Thomas Hely (1583–1596) four out of every ten children were baptised with such names.

This was a reaction against the failings of the late sixteenth-century Church. Chichester was one of the poorest dioceses in the kingdom and many of its benefices were insufficient to support the clergy. Seventeenth-century visitation reports reveal the extent of the neglect and decay: at Lancing, for instance, pigeons were nesting in the church through an unrepaired window, many furnishings were in disrepair or simply inadequate. At Westhampnett 'they christen in a buckett' and the collapse of parts of the church was predicted at Chidham, Stoughton, Funtington and Washington. Many of the clergy were non-resident and neglectful though few were perhaps as bad as the incumbent of Herstmonceux in the 1580s 'one Jones who cometh so seldomly there that it is thought that there be very few of the people that know his face'. The Puritan demand was for a 'learned, godly and resident ministry' within the Established Church and some improvements were achieved under Bishop Curteys (1570–1582). Amongst the town corporations, which were clearly more radical in outlook than the Church authorities, Rye and Lewes (E) led the way in appointing town lecturers to preach and educate the people, with Horsham following suit in the 1630s and Midhurst in 1642.

During this period there was undoubtedly a good deal of clerical Non-Conformity within the Established Church, but relatively few cases reached the ecclesiastical courts, probably because the churchwardens were in sympathy with their Puritan ministers over such matters as not bowing at the name of Jesus or standing during the gospel reading. In 1621 the curate of Rye, Thomas Warren, was charged with administering the sacrament to men sitting not kneeling, and others were presented for continuing to wear the Genevan gown rather than the surplice as ordered in the 1604 Injunctions. John Waterhouse, vicar of Cowfold (W), was accused in 1605 of 'not wearing the surplice, nor using the crosse in baptisme'. In 1611 one minister stated his opposition to ecclesiastical vestments in blunt terms: 'Hee had as leefe see a sowe weare a Saddell as see a minister weare a surplice'. The leaders of this militant Puritanism were not the clergy but the gentry.

During the 1620s a reaction set in against this Puritanism and its Calvinistic theology which held that only a predestined elect could obtain eternal salvation. When

William Laud became Archbishop of Canterbury in 1633 and Richard Montague obtained the see of Chichester in 1628, they commenced a programme of re-introducing ceremonial and re-emphasising the sanctity of both the priesthood and the chancel itself. They laid emphasis on the re-positioning of the communion table at the east end of the chancel enclosed within rails placed north-south across the chancel enclosure such as can still be seen at Edburton (W). At Northiam (E) both the table and rails were provided by the local squire, Thankful Frewen in 1638, whose Puritan views as suggested by his name, probably explain the compromise three-sided rails (see p. 101). The eastern half of the county was slow to adopt such practices and some places expressed blatant opposition. At Rye the churchwardens in 1636 claimed 'our communion table standeth where it formerly stood tyme out of mynde'. Two years later at Chiddingly (E) wardens could state that their table 'stands in the midst of the chancell and without ralles'. Often such opposition was led by the local gentry, as at Warbleton (E) where the rector complains in 1638 that the 'greatest men', including Herbert and William Roberts, the lords of the manor, wore their hats during sermons.

This Laudian dominance was, however, short-lived and the period which followed the fall of Chichester to the Parliamentary forces in 1642 until the restoration of Charles II in 1660 saw the Sussex Church hierarchy dominated by the Presbyterians and their leading minister in Sussex, Francis Cheynel, rector of Petworth. He was described by some contemporaries as acting like the Bishop of Chichester. A number of benefices (seventy-six out of 276) were seized and unsuitable ministers (i.e. those with Royalist or Laudian sympathies) were replaced. Yet despite this the Church during the Commonwealth probably encompassed as wide a range of theological viewpoints as it has ever done. Future Congregationalists like Samuel Wilmer of Clapham, Robert Parke of East Lavant and John Stonestreet of Lindfield were accepted as ministers of the Established Church.

There were, however, growing numbers who remained outside this broad church, particularly the Congregationalists and General Baptists. The gradual withdrawal of small groups of people who chose to attend their own meetings rather than the parish church can be traced through the churchwardens' presentments to the ecclesiastical courts, as at West Wittering (W) where in 1640 eight Anabaptists were presented for attending their own conventicle. Such conventicles would be held in a variety of private buildings around the locality. Non-Conformity was more than just regular meetings in a chapel, it concerned a community of believers who could worship wherever they gathered together. Their religion was represented not by bricks and mortar but by its members' faith. Many of the early meetings could describe themselves in terms similar to those used by the Ditchling General Baptists in 1645: 'The Church of our Lord Jesus Christ meeting in and about Ditchelling'. This congregation continued to meet in a variety of farm buildings until about 1740 when it erected a chapel in Ditchling itself, discreetly hidden away and approached by means of a small twitten. The sixteenth and seventeenth centuries see the increasing fragmentation of the Established Church. The all-embracing medieval church was replaced by a multitude of competing sects. By 1676 there were important Non-Conformist congregations in many parts of Sussex.

Strict definitions of the main dissenting denominations are difficult as boundaries were flexible and changed over time and during the era of the penal laws it is wise to be wary of labels placed on the dissenters by Anglican ministers or churchwardens. Baptists believed in the baptism of adult believers, their chapels therefore included

CHICHESTER, PROVIDENCE CHAPEL (W): Interior showing pulpit, reading desk and railed communion area

baptistries that allowed for total adult immersion and not simply a symbolic sprinkling of infants, although initially at least baptism was liable to take place in nearby streams or ponds as occurred at Ditchling and Pell Green, Wadhurst. The Baptists placed great emphasis on the New Testament to regulate church practice and rejected the services of the Anglican Book of Common Prayer. They believed in congregational independence but their organisational links were rather more formal than the Congregationalists who believed in the total independence of each congregation and in the complete separation of Church and State. By contrast the Presbyterians favoured a hierarchical form of church organisation and worked within the Church of England until the 1662 Act of Uniformity led to the widespread expulsion of Protestant dissenting ministers who refused to accept the re-imposition of episcopal authority and the return of the Book of Common Prayer (replacing the Puritan Directory of Public Worship issued in 1644). Others decided to conform in order to retain their livings, George Vinter, vicar of Cowfold, was one who seemed to change his religious views to suit the prevailing wind. A 'zealous loyalist' in 1641, he favoured the Presbyterians from 1642 until 1657 when he expressed strong Congregationalist sentiments. In 1662, after advising others to refuse, he chose to conform himself and was in sympathy with the Catholic position towards the end of Charles II's reign. Sixty-five ministers were ejected in Sussex and many went on to lead Non-Conformist meetings, including men like Edward Newton, the incumbent of St. Anne's, Lewes, who ten years later applied to preach to a Presbyterian meeting in the town.

Following the Act of Uniformity legislation was passed to prevent meetings for public worship and the organisation of religious education outside the Established Church. These penal laws included a fine of 5s. for those attending dissenting

BILLINGSHURST, UNITARIAN CHURCH (W): The small chapel, erected in 1754 and looking like a cottage is set back from the main street and partially hidden

conventicles; a £20 fine for the preacher, which if he was not detained, was added to the fines of those present. Conviction could be obtained merely on the word of a single informer who received one-third of any resulting fines as a reward. By 1669 forty-nine conventicles are listed in Sussex of a variety of persuasions. These included the congregation at Ditchling led by Mr. Lulham who had been the Anglican incumbent there between 1653 and 1658. In 1672 Non-Conformists could apply to licence meeting houses in a short-lived measure of toleration that was repealed the following year. Those applying in Sussex included nineteen Presbyterian, eleven Congregationalist or Independent and four Baptist conventicles (or meetings). Some degree of relief came with the Toleration Act in 1689 which suspended the penal laws and therefore allowed meetings for public worship on licensed premises and for the creation of schools and theological colleges. It still did not allow Non-Conformists access to Oxford or Cambridge universities, to public office or to most of the professions.

One of the most successful groups of dissenters in Sussex in these early years were the Quakers. Within eight years of George Fox first 'declaring the truth' in Nottinghamshire in 1647 the first Quaker missionaries or 'publishers of truth' had arrived in Sussex. The term Quaker was a term of abuse first coined in 1650 by a magistrate in Derby whom Fox claimed ought 'to tremble at the Word of the Lord'. Before the end of the eighteenth century, when the term Society of Friends first appears, the Quakers seem to have simply referred to themselves as 'Children of the Light'. Believers rejected ordained ministers, regarding them as paid hirelings and not men of faith, and organised services which favoured an informal structure. Meetings consisted of spontaneous prayer mixed with periods of silence and individual exhortation. The requirements of a Quaker Meeting House were therefore very simple. Unlike a chapel or church, where the focus of attention was the pulpit or chancel, speaking was encouraged from all parts of the floor so that an uncluttered and acoustically clear open space was required. Nowhere can this be better seen than at the Blue Idol Meeting House near Coolham (W).

The strange name probably refers to the period between 1793 and 1869 when the meeting house was not in use (idle) and apparently painted blue. Originally a sixteenth-century farmhouse, one end of the timber-framed structure was converted in 1691 by the removal of partitions and floors to create an empty interior whilst retaining an adjacent first floor room as a gallery. The plain, whitewashed walls and ceiling, the unpolished deal panelling and the absence of any form of decoration or embellishment creates a very simple and moving interior. The only fitting breaking this austerity is the so-called 'minister's stand', a slightly raised platform set aside for the elders, and just in front of it a simple table and bible box. There was probably no form of heating since it was generally felt that this was 'detrimental to both devotional feeling and to animal respiration' and 'conducive to unseemly somnolence to those sleeping near'. Later in the nineteenth century opinions softened and stoves appeared; a heating pipe is certainly visible in the earliest photograph of Blue Idol which dates from 1882. The women often met in a separate adjoining room and the dividing partition can still be seen at the meeting house at Ifield (W, erected in 1676). The only evidence of this at Blue Idol is an apparently blocked opening behind the minister's stand. Initially Quakers were refused burial in churchyards and so they often set aside small enclosures for their own use. Individual burials were often unmarked since throughout the eighteenth century and beginning of the nineteenth century many Quakers rejected displays of personal ostentation. There are two small burial grounds associated with Blue Idol, one adjacent to the meeting house, and another about a quarter of a mile away. The headstones are simple and plain, usually recording no more than the name and dates of birth and death.

In March 1655 the first three Quaker missionaries were met with both mockery and violence when they spoke in Horsham market place. Despite this, converts were readily obtained and following a tour of the county by George Fox, a number of regular meeting places were established, the first being in the house of Richard Bax in Ifield. By 1668 regular meeting places (i.e. safe private houses and farm buildings, not purpose-built meeting houses) existed in Chichester, Arundel, Steyning, Wiston, Shipley, East Grinstead, Ifield, Horsham, Lewes, Blatchington, Rottingdean, Warbleton and Alfriston. The first reference to a meeting at Blue Idol is in 1682 when a monthly meeting is held in the house of John Shawes, attended by (amongst others) the most famous Quaker associated with Sussex, William Penn, who lived at Warminghurst for fifteen years before emigrating to America. Penn was described in the court records as 'a factious and seditious person [who] doth frequently entertain and Keepe unlawfull assemblye and conventicle in his dwelling house at Warminghurst' attracting, it was claimed, between one and two hundred people. The early success of the Quakers was achieved by an active missionary zeal which gained them few friends amongst rival dissenting groups. The leading Baptist in the county, Matthew Caffyn Senior of Horsham, was a particularly vehement opponent, publishing in 1656 a scathing attack entitled *The Deceived and Deceiving Quakers Discovered.* On one particular occasion he and George Fox confronted one another in Nuthurst parish in what must have been a memorable encounter between these two larger-than-life characters.

Records of Quaker meetings and the persecution and vilification they often

HEATHFIELD, CADE STREET CHAPEL (E)

suffered survive from the seventeenth century. It is perhaps difficult today to understand the ill-feeling raised by the Friends, but the archetypical nineteenth and twentieth-century Quaker – honest and faithful, a non-violent pillar of society – was not an image held by contemporaries in the seventeenth century who saw a socially disruptive group who refused to swear oaths, rejected the payment of tithes (dismissed as 'steeple-house rates') and who interrupted the parish priest to question or verbally assault him. Such tactics invariably led to arrest, fines and ultimately prison, as in the case of one of the original missionaries, Thomas Lawcock, who was jailed in 1655 after he accosted the Horsham minister, John Chatfield 'before he was come out of the pulpit and poynting to him sayd Thou lyor and that he was a ravening wolfe in sheepes cloathing'. In Ifield church in 1658 Thomas Patching stood on a pew and, according to the minister's servant, 'delivered with an audible voyce a greate deale of nonscence, concerninge a newe light as he sayd he would hold out to them'. In Lewes such evangelical zeal created ill-feeling amongst the local populace and violent intimidation was frequently the result. When the Quaker John Pellet had the temerity to tell the magistrates in the course of his trial that 'he was not convinced of any ill-behaviour that he had committed' a mob hauled him from the court and dragged him off to the house of correction. Quaker services were interrupted on occasions by armed mobs and water, dirt, fire and cow dung was liable to be thrown into their meetings.

Although the Toleration Act brought the Quakers freedom of worship and the legal ending of compulsory church attendance, the payment of tithes remained and the resulting confiscation of property and goods in lieu of non-payment often saw the removal of goods worth substantially more than the fine. In May 1718/19 Elias Ellis of the Cliffe, Lewes, upon refusing a tithe demand of £1.12s. lost five pewter dishes and a copper pot subsequently sold for £7.11s.3d. In 1670 Ambrose Galloway was refused 8s. payment owed to him by the Minister of All Hallows for two waistcoats as Galloway owed 2s.8d. in tithes.

In Sussex the Quakers never really developed from these strong beginnings and once the era of missionary zeal and the penal laws passed they faced a long period of retrenchment with stagnant, even declining, membership. By 1751 there were only five families attending the meeting at Blue Idol and by 1786 this had fallen to only ten people. The following year closure was discussed and in 1793 regular meetings ceased, not to be revived until 1869. Like many dissenting groups it came to be maintained by intermarriage amongst a small group of families, Quakers being more likely to be born into a Quaker family than converted. As the emphasis on hard work, thrift and honesty led to worldly success so the Quakers came to be accepted as respectable pillars of the community and the Society of Friends developed as a passive, contemplative religion, untouched by the eighteenth-century evangelical revival, its members tolerated by a state more concerned with social order than with religious controversy.

A similar pattern of decline can be traced in almost all of the denominations of Old Dissent in the first half of the eighteenth century. Some, like the General Baptists, fared rather better, since they used ordained laymen rather than full-time ministers and therefore did not require the payment of a stipend impoverished chapel-attenders could ill afford.

In the country as a whole the second half of the eighteenth century saw a revival in Non-Conformist fortunes based on the New Dissent of Evangelical Methodism. In Sussex the revival was due less to John and Charles Wesley than to the Calvinist Methodism of George Whitefield which was expounded most successfully by George Gilbert of Heathfield and Selina, Countess of Huntingdon. Methodism was never as strong in eighteenth-century Sussex as it was in many other counties. The Sussex Circuit in 1767 boasted only 176 members in contrast with that of Cornwall which had over two thousand. Caplan has argued that this can be explained by the 'unbroken front of open hostility or cold indifference' presented by the Anglican clergy in Sussex which sharply contrasted with many other areas of England. The Countess of Huntingdon first came to Brighton in 1755 searching for a cure for her ailing younger son. Following his death she was converted to Methodism and in 1760 invited Whitefield to preach in Brighton and a chapel opened in 1761. This was the first of a number of churches of 'Lady Huntingdon's Connexion' built around the country. In Sussex others followed at Ote Hall, Chichester, Lewes, and Petworth, whilst the North Street Chapel in Brighton went through several phases of rebuilding, culminating in a Gothic church in 1871, which was demolished in 1968. The development of the Sussex seaside resorts provided a ready congregation for a variety of dissenting causes. Rapidly growing populations, substantial numbers of wealthy visitors able to indulge their religious whims and a socially dislocated population outgrowing the provision of places of worship provided the ideal conditions for the spread of Non-Conformity.

Other sects achieved a short-lived success during the nineteenth century. The Bible Christians established themselves around Chichester in the 1830s and are of interest as a number of their early preachers were women, including Mary Toms, who first brought the Word into Sussex. A typical example of one of their chapels can be seen in Selsey, where the brick and flint building erected in 1867 is now a Methodist Chapel. At the end of the eighteenth century the Unitarians (who disavow the existence of the Trinity) were emerging as a force in their own right, to a large extent replacing the English Presbyterian tradition and incorporating many former General Baptist congregations (the latter tended to split between the Unitarians and the Calvinist Strict Baptists). The 1813 Trinity Act legalised Unitarian belief and their chapels can be architecturally impressive, none more so than the Unitarian Church in New Road, Brighton, designed in 1820 by Amon Henry Wilds with a Greek Revival façade based upon the Thesaeum in Athens.

By the middle of the Victorian age worshippers were faced with a bewildering array of chapels from which to select. In Lewes alone there were dissenting congregations representing both the Wesleyan and Primitive Methodists, Presbyterians, Congregationalists, Baptists, Unitarians and Quakers as well as three Independent Chapels. In isolated rural areas small local sects are often found. A good example of these 'rural peculiars' is the Society of Dependents, or 'Cokelers' as they were known. Centred on Loxwood in the north of the county, Roger Homan has shown that they were founded by John Sirgood, a Gloucestershire bootmaker who entered the area in 1850. The first chapel was built eleven years later and although no longer used by them, it still stands in Spy Lane, Loxwood (W). Other chapels followed at Lord's Hill, North Chapel, Plaistow, Warnham and as far afield as Chichester, Hove and even South London. Never numerous, by Sirgood's death in 1885 there were some two thousand Dependents. Predominantly working class, the men worked on the land and the women were in domestic service. The sect had strong Calvinist beliefs and came to operate its own village stores (at least partly to provide work for its members) and followed a strict moral code that rejected listening to any secular music or reading any published work other than the Bible. The 'Cokelers' did not play games, smoke or drink and were confirmed pacifists. Like many other dissenting sects they believed that theirs was the true religion; as one Dependent said in 1905 'We are the holiest people in the world'. Their services were simple affairs with their own hymns sung unaccompanied by any instrument. A Bible-reading from the platform was followed by those present commenting on the passage and quoting personal experiences, in between which hymns would be sung. The services closed with a spontaneous prayer, for the Dependents did not use the Lord's Prayer. As one stated in 1947 'We close our meeting with a prayer from the heart, not one written from a book'.

During the reign of Queen Victoria the growing confidence of Non-Conformists as they became increasingly accepted is reflected in the architecture of their chapels. Their places of worship were no longer discreet back street chapels but prominent High Street edifices designed in the latest architectural fashions. The Southgate Methodist Chapel in Chichester (now demolished), was built in 1876 in an Italianate style, and five years later a Renaissance design was adopted by Thomas Elworthy in the Congregational–Methodist Chapel in Robertsbridge (E). It was, however, the Gothic Revival which came to dominate both church and chapel architecture. It was adopted, for example, by the Eastbourne Congregationalists in 1882 and by the Eastbourne Baptists at Ceylon Place four years later. In Brighton the Dials Congregational Chapel with its 130-foot tower (erected in 1870 and demolished 1972), symbolised the new-found confidence of Non-Conformity. Examples of late classicism can be seen, as at Burgess Hill (E) where the Congregational Chapel of 1881 was built with a Tuscan portico, but many previously classical chapels were rebuilt according to the precepts of the Gothic Revival such as the Countess of Huntingdon Chapel in Brighton of 1871. Many of the later Victorian chapels incorporated schoolrooms or church halls such as the Methodists at Dorset Gardens in Brighton (D. Elleray, *The Victorian Churches of Sussex*). In rural areas where money was scarce and congregations were smaller, chapels continued to be more domestic in scale. The most attractive are in the Weald, timber-framed and either weather boarded or tile hung like the two disused chapels near Wadhurst, at Shover's Green and the 'Rehobeth' at Pell Green (1824) (E).

Internally early nineteenth-century churches and chapels were often virtually

PELL GREEN, REHOBETH CHAPEL (E): A typical Wealden chapel, attractively weather-boarded and shuttered

indistinguishable, as can be seen by comparing the Calvinist Independent Jireh Chapel in Lewes (built in 1805) with the low Anglican St. John's Church in Chichester erected some seven years later. Both have simple exteriors with galleried interiors. The pulpit dominates both church and chapel; at Jireh a suspended octagonal pulpit entered from the first-floor minister's gallery, whilst at St. John's a towering three-decker shields the small railed sanctuary. The Jireh Chapel is a particularly important unspoilt example of nineteenth-century chapel architecture. Erected by the supporters of the Reverend Jenkin Jenkins following his expulsion from the Cliffe Chapel, it was enlarged in 1827. Timber-framed, the walls are clad with mathematical tiles to give the impression of brickwork but at considerably lower cost. The barrel-vaulted and galleried interior has hat pegs on whitewashed walls. Below the dominating pulpit is the clerk's desk and railed communion area from where the chapel clerk led the singing, setting the note with the still surviving pitchpipe and then 'lining-out' the hymns, two lines at a time. Behind the pulpit, shutters give access to a large ground-floor vestry above which two smaller rooms serve as vestries for the deacons and minister respectively.

Non-Conformists were always in a minority in Sussex; Caplan estimates that they never formed more than ten or eleven per cent of the population, although this obviously disguises great local variations. The Compton Religious Census of 1676 lists 2,452 Non-Conformists across the county, but the strongholds were clearly the towns and particularly Rye where Anglicans and Dissenters were divided in roughly equal proportions. Otherwise the figures illustrate the stronger hold dissent held on the east of the county, where over eighty per cent of the parishes had a Non-Conformist presence as against only fifty-four per cent in the west. Similarly, two-thirds of the 1662 ejections occurred in East Sussex and the variations between the two parts of the county were maintained into the nineteenth century, for in 1829 two-thirds of the Non-Conformist places of worship listed lay in the eastern half of the county. Within West Sussex dissent was stronger in the urban centres like Chichester and Arundel and in the isolated north-west.

The relative strength of Non-Conformity was strongly influenced by local factors of settlement, economy, social structure and topography. Dissent was likely to succeed where the Church of England was weak and so it was more liable to be found in parishes with a loose manorial structure and a scattered pattern of settlement spread over a large parish. A social structure of small freeholders had a greater degree of economic independence upon which to base their religious freedom than those living in small nucleated villages and relying for their livelihoods upon a single dominant landowner. This was likely to be the case in the Downland villages which were reliant on a system of sheep and corn husbandry utilising a small workforce of unmarried living-in labourers and cottagers who had few opportunities for by-employment to supplement their existence and enhance their independence. Here the rector was better able to supervise his flock. The 1664–5 Hearth Tax returns show that these were not heavily populated parishes, Aldrington had only three hearths, Ovingdean one and Lullington only five. It was this sparsity of population that led the Established Church to unite benefices in order to raise an adequate stipend for the vicar. This occurred in 1657 when Ovingdean was joined to Brighton and other examples include Ford and Climping, Tortington and Arundel and Tangmere and Boxgrove. On the Downland village populations were liable to be kept low by a dominant landlord concerned with excluding undesirable elements – the itinerant, the unemployed, the single parent and the poor. It is significant that of the parishes applying for licenses to build poorhouses in the seventeenth century, almost all were in the Weald, with only one (Iford) on the Downs following suit. Arthur Young's description of Glynde could equally well apply to many of the Downland parishes: 'We have no tradesmen or artificers but what are connected with and dependant on agriculture, as carpenters, wheelwrights, blacksmiths, bricklayers etc.'.

West Firle, for instance, had less than half the acreage of Wealden parishes like Burwash and Buxted. The Downland was never fertile ground for Non-Conformity and attempts by groups like the aptly named 'Society for Spreading the Light of the Gospel in the Dark Towns and Villages of Sussex', to evangelise the area in the early nineteenth century met with little success. The Sussex Missionary Society, established in Brighton in 1809, largely failed in its attempts to appoint home missionaries and lay preachers and to establish preaching stations on the Downs, although it was rather more successful in encouraging the erection of new chapels by giving enabling grants, as with the chapel at Lindfield in 1813.

By contrast the larger Wealden parishes were both more populous and had complex social structures with individual freeholders sustained by a range of work which included weaving, tanning, pottery and iron working. For instance, Forest Fold Baptist Chapel, founded in 1832 by George Doggott a Withyham farmer, was in an area of independent charcoal burners and iron ore diggers. William Cobbett succinctly summarised the difference between the Weald and the Downs when describing the area between Worth and Tunbridge Wells: 'The labouring people look pretty well. They have pigs. They invariably do best in the woodland and forest, and wild countries. Where the mighty grasper has all under his eye, they can get little'. It was in the wastes and commons of the Weald that illicit cottage-building could take place on isolated sites near parish boundaries where parochial and manorial authority was invariably weak and religious freedom was more likely to gain root. The authorities at Slaugham reported in 1638 'Some of the poore of St. Leonards Forest resort to our church' rather than attend their parish church which was nearly ten miles distant.

CHICHESTER, PROVIDENCE CHAPEL (W): The chapel and minister's house (visible at the rear) were erected in 1809. The brick wall has now been replaced by iron railings

Such a settlement of squatters was Punnett's Town which grew up on part of 4,000 acres of heathland on the borders of Heathfield parish in the late eighteenth century. A Non-Conformist chapel was first erected here by George Gilbert in 1767, replaced by the present Cade Street Chapel in 1809. Non-Conformity flourished in market towns like Lewes, Ditchling, Cuckfield and East Grinstead which were natural meeting places at the centre of established trading and communication networks, amenable to new ideas and where the population was sufficient to support a meeting and the social structure allowed a greater degree of economic and religious freedom. Non-Conformity does not have to exist in any parish meeting these criteria, but they provided the conditions for it to flourish. Whether it did or not depended upon the dedication of the dissenters and ministers concerned.

That dissenters tended to come from the ranks of the small tradesmen and craftsmen was recognised by contemporaries and visible evidence of the trading activities of many of the Quakers of Lewes can be found in the surviving seventeenth-century trade tokens for families like Akehurst and Galloway. Chapel members set themselves apart from what they perceived as a hostile world. Any single village was likely to include only a few dissenters and so rural chapels drew their membership from over a wide area across parish and county boundaries. The Ditchling Chapel minute books list members from as far afield as Billingshurst, Balcombe, Ringmer, Henfield, Cuckfield, Lindfield, Falmer, Battle, Clayton, Wivelsfield, Southover, Lewes and Chiddingly. It was normal to travel long distances to a meeting and service times altered with the seasons to allow the brethren to return in daylight and packed lunches were brought to eat between morning and afternoon meetings.

Individual believers were inclined to be isolated from many of the social activities of their local communities. Such isolation was a constant weakener of religious faith, particularly among the elderly and infirm who were unable to travel to meetings. Much Non-Conformist belief only served to reinforce doubts in the individual about his or her worthiness. Spiritual diaries like those by James Nye or the letters of John Burgess are a catalogue of niggling self-doubt and reassessment. The Non-Conformist path to spiritual fulfilment was never easy. The chapel brethren provided a separate structure of support and recreation to that offered by the parish authorities and denied to the believers. To keep members on the path of righteousness the chapels regulated the lives of their members. Centres for the Temperance Movement, the chapels were also hostile to gambling and maintained strict sexual morals. The Ditchling minute books reveal the case of John Vincent, expelled from chapel membership in 1757: 'whereas he had been admonished several times and has promised a reformation and still remains in a careless way, and seldom goes to any hearing of a Sunday, and follows gaming and keeping bad company and breaks his promises in regard to making good his payment, therefore we agree to withdraw him for such disorderly walking'. The chapel attenders were also active educators who sought to improve their lot by means of adult classes, Sunday schools, chapel libraries, debating societies, choirs and orchestras. Examples of these and the clothing clubs, sewing classes, benevolent societies, soup kitchens provided in hard times and teas given for children at Christmas can be found in most chapel records.

Links across the religious divide were always present: the graveyard of the parish church at Twineham was partly given over to a Quaker burial ground between 1694 to 1732 as a result of the vicar's daughter marrying a Quaker. By the eighteenth century Non-Conformists were playing an important and accepted rôle in their communities whether it was the Quaker trading community of the Cliffe, Lewes, or some form of public service such as was actively encouraged by the Unitarians, who regarded service to the community as an active part of their religious commitment. Benjamin Potter and John Agate were both trustees of the Horsham meeting house and yet served as overseers of the poor for the parish of Warnham in 1778–9 and 1780–1.

Today as redundant chapels increasingly face the threat of demolition or inappropriate conversion it is surely time to take note of our Non-Conformist heritage. The chapels were above all buildings intended for worship, and perhaps the final word should be this charming nineteenth-century description of the chapel at Billingshurst: 'A delightful plain rural chapel, with the men and women sitting on different sides, the deacons crouching around a table at front of the pulpit, the singers in the gallery, the hymns introduced by the wail of a pitchpipe'.

J.R.

Six

CHURCHES AND CHURCH ARCHITECTURE *c.* 1600–1900

THE seventeenth and eighteenth centuries were a fallow period as far as church building in Sussex is concerned. The distribution of parishes was found to be adequate and church building consisted of repairs and renewals of existing structures. New churches were only erected when existing buildings had become ruinous. Egdean (W) was rebuilt in 1622 in a Tudor Gothic style of which little remains following the nineteenth-century restoration. South Malling (E) was substantially altered in 1626–8; one of the foundation stones was laid by the diarist John Evelyn. Ford (W) benefited from the addition of a brick porch in 1637. Much more important was the rebuilding of Ashburnham (E) between 1665–67 in a style which has been christened 'Gothic Survival'. The nave and chancel were rebuilt on 'a noble scale and in the ancient style' at the expense of John Ashburnham (1603–71), Groom of the Bedchamber to Charles I. The window tracery in the nave looks authentically medieval at a distance, but the mullions are made of oak. The interior contains virtually all its late Stuart fittings including the pulpit, west gallery, font and cover, and locally made wrought iron screens to the tower, chancel and chapels. The box pews survive in a mutilated state, having been cut down in 1893. Around the altar is a three-sided communion rail which was probably added in the 1680s (see p. 101). On the south wall is a remarkable reredos dated 1676 which formerly hung behind the altar. It consists of painted panels of Moses and Aaron flanking the Ten Commandments which are taken not from the 1611 Authorised Version of the Bible but an earlier translation. Since Moses was the human agent of God's law he was thought to be a suitable adjunct to the Decalogue; his brother Aaron was a natural companion figure. South of the chancel is the former Ashburnham family pew, a rare survival, although its former function is disguised by the fact that the opening from the pew to the chancel has been filled in to create a room. In 1968 it was reported that within living memory a footman was placed in the chancel beneath the pew to inform the vicar when the Ashburnham family was ready for the service to start (*Sussex Life,* July 1968).

Other seventeenth-century alterations worth recording include the tower added to Stedham (W) in 1673 and the more substantial rebuilding of Withyham (E) between 1663–72 after the church had been 'burnt down by a tempest of thunder and lightning'. The rebuilding followed traditional Gothic forms.

The eighteenth century has little more to offer. Churches continued to be repaired and, in the contemporary term, 'beautified'. Under the terms of Canon 85 of the 1604 *Canons Ecclesiastical of the Church of England* the churchwardens were

ASHBURNHAM (E): View of the north side

responsible for the maintenance of the fabric of the nave while the chancel remained the responsibility of the rector. This codified a well-established tradition going back to the medieval period. Warminghurst (W) escaped restoration in the nineteenth century and survives to show the type of repairs undertaken. Bishop Bower's Visitation of 1724 reported: 'Church in extraordinarily good repair by the Expence of James Butler Esq.'. It was probably Butler who paid for the heads of the lancet windows to be rebuilt in brick and made semi-circular and for the west window to be blocked and replaced. A triple arched screen with the painted Arms of Queen Anne on the tympanum was inserted to separate nave from chancel; Rusper (W) had a similar screen before about 1855 and Racton (W) still possesses one. The other fittings at Warminghurst were added in about 1770. At Itchingfield (W) the 1724 Visitation remarked: 'Chancel better in repair than ordinary at the Expence of Mr. Hay. Chancel rebuilt'. It is interesting to note that the twelfth-century windows were re-used. Brightling (E) still has a 1749 porch with typical quatrefoil decoration, and the chancel at Laughton (E) was rebuilt in about 1760. However, most repairs and additions made in the eighteenth century were swept away during the great wave of church restorations in the next century.

Only four surviving churches were completely rebuilt in the eighteenth century: Crowborough (1744), St. Pancras, Chichester (1750), Glynde (1763–5), and East Grinstead (1789–1813). Crowborough (E) was enlarged out of recognition in 1881–3; only the tower remains untouched. St. Pancras (W) was built in a rustic 'Gothick' style by William Ryde, surveyor to the Duke of Richmond; it was mercilessly restored by G. M. Hills in 1868. East Grinstead (E) was rebuilt by James Wyatt after the tower of the previous church had collapsed into the nave in 1785. The tower of the new church was designed by J. T. Groves in 1811 and executed after Groves's death by H. W. and W. Inwood. Wyatt's church is in a minimal Perpendicular Gothic style but with wheel windows in the clerestory; the south side of the nave incorporates a few piers from the earlier church. Before its restoration by J. M. Hooker in 1874 the church had high box pews and the liturgical emphasis was on the

CHICHESTER, St. JOHN (W): Interior looking east

pulpit. It is, however, notable as a good Sussex example of consciously revived Gothic.

Glynde is the most important church built in the county in the eighteenth century. The old church was pulled down in 1763 and its replacement was paid for by Richard Trevor, Bishop of Durham, the owner of Glynde place. Trevor's architect was Sir Thomas Robinson, an accomplished amateur who may also have built the stable block of Glynde Place. The design was executed by John Morris, a Lewes architect and stonemason. The plan of this classical church is similar to that used by Inigo Jones in 1623 for the Queen's chapel at St. James's Palace, Westminster and it departs radically from any medieval prototypes. It is a single oblong room with no separation between nave and chancel. In a letter dated 12 July 1763 Bishop Trevor's agent wrote to the Patrons of the Benefice, the Dean and Chapter of Windsor, that the church was to be without 'any formal chancel to it'. There is a Venetian window at the east end, a pedimented west end containing the Bishop's Arms (which cost £26), and a projecting pedimented porch. It is the first example in Sussex of a new church built entirely on the auditory principle, that is, with the emphasis on the pulpit rather than the altar. Sir Christopher Wren explained the planning of many eighteenth-century churches in a letter written in 1708: 'it is enough if they (the Roman Catholics) hear the murmur of the Mass and see the elevation of the Host, but ours are to be fitted for Auditories'. Glynde perfectly exemplifies this Protestant plan with the pulpit raised above the high box pews. The church was built for a reasoned, unmystical religion nicely summed-up by T. W. Horsfield's remarks in his *History of Sussex* (1835): 'The interior is exquisitely neat . . . every part of the edifice is alike distinguished by an elegant simplicity, which affords a striking contrast to the barbaric gloom . . . which characterises the great majority of Sussex churches'.

St. Mary's, Glynde, resembles a private chapel rather than a parish church. Stansted chapel (W) was indeed a private chapel but it deserves mention as one of the most delightful Regency Gothic buildings in Sussex. The chapel, formed from remains of the late Tudor Stansted House, was constructed in 1812 at the behest of Lewis Way (1772–1840) whose mission was to convert the Jews to Christianity. Towers, battlements, pinnacles, 'Gothick' windows and plaster vaults combine to form a remarkably playful example of this architectural style. The extraordinary stained glass is discussed on p. 94.

By the early years of the nineteenth century additional churches, especially in the larger towns, were increasingly necessary. An expanding population, the Evangelical Revival within the Church of England, the competition of the dissenters, and the fear of atheism and revolution following the end of the Napoleonic wars in 1815 gave rise to an unprecedented wave of church building. In 1818 the Church Building Act was passed; this set aside £1,000,000 to be allocated by specially appointed Commissioners empowered to make grants. In 1824 there was a further grant of £500,000. St. Peter's church, Brighton (E), was partly financed by the Commissioners. Money was also dispensed from donations made to the Incorporated Society for Promoting the Enlargement, Building, and Repair of Churches and Chapels. In Sussex the Chichester Diocesan Association, founded in 1838 to build and improve churches, spent £88,000 between 1838 and 1881 (W. R. W. Stephens, *The South Saxon Diocese,* 1881).

A further method of raising money for churches was particularly prevalent in the coastal towns of Sussex. This was the proprietary system by which pews or 'sittings' were allocated according to the number of shares in the new building bought by each shareholder or 'proprietor'. The pews then became the property of the shareholder and could, if wished, be rented or sold. In addition, sufficient pews were set aside to produce an annual pew rent to provide an income for the curate and clerk. An admission charge of one shilling was levied on visitors who did not buy or rent a pew. The diocese was involved only in approving the proposed incumbent and the site on which the church was to be built; a sufficient number of seats also had to be set aside for the use of the poor. A private Act of Parliament usually had to be passed to enable building to proceed.

The architectural results of this system depended to some extent on the amount of money initially raised. The promoters of St. John's chapel (later church) in Chichester (W) employed James Elmes (1782–1862) as architect in 1812. He designed a Greek Revival building on an octagonal plan. Significantly, the Nonconformists, and in particular John Wesley, favoured octagonally planned chapels; the earliest is the Octagon chapel in Norwich (1754) built by Thomas Ivory for the Presbyterians. It is typical of church building of the time that no distinction was made between an Anglican church and a dissenting chapel. The interior of St. John's represents a unique survival of a type of plan common in the early nineteenth century but now rare. A massive three-decker pulpit is placed immediately in front of the altar; galleries are ranged on four sides. The pews in the galleries and aisles were privately appropriated and on the ground floor the free seats for the poor were separated from those for which rent was charged. Out of a total of 622 seats 250 were free. The plan is that of an auditory church; the altar is reduced to insignificance.

The auditory principle dominated both proprietary chapels and churches built at this time. Many of these were later given parishes and put under the control of the diocese. St. Paul's church, Worthing (W), was built as a proprietary chapel by J. B. Rebecca in 1812. Like St. John's, Chichester, it is Greek Revival with a tetrastyle

HASTINGS, St. MARY-IN-THE-CASTLE (E): Watercolour by W. H. Brooke

(i.e. four-columned) Tuscan portico. The original auditory interior was altered in 1893. In the same style is St. Mary-in-the-Castle, Hastings (E), built in 1824–28 by Joseph Kay for the Earl of Chichester. The Greek Ionic portico dominates Pelham Crescent whilst the interior, with its D-shaped auditorium, resembles a theatre rather than a church. The altar is behind the portico. Particularly remarkable was the baptistry where, in addition to the normal font, a tank, fed by a natural spring, was provided for total immersion. No less than six proprietary chapels were built in Brighton (E), the fastest growing resort town. All were built in the classical style on an auditory plan. St. George's, Kemp Town, is the best surviving example,

By the 1840s, however, both the style and methods of financing such churches began to seem improper, even immoral. The arch-theorist of the Gothic Revival, A. W. N. Pugin (see p. 69) wrote of them in vitriolic terms in *The Present State of Ecclesiastical Architecture in England* (1843): 'Churches are now built on exactly the same principle as theatres . . . and the only difference . . . is the substitution of an altar for the proscenium and drop-scene . . . they are filled and emptied like dissenting meeting houses. The worshipper is either in a mob, or in the odious and Protestant distinction of a private pew'. The Cambridge Camden Society's periodical, the *Ecclesiologist,* satirised the internal arrangements of a 'Proprietary chapel in a Fashionable Watering Place' (almost certainly Brighton) in 1845. The reading desk and pulpit were fastened to the wall with no visible support: 'should the preacher be weighty in person, and vehement in action, he will in falling cause these deformities to break from their moorings'. Twin pulpits became something of a Brighton speciality; none now survives but they were formerly in the churches of St. Mary, St. John, St. Stephen, and St. Andrew's, Hove.

The churches built by the Anglican Establishment after 1818 tended to be Gothic because the style was associated with churches but mostly because it was usually cheap. The Commissioners appointed to administer the Church Building Act advised Gothic because expensive stone was usually necessary for a classical church. The churches built were designed to accommodate 'the greatest number of persons at the smallest expense within the compass of an ordinary voice'; like the proprietary chapels, they were to be preaching houses. St. Peter's church, Brighton (1824–28) is a particularly striking example of an early Gothic Revival Commissioners' church. Designed by Charles Barry, the church is unusual in several respects. It was expensive (£20,365) partly because it was built of Portland stone and partly because Barry designed an ambitious tower to provide a grand termination to the north end of the Steyne. A spire was projected but never built. The lower part of the tower walls are encased with a buttressed screen with flying buttresses at the corners. This enabled Barry to provide three enormously high entrances which otherwise would have rendered the structure unstable. The tower contrasts tellingly with the thinly detailed west towers of other Commissioners' churches, for instance, Lewis Vulliamy's St. Bartholomew's, Sydenham, London (1827–32). The Perpendicular Gothic details of the church are used in a way no medieval architect would have countenanced. In later life Barry himself, according to his son, 'felt dissatisfied with the faults of detail and the mixture of styles'. The interior was much less inventive than the exterior; it followed the normal auditory plan tricked out with Gothic detail. There were north, south, and west galleries, a pair of pulpits, one for the service and one for the sermon, and no distinct chancel but a small apsidal projection containing

GLYNDE (E): The west front

BRIGHTON, St. PETER (E): Watercolour by Delamotte showing Barry's original apse. Note the twin pulpits

an altar table. The Commissioners gave a grant of £5,000 and a loan of £15,000 towards the cost of St. Peter's; rented pews went some way towards repaying the loan but there were 1,100 free seats, later reduced to 900. In 1898–1906 Barry's apse was demolished when a new chancel was built by Somers Clarke and J. T. Micklethwaite.

The decorative possibilities of Perpendicular Gothic were also exploited at Frant church (E), rebuilt in 1819–22 by John Montier, a builder and architect from Tunbridge Wells. Montier used cast iron tracery and cast iron piers, materials that were to be condemned by Pugin and the Ecclesiologists because they were cheap and had no medieval precedent. Internally, Montier's Perpendicular detail is remarkably accurate for its date, however. The original pulpit, now destroyed, stood in the middle of the church in front of the sanctuary.

By the 1840s the influence of the Oxford Movement, the Cambridge Camden Society (from 1845 the Ecclesiological Society), and the writings of A. W. N. Pugin changed the whole character of church building (see p. 69). Gothic was no longer just one of many available styles, it was the *only* style suitable for churches. Perpendicular and Early English or 'lancet' Gothic was the favoured style of the Commissioners, but Pugin and the Ecclesiologists favoured 'Middle Pointed' or Decorated. In 1843 J. M. Neale and B. Webb wrote an introduction to William Durandus's *The Symbolism of Churches and Church Ornaments*. Here it was stated that the architect must not only have 'a more elevated and directly religious habit of mind', but he 'must design in one style and one style only', late thirteenth and early fourteenth-century Gothic. Ideally he should be 'a single pious and laborious artist alone, pondering deeply over his duty to do his upmost for the service of God's Holy Religion'. Above all, 'every church of whatever kind, size, or shape, should have a . . . chancel *at least* one third of the length of the Nave'. As chancels were only employed for Communion and the marriage service a use had to be found for them, however. The answer was provided for the Ecclesiologists by Walter Hook, Rector of Leeds and later Dean of Chichester, who in 1841 introduced a cathedral form of choral service and placed a choir of laymen in the chancel of St. Peter's, Leeds. Hook took advice from John Jebb, canon of Hereford, though Jebb would have objected to the later practice of having female choristers as 'inconsistent with that retiring, dependent, and domestic character so proper to all Christian women'. So churches should have deep chancels filled with a lay choir, they should be built in Decorated Gothic, and (*Ecclesiologist,* 1841) 'the most important requisite in erecting a church is that it be built in such a way that the Rubricks and Canons of the Church of England may be Consistently observed, and the Sacraments rubrically and decently administered'. In a pamphlet on *Church Enlargement and Church Arrangement* (1843), Neale pictured his ideal church as one in which every window was filled with stained glass, the floor was covered with encaustic tiles, and the roodscreen, walls and roof were all painted and frescoed.

The Ecclesiologists found much to object to and little to praise in the early Gothic Revival churches in Sussex. The first Gothic Revival church in Worthing (W), Christ Church (1840–43), was built by John Elliot of Chichester in an Early English style. The *Ecclesiologist* commented in 1842: 'the whole is of the most lean and hungry description, and much more nearly resembles a railroad station than a church'. Elliott had contracted to build the church for £3,000 but the alterations made after the Camden Society's criticisms cost so much that he went bankrupt. It is a notable example of the almost tyrannical authority wielded by the Society.

In Brighton, however, the Society found a church it could praise almost unreservedly: St. Paul's, West Street (1846–48). The architect was Richard Cromwell Carpenter, one of the Camden Society's favourite church builders. The church is a sophisticated essay in the 'Middle Pointed' or Decorated Style, and was built, appropriately enough, on the site of a dissenters' chapel. It was erected for Arthur Wagner, son of Henry Wagner, vicar of Brighton, and was intended to minister to the poor fishermen then living in West Street. The Wagner family contributed £2,738 towards the total cost of £12,000.

Today St. Paul's is regarded as a 'typical' Victorian church, but, though some of its seats were still rented (460 out of 1,200), the type of building and the worship within it were a radical departure from that in the other churches we have been examining. The *Ecclesiologist* wrote in 1846: 'At last Brighton is to have its part in the revival of church architecture; and its hideous chapels are to be shamed by a real church'. The 'real church' was distinguished by an east window designed by Pugin, side windows containing stained glass figures of the Apostles, metalwork by Hardman of Birmingham (Pugin's favourite firm) and fittings designed by Carpenter. The *Ecclesiologist* could still find fault (in 1848) with seats which had doors, the pulpit on the wrong side of the chancel arch, and that the nave was of six bays, 'an unusual, and certainly an undesirable number'. Yet the Society knew that its principles had triumphed.

St. Paul's has introduced the Wagner family, the greatest patrons of church architecture that the nineteenth century produced. Henry Wagner was vicar of Brighton from 1824–70 and was responsible for the building of six new churches, only two of which survive (St. John's, Carlton Hill and St. Paul's). Wagner used local Brighton builders for all his churches except All Saints, Clifton Road (1852) and St. Paul's, both by R. C. Carpenter. The 'Middle Pointed' style of the latter two churches reflects the influence of Henry's son, Arthur Wagner (1824–1902), the famous High Church ritualist. Arthur Wagner probably knew the Camden Society when he was an undergraduate at Cambridge and he was certainly aware of their work and opinions.

Arthur Wagner's vision was a pre-Reformation ideal of a church as a mystical body infused by God's power; a priesthood raised to union with God through the sacraments. Worship should reflect these mysteries and at St. Paul's many of the so called 'Six Points' of ritual observance were practised: the eastward position for consecration of the Host, wafer bread, the mixed chalice (i.e. water and wine together), candles, vestments, and incense. The church became notorious for its 'advanced' services. Clergy wore vestments of the appropriate colour for the different seasons of the liturgical year and the *Brighton Gazette* reported in 1874 that the congregation bowed to the altar when entering or leaving and even made the sign of the Cross. Hostile placards proclaimed 'The Morning Opera' at St. Paul's, questions were asked in Parliament, and in 1867 Wagner was summoned to give evidence before a Royal Commission on ritual. During building work at one Brighton church, probably St. Paul's, one of the workmen declared: 'I publish the banns of matrimony between this church and the Church of Rome'. 'And I forbid the banns', replied another. 'On what grounds'. 'Cos the parties is too near akin' (P. Ferriday, 1964).

In spite of Henry Wagner's new churches the 1851 Religious Census revealed that in the south-east only two other places, Gravesend and Portsea, were worse off for church accommodation than Brighton. The existing Brighton churches could provide places for only 20.6 per cent of the people; this was due to exceptionally rapid population growth. At his own expense Arthur Wagner sought to remedy the situation by building four new churches: St. Mary Magdalene (1862), by G. F. Bodley, the Annunciation (1864), by William Dancy, a local surveyor, St. Bartholomew's (1872–74), by Edmund Scott, a local architect, and the Resurrection (1876–7), by R. H. Carpenter. St. Martin's (1872–75), by Somers Clarke, was jointly financed by Arthur Wagner and his half brothers. Wagner paid for one other church, St. Mary, Buxted (1885–6), by Edmund Scott and F. Cawthorn.

Of these churches St. Bartholomew's and St. Martin's are of national importance. St. Bartholomew's is an example of a minor architect inspired by the wealth and vision of his patron into designing one of the great churches of the nineteenth century, a grandiose statement of the faith of Arthur Wagner. Built of stock brick, the church is four feet higher than Westminster Abbey and probably the tallest parish church in England; John Betjeman once imagined the clergy entering on elephants. Somers Clarke suggested in a letter written to the *Architectural Review* in 1919 that both St. Bartholomew's and St. Martin's were influenced by a visit Wagner had made to Spain. Wagner admired vast Spanish reredoses (the east wall of St. Bartholomew's was left plain for a huge reredos), high windows, and thick walls. 'He was very appreciative of simplicity and dignity gained by height . . . (and) would sooner have a few feet more of height than all the little mouldings and marble pillars in the

BRIGHTON, St. PAUL (E): Lithograph of the interior looking towards the chancel

THE CHICHESTER EXTINGUISHER: Engraving from *Punch*, October 24, 1868. A satire on the ritual innovations of the Rev. James Purchas at St. James's Chapel, Brighton. The text reads: 'Go! Go! You insolent, rebellious boy. What with your nonsense and incense and candles you'll be setting the church on fire'

world.' The church owes little to precedent and in this reflects the eclecticism and more original treatment of medieval sources current from the 1850s. The overall height may have been inspired not only by Spanish Catalan architecture and the brick churches of James Brooks but also by the thirteenth-century Italian friars' churches. The strikingly stark interior was embellished by magnificent fittings designed by Henry Wilson between 1895 and 1908. The church was characterised by 'extreme' ritual from the beginning. There were no pews, but 1500 chairs (made by H. Nye of Brighton) similar to those in Continental Catholic churches. Vestments were used from 1874, the confessionals date from 1880, the Stations of the Cross were added in 1881, and the Sacrament was reserved from 1896. Wagner hoped that the solemn ritual of the services would attract the poor and the deprived for whom the church was built. A soup kitchen, school, blanket-lending club and carefully organised pastoral work also had this end in view.

St. Martin's was built by Somers Clarke at the same time as St. Bartholomew's as a memorial to Henry Wagner, who died in 1870. Like the latter church it is built of brick and the sheer scale of the building owes as much to Wagner as it does to the architect. The exterior of the church is in a severe Early English style characteristic of the reaction which took place in the 1860s to the prettiness of 'Middle Pointed'. The interior consists of chancel, nave, and aisles; the low chancel screen allows the vast interior space (173 feet long) to be seen to its maximum advantage. The most important of the extraordinary interior fittings were designed by Somers Clarke; these include the vast reredos, suggested by Arthur Wagner, the font and font canopy, and the pulpit, the base of which is inlaid with olive wood from the Mount of Olives. The roof is painted with seventy panels representing the expansion of the Anglican communion: Colonial sees are painted on one side, and American sees on the other. The church was the first in this country to be provided with a wood block parquet floor.

The most important of the Brighton churches not financed by Arthur Wagner is St. Michael and All Angels, and yet it has a Wagner connection because the church was built for the Rev. Charles Beanlands, one of Wagner's curates at St. Paul's. The original church was designed by G. F. Bodley in 1858 and built in 1860–62. Bodley was a pupil of Gilbert Scott but at St. Michael's he reacted against what he took to be Scott's smooth, mechanically produced detail to produce a church influenced by the High Victorian muscularity of G. E. Street and William Butterfield and the Gothic characteristic of northern Italy. Street advocated a departure from pure English Gothic and suggested a mixture of other medieval styles, most notably north Italian Gothic, a style also favoured by John Ruskin in *The Stones of Venice.* The Ecclesiological Society had also moved in this direction and in 1859 its journal the *Ecclesiologist* commented that 'the design . . . has pleased us much by its power and originality'. In 1896 Bodley, who had moved towards a revival of English Perpendicular, called his church a 'boyish, antagonistic effort . . . not believing in what one saw at Scott's one went in for a violent reaction'. The interior of Bodley's church is characterised by stark, almost primitive forms admirably set off by the stunning pre-Raphaelite stained glass (see p. 95). Into this setting Beanlands introduced some of the most ritualistic services in Brighton: vestments were in use from the start and sung masses by Mozart and Gounod were accompanied by kettle-drums. Vast congregations were attracted and, in order to accommodate them, Beanlands soon asked his friend, William Burges, to draw up plans which would eventually dwarf Bodley's church.

Burges's scheme dates from 1868 and involved building a vast new nave of cathedral proportions, a north aisle, vestries, north and south porches, a cloister, and a campanile or bell tower. Bodley's original church became the south aisle. Insufficient funds were forthcoming for such an elaborate scheme and when building began in 1893 the campanile and cloister had to be omitted. What was built is impressive enough, however. The nave is lined with stone and marble, the clerestory has double plate tracery, and to the west is a huge rose window. The style chosen was early thirteenth-century French Gothic. The critic Goodhart-Rendel wrote: 'Magnificent in conception and noble in size, the new church is . . . perhaps the finest of those few precious works that testify for all time to the genius of William Burges'.

Both Bodley and Burges designed other churches in Sussex. Bodley's St. Wilfred's, Haywards Heath (1863–5), is a minor work, however, and All Saints, Danehill (E), was designed in 1892 with his partner, Thomas Garner, in a conservative Decorated style. Burges designed a long demolished temporary mission hall for Arthur Wagner near St. Martin's church. The style was early French Gothic. In 1867–8 he built St. Michael's, Lowfield Heath (W); the church has been described by J. Mordaunt-Crook as 'a veritable anthology of Burgesian "dodges"'. The style is again based on thirteenth-century French Gothic.

Most of the great names in Victorian church architecture are represented in Sussex. G. E. Street's St. Saviour's, Eastbourne (1865–72), is in red brick and dominates its surroundings. Here Street emphasised the chancel by narrowing the building towards this focal point, a device he had learnt from his study of Spanish churches. St. Peter's, Hastings (E), by James Brooks, is an excellent example of the type of town church favoured by the Ecclesiologists in the 1860s. Built in a poor area,

BRIGHTON, St. BARTHOLOMEW (E): Engraving from the *Builder*, October 31, 1874

BRIGHTON, St. MICHAEL (E): The nave. Note the double-plate tracery in the clerestory

the church has a simple plan and clear uninterrupted spaces with the architectural elements reduced to basic geometry. J. L. Pearson is represented by St. Barnabus, Hove (1882–3), St. Matthew's, Hastings (1884–5) and All Saints, Hove (1889–1901). All Saints (E) is one of Pearson's finest churches. Built in Sussex sandstone in the Early English style, the church is constructed on a cathedral scale with the chancel differentiated by being built a little lower and narrower than the nave. It was Pearson's last church and cost £40,000. H. Goodhart-Rendel wrote that here Pearson 'gave of his best . . . the chancel is as nearly perfect as can be'. St. Matthew's (E) and St. Barnabus (E) were both what Pearson called his 'cheap churches'. St. Barnabus is in flint and red brick and cost £8,000 while St. Matthew's, which was built after the vicar had seen St. Barnabus, is of similar design. It cost £11,000. Both churches rely for their effect on simple geometrical forms largely devoid of ornament. Apart from his restorations Samuel Sanders Teulon built three new churches in Sussex: Holy Spirit, Rye harbour (1849–50), St. John's, Netherfield (1855), and Holy Trinity, Hastings (1857–62). All are characterised by Teulon's enjoyably eccentric mannerisms. He has become known as a 'rogue architect', the analogy being to a 'rogue elephant', because of his freedom from convention and lack of restraint. William Butterfield's St. Mary Magdalen, West Lavington (1849–50) was built for the incumbent, Henry Manning, who went over to Rome before he could hold services in it. It is a church of extraordinary vigour, but the *Ecclesiologist* (1849) detected heresy on the part of one of its favourite architects in his use of Perpendicular Gothic forms: 'We can enter into the temptation an architect must feel to depart from the beaten track in design: but we must anxiously watch any such departure. In this case we have an interesting and excellent design deprived of much of its beauty by what we can consider little better than the *crotchets* of its author'.

The churches mentioned above are only the most distinguished amongst the vast number of ecclesiastical buildings erected in the nineteenth century. D. R. Elleray has calculated that 600 churches and chapels were built in Sussex between 1810–1914; in 1881 a new church or chapel was opened every two or three weeks. It is a remarkable testimony to the piety of what has been called the last great age of faith.

D.B.

Seven

NINETEENTH-CENTURY CHURCH RESTORATION IN SUSSEX

The Church's Restoration
In eighteen-eighty three
Has left for contemplation
Not what there used to be,
How well the ancient woodwork
Looks round the Rect'ry hall,
Memorial of the good work
Of him who plann'd it all

JOHN Betjeman's *Hymn* neatly expresses the feelings of many visitors to ancient parish churches in Sussex and elsewhere. As early as June 1866 a letter was written to the *Ecclesiologist* in which the writer condemns the practice of recutting medieval tombs and scraping walls bare of whitewash and plaster: 'Let anyone . . . take the old Sussex Churches, which used to be so interesting because, happily, they had been left in their original state, probably through the poverty of the Downs Country. How is it now? Almost without exception, those that have been touched have been ruined. Sompting, Broadwater, Old Shoreham, and a host of others have scarcely a vestige of original antiquity about them . . . How heartily our grandchildren will hate this generation! Our own objection to Puritans and Church wardens is as nothing when compared with what must be the contempt which will be felt for the nineteenth-century spoilers'. The author went on to condemn 'the stupid ignorance which characterises so many of the Sussex restorations'. In similar vein A. Nesbitt (see Bibliography) remarked in 1883: 'Who would not be attracted by the idea of restoring a beautiful but neglected church to its pristine glories? Could anyone blame such a project? Yet as events have shown, the mischief done by "restoration" has been so enormous that the word has become a word of fear and shame . . . a very by-word and reproach'.

How was it that so many Sussex churches were so mercilessly restored? The early generation of church restorers delighted in horror stories as to the degenerate state of churches in the years prior to the great series of restorations lasting from the late 1840s to the 1870s. The north aisle of Kingston Buci (W), was, until 1844, used as a potato cellar; at St. Nicholas, Arundel (W), the *Ecclesiologist* reported in October 1857 that 'the building shows on every side traces of that incredible barbarism of the eighteenth-century . . . [the] eastern portion of the nave aisles are choked up by

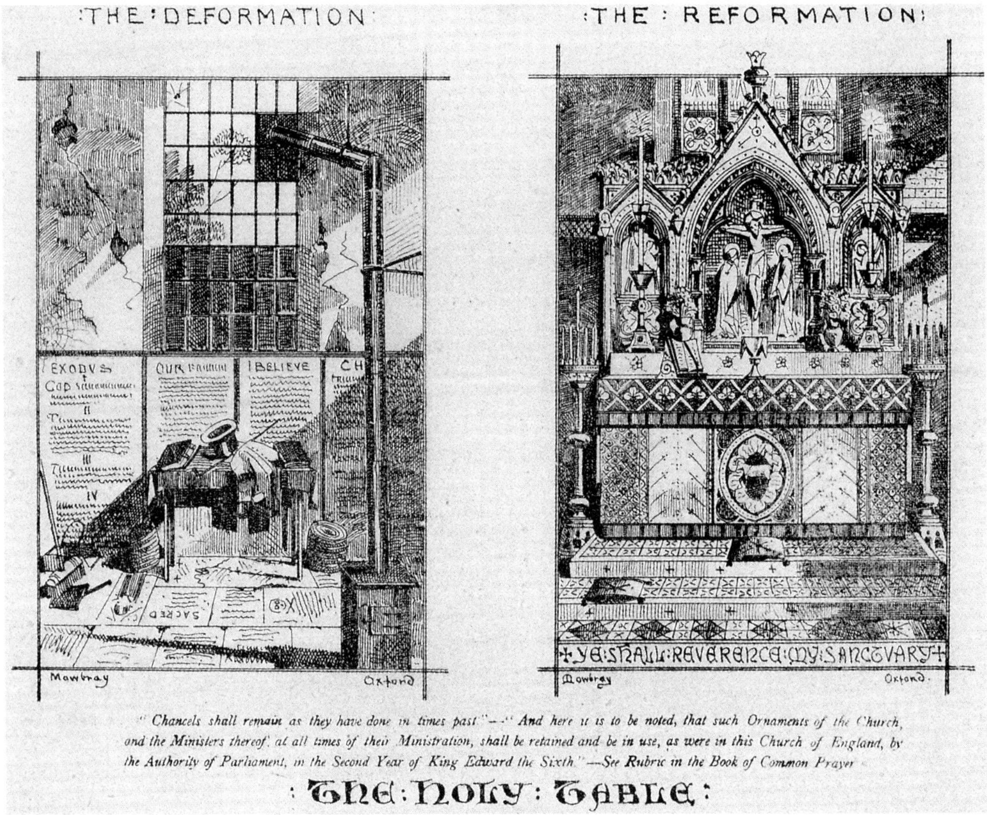

THE HOLY TABLE: Lithograph from A. R. Mowbray, *The Deformation and the Reformation,* 1873. Note the top hat on the altar table, the commandment boards and the heating pipe going through the east window. The contrasted view shows the same church after restoration

galleries, but a rostrum of more than usual absurdity still rises in the middle composed of a pulpit . . . flanked by matching tubs for the reader and clerk. To complete the affair, the old . . . stone pulpit . . . [is] cushioned up as a private box . . . for a single individual'; at Clayton (E) in 1838 (*Ecclesiologist,* May 1847) the east window was filled with a piece of red calico and the side windows with pink calico, the font was placed in the centre of the chancel and the tops of the nave windows had pieces of wood cut to imitate tracery; in 1841, John Mason Neale described St. Nicholas's, Old Shoreham (W) as being in such an appalling state of decay that the visitor might 'imagine that he was descending into the dungeon of a criminal rather than going into the house of the Lord'.

Churches in Sussex were probably rather better cared for than those elsewhere, however. Bishop Bower's *Visitation of the Diocese of Chichester* in 1724 suggests that of 257 parish churches only fifteen per cent were in a poor state of repair. The Deanery of Arundel was certainly the worst where fourteen out of twenty-six churches were in bad or fair condition. In 1817, the deans of Graffham, Rye and Ashburnham reported that the churches in their deanery were all in good order; only Selsey deanery had churches which needed attention (B. F. L. Clarke, *c.* 1976). Further evidence is provided by Sir Stephen Glynn, a founder member of the Ecclesiological Society, who visited 181 churches in Sussex between 1825 and 1874. The early descriptions in 1825 show that churches were generally in good condition: Patcham (E) was 'decently fitted up'; Portslade (E) was 'kept in a state of great neatness and respectability'; the windows at St. Thomas Becket, Lewes (E), were however (in 1826) in a state of 'barbarous mutilation' with 'many frightful modern ones . . . introduced'.

Under the influence of the nineteenth-century Church Revival the piecemeal methods of repair current in the eighteenth century began to seem unprincipled. The reinstitution of resident clergy meant that there was often an enthusiastic vicar for whom the restoration of his parish church became an abiding passion. The eighteenth-century churchman valued neatness and simplicity; his mid nineteenth-century counterpart insisted on reverential worship conducted in churches restored to what was thought to be their medieval glory. The change came about through two related ideologies within the Anglican church: the Oxford Movement and the Cambridge Camden Society.

On 14 July 1833 John Keble preached a sermon on 'National Apostasy' (i.e. the abandonment of religious faith) at St. Mary's church, Oxford. Keble aimed to protect the Church against the government's action in suppressing ten Irish bishoprics. This sermon is usually regarded as the beginning of the Oxford Movement, the chief object of which was the defence of the Church as the guardian of the Apostolic Succession, a trust handed down from Christ through the Apostles and the early Fathers of the Church and which had been emphasised by Archbishop Laud in the seventeenth century but subsequently lost. The Church was an instrument of the will of God; no secular institution could touch it. The theorists of the Oxford Movement laid emphasis on the inherited traditions of the Church; it was 'Catholic but not Roman', and aimed to recall Anglicanism back to its historic roots. This theological emphasis was expressed architecturally and liturgically by the Cambridge Camden Society.

The threefold aims of the Camden Society can be summarised as the reintroduction of Catholic ritual, the restoration of medieval churches, and the supervision of new church building. Founded in 1839 by John Mason Neale (1818–1866), later to become warden of Sackville College, East Grinstead (E), and Benjamin Webb (1819–1885), by 1843 the Society could number two Archbishops, sixteen Bishops and twenty-one Archdeacons among its members. A powerful influence on the Society was provided by the Catholic convert, architect, and theorist Augustus Welby Northmore Pugin (1812–1852). In *Contrasts* (1836) Pugin lampooned modern architecture as contrasted with the glories of the medieval past, and in *The True Principles of Pointed or Christian Architecture* (1841) he wrote: 'We can never successfully deviate one tittle from the spirit and principles of pointed (i.e. Gothic) architecture'. Pugin and the Camdenians, or Ecclesiologists, as they became known, after their periodical, the *Ecclesiologist,* also agreed on the necessity of long chancels, the separation of nave from chancel, bell towers, fonts placed in their original position by the south door, a pulpit placed to one side of the chancel arch, a chancel screen, and the necessity of sacred symbols and ornaments. To them the pure Gothic stream had been polluted by the revival of Pagan classicism during the Renaissance. What Pugin called 'thrice cooked hashes of pagan fragments' were inadmissible in a Christian church.

With such an ideology allied to a romantic view of the medieval past the stage was set for defining the principles of church restoration. The first volume of the *Ecclesiologist* (1841–2) stated that 'we must, whether from existing evidences or from supposition, recover the original scheme of the edifice as conceived by the first builder, or as begun by him and developed by his immediate successors'. Certain allowance was to be made for the 'age and purity' of later work. The Ecclesiologists, influenced by Pugin, were already agreed that the climax of English church architecture was the Decorated Gothic style of the late thirteenth and early fourteenth centuries. In practice, therefore, if a choice had to be made as to the 'right period' to which a church of several styles should be restored, the Ecclesiologists recommended the favoured Decorated style. In 1847 a rather more subtle approach was adopted. In a review of E. A. Freeman's pamphlet *Principles of Church Restoration* (1846), the reviewer put forward three theories of restoration: destructive, conservative, and eclectic. A destructive restoration meant rebuilding the church in 'the best style of art', that is, Decorated Gothic; a conservative restoration would restore and keep 'every piece of ancient work . . . Norman, First-Pointed, and Middle-Pointed (and) Tudor work'. First Pointed and Middle Pointed were the terms the Ecclesiologists used for Early English and Decorated Gothic. Georgian additions were not even mentioned: it was simply assumed that such debased work would go. As Julius Hare, Archdeacon of Lewes, wrote in 1842: 'I seldom enter an old church but a wish arises to sweep away almost everything that is in it . . . hardly anything has been put up . . . during the last 200 years which is not objectionable in taste, and few things that are not reprehensible in spirit'. The third theory, the eclectic, meant restoring in some cases and remodelling in others; it was this theory the Ecclesiologists favoured. Remodelling rather than restoration tended to be the practical result, however. This classification meant that the extremely destructive 'restoration' of St. Nicholas's, Brighton (E), was called 'conservative' by the *Ecclesiologist* in 1854 because although the church was virtually rebuilt the 'debased' early Perpendicular windows in the aisles were reproduced and not replaced during R. C. Carpenter's remodelling of 1852–4. Only the tower, nave arcades, chancel arch, and part of the chancel walls survive from the original building.

By the 1850s all church restorations involved the removal of pews, galleries, plaster ceilings, 'debased' classical work, and sash windows and dormers. Only in exceptional cases were Perpendicular windows preserved and the roof was often raised to what was taken to be its original height. A vestry was frequently added, heating provided, and the windows filled with stained glass. As Gilbert Scott wrote in *A Plea for the Faithful Restoration of Our Ancient Churches* (1850), 'the great difficulty is to know where to stop'.

The first stage in a restoration was the removal of box pews, or 'pues' as the Ecclesiologists called them. A pew in the nineteenth-century sense is almost forgotten today, so successful was the campaign against them. Good examples still exist at Rotherfield (E) and Warminghurst (W). A pew was either privately owned and attached to a family or house or rented by the year; it was often enclosed on all four sides and had lockable doors while the more elaborate of them such as the squire's pew at Parham (W), had fireplaces and comfortable cushions. They reflected a rigid class structure with the poor placed at the back of the church, in galleries, or on benches in the aisles. The 1851 religious census revealed that fifty-three per cent of seats in parish churches throughout the country were privately appropriated; the figures for Sussex reveal a similar story. For instance of the 13,491 sittings in Brighton, 6,952 were appropriated. The Camden Society's campaign against pews started in 1841 with the publication of J. M. Neale's *A History of Pews*. Neale spoke of them as 'lidless boxes, painted every colour and all colours, these cattleless pens inferior to those at Smithfield, that they are never cleaned, but harbour in their

BRIGHTON, St. NICHOLAS (E): Drawing by W. T. Quartermain of the church under restoration

tattered green baize the dust and corruption of a century'. A year later Neale wrote in *The Statistics of Pews* of 'the open bribery and traffic, at once illegal, irreverent, and abominable . . . this turning of GOD'S HOUSE into a place of merchandise'. Pews, he went on, were selfish, exclusive, gave rise to 'wicked practices', were dirty, Protestant and Puritan and were 'invented by people who thought themselves too good to pray by the side of their neighbours'. Neale spoke with approval of 'how pues fell before the Archdeacons of East and West Sussex like heroes in Homer before Achilles'. In 1841 the Archdeacon of Chichester was Henry Edward Manning (1803–1892), Rector of Graffham and Lavington (W), and the Archdeacon of Lewes was Julius Charles Hare (1795–1855) rector of Herstmonceux (E). In 1851 Manning went over to Rome and in 1875 he was made a Cardinal. Hare was one of the first Sussex clergymen to make a systematic attack on the pew system. In his *Charges to the Archdeaconry of Lewes,* delivered in 1840, he wrote: 'the first measure I would recommend is to alter the distribution of seats by getting rid of those eyesores and heartsores, pews, and substituting open benches with backs in their stead'. But a new spirit was abroad. Hare wrote with approval that pews had been converted to open seats at Kingston by Sea (Kingston Buci (W)) and at Graffham (W) the pews had been removed from the centre of the church. It is scarcely surprising that few box pews surviveed this onslaught. In 1852 the pew system in Sussex received national attention during the Horsham Pew Case which tried the churchwardens' claim to treat pews as belonging to private houses. It was revealed that at Whitsun 1851 eight people occupied pews that would seat thirty-six. Pews had been illegally bought and sold for fifty years and the judge ruled that they were only legal with a faculty, i.e. a Bishop's license, but that as a general principle there could be no property in seats. In virtually every Sussex church restoration the pews disappeared. Needless to say, much fine seventeenth and eighteenth-century woodwork was destroyed. The mass produced deal, pitch pine, or oak benches were no substitute.

The restorers linked pews and galleries together as post-Reformation abominations tending towards exclusivity in worship. Manning believed that galleries and pews would 'one day . . . be rejected as incredible, or believed only as the act of some few mutilators of things sacred to God'. Galleries had been added to churches to provide extra accommodation; west galleries were often used by the village choir bands. In 1841 the Cambridge Camden Society issued a Pamphlet entitled *A Few Words to Churchwardens on Churches and Church Ornaments: No. 1. Suited to Country Parishes.* The pamphlet was writen by J. M. Neale and sold 5,000 copies in six weeks. It roundly condemned pews, galleries, and three-decker pulpits. The second issue, devoted to *Town and Manufacturing Parishes,* stressed the 'devastation' caused by galleries being built against medieval windows and needing separate external doors. In *A Few Words to Church Builders* (1841) Neale wrote: 'If everything else is forgotten, and two points only remembered, THE ABSOLUTE NECESSITY OF A DISTINCT AND SPACIOUS CHANCEL, and THE ABSOLUTE INADMISSIBILITY OF PUES AND GALLERIES'. Two years later Neale spelt out

BRIGHTON, St. NICHOLAS (E): Engraving of the interior after restoration

HERSTMONCEUX (E): Drawing of the church from the west gallery. This early 19th-century illustration shows how many churches must have looked before the Victorian restorers

his opposition to galleries in a pamphlet entitled *Church Enlargement.* Their 'proud height . . . seclusion . . . (and) separation from the rest of the congregation' give rise to 'wandering thoughts' and 'their theatrical appearance' was out of place in the house of God. Today galleries are almost as scarce as pews in Sussex churches; an extremely rare galleried squire's pew still survives at Warbleton (E) and Worth (E) still has its west gallery.

The Ecclesiologists were determined to change the liturgical emphasis away from the pulpit and towards the altar. This meant dismantling three-decker pulpits, especially if they were centrally placed under the chancel arch (see p. 104). Neale wrote in *A Few Words to Church Builders* (1841) that they were 'symbolic of the age, which puts preaching before praying, the word of man before the ordinances of God'. Archdeacon Hare in his *Charges to the Archdeaconry of Lewes* wrote that a centrally placed pulpit implied that 'the mysteries of religion were still to be hidden from the multitude; as though the chief object of our commission were to keep people dangling in the outer court of the intellect'. Above all the primary idea of a church was as a house of prayer not a house of preaching. The latter function was more proper to a dissenters' meeting house. The three-deckers only survived in unrestored churches: St. John's church, Chichester (W), retains a towering centrally placed example. Others can often be seen in prints and photographs of churches before restoration.

The destruction of pews, galleries, and three-decker pulpits was the inevitable concomitant of most church restorations. Although restoring architects such as G. E. Street and Gilbert Scott deplored it, there was also a tendency to hack off whitewash and plaster. All church interiors were whitewashed in the eighteenth century and earlier but the early restorers felt vehemently that a church interior should be 'real', and this meant that stonework should be revealed. Neale wrote in *Church Enlargement* (1843) that the stonework in the chancel should be free of whitewash, paint, and stucco and every beam of the roof should be visible. There should be no 'deceptions'. Archdeacon Hare wondered about the origin of whitewash: 'Was it', he wrote, 'one of the rats that swam over in the train of William III . . . There is hardly a church that has not been defaced by this architectural basting . . . and most earnestly would I entreat the clergy and church wardens . . . to strip off this white shroud in which the limbs of our churches have been wrapt up'. Unfortunately the removal of whitewash often meant the removal of plaster decorated with medieval wall paintings. T. Gambier Parry in a letter to the *Ecclesiologist* in February 1858 entitled 'Whitewash and Yellow Dab' pointed out the dangers: 'Those children of the generation of whitewash, the Puritans, have done us good service. It is the friends of the Church who are now doing us an injury – injury which is irremediable. Walls are to be cleaned – churches to be restored – away goes everything down to the bare stone . . . where walls never intended to be bare were built rough, to be coated with plaster, and then fresco painted – but away it has all gone, frescoes, powderings, diapers, scrollage, symbols, inscriptions, everything'. At St. Leonard's, Hollington (E) the nave walls were so mercilessly scraped during William Slater's restoration of 1865 that even the *Ecclesiologist* could pronounce that 'all vestiges of antiquity have nearly disappeared from the existing structure'. After the 1870s architects' specifications usually insisted on the retention of plaster, although whitewash continued to be removed, often destroying layers of plaster beneath it. As late as 1876 the whitewash at New Shoreham was removed with crowbars, rasps, and chisels (P. Ferriday, 1964).

A scrapbook recording the restoration of St. Pancras, Arlington (E) is preserved in the East Sussex Record Office (PAR/232/7/7). The scrapbook illustrates the way in which the vicar involved the local community in the restoration of its church and it also shows the more conservative approach adopted towards the end of the century. The first stage was the distribution of a printed appeal written by the vicar, the Rev. T. Bunston, in August 1889. Thirteen years previously the church was evidently in poor condition and R. H. Carpenter's survey is cited: 'The whole fabric has been disfigured by plaster ceilings, whitewash, common deal pews and west gallery blocking up the tower arch, and the driving rain has caused decay in woodwork and damp in walls'. Since then, the vicar went on, 'decay has gone unchecked and now the tower buttresses are falling to pieces, the rain pours unhindered through the gaping shingles of the spire . . . (there is) green slime covering the walls, and the broad sill of the west window a bed of weeds . . . The rest of the interior of the church is dreary in the extreme, common deal pews, high and square, the seats high, narrow, and uncomfortable, and kneeling almost impossible . . . large portions of the plaster ceilings have fallen and admit the wind . . .'. The church had been surveyed by the architect Charles E. Powell and the cost of restoration was £1,800. 'Every feature and detail of ancient work will be most reverently and jealously preserved'. The appeal ended with a commendation from the Bishop of Chichester: 'I earnestly commend this appeal to the charitable consideration of Christ's people'. By 1891 all but £600 had been raised and a second appeal leaflet was printed. The Vicar stressed that for a quarter of a century Arlington had been the '*most neglected* parish in the Diocese', that congregations often consisted 'of 2 or 3, often none' and that the church was 'in the worst state – of dirt, decay, and ruin – of *any in Sussex* . . .' Money had been donated by the Archdeacons of East and West Sussex and the Diocesan Church Building Association had made three grants amounting to £190. Smaller sums of money had been raised by the Arlington Vicarage working party, a sale of work at Warbleton Rectory, a concert at Dicker School and the offertory at Arlington Church Harvest Thanksgiving (£1 7s 3d.). Special donations had been received for furniture for the Sanctuary, tiles for the Sanctuary (£10 – in memory of Col. Sir John Steward Wood, K.C.B. and Lady Wood), and the vicar's daughter, Miss M. A. Bunston, had given £5 for an altar frontal. But the problem of raising money was still serious as Arlington was an isolated country parish with a population of 648 in 1891: 'The Parish, alas! is one of the very poorest, *No* gentry'.

Fund raising went on apace. A loan exhibition was held at the Corn Exchange, Hailsham. The committee invited 'the loan of articles from all classes'. A Fancy Dress Bazaar was also held at Hailsham Corn Exchange. The event was marked by 'its brotherliness, in the richer parish of Hailsham, coming forward so heartily to the assistance of our own poor parish'. Further sums were donated by individual clergy; the Duke of Devonshire gave £750; the Chichester Diocesan Association £300; the Incorporated Church Building Society £75; a Bazaar at Warbleton Rectory raised £28. 11s; and a fund raising concert brought a further £115 17s 6d. There were further individual donations for church fittings.

Work could now proceed. The floor was levelled and an earth layer eighteen inches thick removed. The walls were cleaned of whitewash; this brought to light a painting of St. Christopher and post-Reformation biblical texts which rapidly deteriorated. The tower gallery was removed, the north wall rebuilt, and a new aisle roof provided. A bricked up window west of the south door was unblocked and a new Decorated window inserted. The Decorated east window of the Norman chapel was taken down and the tracery replaced. The sanctuary was filled with Godwin's tiles and the pews, like victorious trophies, were used to panel the nave and aisles and provide wood for the school cupboards. The original Queen Anne pulpit was stripped bare of paint and then 'carved on the flat to Mr Powell's designs' at the Mayfield carving school. The Jacobean altar table was similarly treated: it was stripped, lengthened, and provided with a new carved top. A new chancel screen, also carved at Mayfield, was provided and the walls and roof of the chancel were stencilled to Powell's designs.

The architect drew up a careful specification. This draws attention to the problems commonly faced by architects and their contractors. The pews and panelling were not to be used 'for making up shelters for . . . material or workmen'; the brick flooring was to be stacked and re-used; and Powell was well aware of the dangers of removing whitewash: 'the plaster . . . is to be carefully cleaned of the whitewash, care being taken not to disturb the old surface or any painting that may be below it . . . the masonry is to be cleaned with hand scrubbing brushes . . . wire cards only to be used to move the surface wash of where the lime has set too hard . . . no old work is to be restored resurfaced or altered in any way'.

The church was closed for restoration between 1891–1893; the re-opening on 5 May 1893 was described 'as the greatest day the parish has seen . . . for generations'. The ninety-two year old Bishop of Chichester led the procession, the sun shone brightly, and the church was full. 'Great praise was given to the Choir . . . and to Miss Wildbore, who played the Harmonium'. Parish tea was held at six o'clock for eighty or ninety people; the tea ended with '"God save the Queen", and hearty cheers for the Vicar and Mrs. Bunston'.

The Arlington example graphically illustrates the way in which the community became involved with restoration of its parish church. Individual parishes raised money in different ways, but in general the first stage in a church restoration was the

ARLINGTON (E): The tower prior to the 1891–3 restoration

ARLINGTON (E): Interior prior to the 1891–3 restoration. Note the box pews and whitewashed walls

appointment of a committee usually composed of the vicar, the local squire or country gentleman and the larger farmers or tradesmen. As A. Nesbitt pointed out in 1883, 'very probably not one of its members has ever given even the slightest attention to architecture in general, or to medieval architecture in particular'. The committee would then obtain an architect's report, obtain a faculty, hear any objections after the granting of the faculty, and then put the work out to tender. The problem with this procedure was that the lay members inevitably would follow the vicar's lead and vote either for what was cheapest or, if money was available, for what was most showy. To quote Nesbit again: 'the incumbent, emulous of the smartness of the neighbouring recently "restored" church, will be quite satisfied if he sees a floor of Minton's tiles, brass railings, . . . machine carved oak seats or pulpit (and) will care nothing for the worn brass or incised slab . . . or for the remains of oak carving, which must be got rid of in order that all may be uniform in the "restored" chancel'. The architect, on the other hand 'thinks he can design a far better doorway or window than those which exist', and the contracting builder 'will almost always if allowed, destroy and replace rather than mend'. Nesbitt suggested that an efficient clerk of the works should always be appointed to ensure that no damage was done by workman or strangers. 'A church under restoration may be open to any pilferer or idle boy who thinks mischief fun'.

Some of the worst excesses of church restoration were due to ignorance. The eighteenth century was almost universally despised; Tudor, Jacobean, and Stuart work was lucky to survive unscathed, but it is tragic that so much medieval work was destroyed by over-zealous architects and incumbents convinced that what they were replacing was superior to the original. The architect and antiquarian P. M. Johnston (1865–1936) discovered that a fourteenth-century screen at Climping (W) had been removed and burnt. 'Who authorised such a barbarous act?', 'Oh, one of the churchwardens', the Vicar said, 'A good riddance to old rubbish'. The chancel at Cocking (W) had been rebuilt in 1896 and, according to P. M. Johnston's *Guide* to the church, the Rector had been assured by the architect, Mr. Pritchett, that the east window was too decayed to repair. A copy was made, the east wall rebuilt, and the contractors, Rattee and Kett of Cambridge, re-erected the original window as a feature in the Rectory garden. A trifling repair, Johnston said, could have restored the window.

The House of Commons printed returns on church building published in 1876 show that between 1840–1876, 180 churches were restored in Sussex at a cost of £682,906. It was an extraordinary achievement. In 30 years well over half the parish churches had been restored. But the artistic and historical cost was enormous. In church after church walls were stripped, ancient tombs cut and retooled, pews and galleries removed, floors levelled and laid with mass produced black and white tiles, and 'debased' Perpendicular features replaced. At Bexhill (E) William Butterfield pulled down the chancel and south aisle in 1878. At Battle (E) he replaced the Perpendicular east window with a triplet of lancets and heightened and widened the chancel arch in 1869; at All Saints, Hastings (E) he renewed the east windows and swept the church clean of pews and galleries in 1870. Butterfield's obituary in the *Journal of the Royal Institute of British Architects* (1900) stated that it was a pity 'he was ever called in to deal with a single ancient fabric'; the writer was 'wrapt in wonder that he could appreciate so much and spare so little'. This was unfair, however, as Butterfield was in advance of his time in his attitude to plaster and seventeenth-century fittings.

LEWES, St. MICHAEL: The church under restoration in 1878

Particularly damaging restorations were perpetrated by Gordon Macdonald Hills (1826–1895), who was, tragically, one of the most prolific of the Sussex restorers. Hills' 'zealous churchman's pick and plane' was let loose on no less than thirty Sussex churches including Amberley (W), Ashurst (W), Birdham, St. Pancras, Chichester, Climping, East and Mid Lavant, Lyminster, Poling, Pulborough, Steyning, Washington, Westhampnett, Wiston (W), East Dean and Ovingdean (E). His obituary in the *Builder* (April 1895) remarked that he had 'an honourable though unostentatious position in the profession' and went on ominously to state that he died of overwork. One of Hills' greatest acts of vandalism was the destruction of the chancel at Steyning in 1863; at Ashurst he renewed part of the chancel walls with 'random snap' flintwork and replaced the nave windows to accord with those in the chantry chapel (*Parish Record,* November 1877–December 1878). At Climping he was more tender, however; the church was swept clean of box pews, but the windows were not recut or replaced.

In justice to the restorers it must be pointed out that many churches, such as Arlington (E), were evidently in poor structural condition and it is likely that some would have collapsed had they not been restored. Box pews and three-decker pulpits now have a picturesque appeal that would have been incomprehensible to a nineteenth-century churchman. Occasionally restoration could add something to a church. Gilbert Scott's restoration of the chancel at Clapham (W) in 1873 provided a very fine tiled chancel with a reredos consisting of Pre-Raphaelite angels against a vine leaf background. Early photographs show magnificent polychrome decoration in the chancel and nave. A very fine brass pulpit and lectern incorporated in a low alabaster screen was added at a later date. At Newick (E), John Oldrid Scott lengthened the nave and restored the chancel in a late thirteenth-century style. J. O. Scott was a careful and painstaking restorer and the chancel was sumptuously decorated with tiling and stencilled decoration. In 1862 the architect Norman Shaw visited Angmering (W) and described it as 'as awful sell as it was totally restored by Teulon in his best manner'. Ian Nairn in the Sussex volume of *The Buildings of England* (1965) remarks: 'Teulon had a field day . . . leaving medieval fragments around like flotsam on a beach . . . Teulon . . . was at his worst in this kind of sack of an old building'. The church was virtually rebuilt in 1855 in a 'middle pointed' style, but it has a remarkable vigour and authority. All the fittings in the chancel were designed by the architect in a spiky, naturalistic style which he made peculiarly his own.

Restorations which contributed something to a church were exceptional. The counter-attack, when it came, owed much to John Ruskin who, in *The Seven Lamps of Architecture* (1849) wrote: 'Restoration, so called, is the worst manner of Destruction . . . Restoration . . . is always a lie . . . It means the most total destruction which a building can suffer . . . it is *impossible,* as impossible as to raise the dead'. For Ruskin 'the greatest glory of a building . . . is its age'. In 1877 William Morris wrote a letter to the *Athenaeum* on the proposed restoration of Tewkesbury that became the manifesto of the Society for the Protection of Ancient Buildings: 'These last fifty years of knowledge and attention have done more for their (ancient buildings) destruction than all the foregoing centuries of revolution, violence, and contempt'. The S.P.A.B. preached Morris's message of staving off decay by daily care and by the 1890s its dictates were increasingly accepted and reparation became more common than restoration. But as late as 1903 Richard Creed performed what Ian Nairn called 'a mulish restoration' on Walberton church. A rare Saxon gable cross was discarded, a Norman arch in the south wall was rebuilt, the west wall was grossly altered, and the font placed on an extraordinary pedestal carved with imitation Runes. This pedestal no longer survives. The Sussex Archaeological Society and the Society of Antiquaries protested to no avail but the 'restoration' led to the setting up of the Diocesan Advisory Committees which helped to preserve the few remaining unrestored churches in the county. Yet, as the *Ecclesiologist* wrote in 1850: 'We are not artists only: we have a duty to consider the comeliness and decency of God's house'. To the architect G. E. Street (1824–1881), who restored Barlavington, Bignor (W), and Rye (E), and virtually rebuilt Graffham (W), the most important consideration was that a church should encourage the 'hearty, loyal, and reverent setting forth of the Prayer Book'. Archaeological and historic considerations were secondary to this. Many incumbents would have agreed with him and the dilemma remains with us still.

D.B.

HARDHAM (W): Murals depicting the *Agnus Dei,* angels and scenes from the early life of Christ on the nave east wall, *c.* 1080–1120

COOMBES (W): Atlas mural figure on the soffit of the chancel arch, *c.* 1080–1120

TICEHURST (E): Fragments of a Last Judgement window, early 15th century

HERSTMONCEUX (E): Exterior from the east. Note the chancel and north chapel rebuilt in brick in 1440

ASHBURNHAM (E): Former reredos, dated 1676. The frame is contemporary

BLUE IDOL, FRIENDS MEETING HOUSE (W): The right-hand side of the farmhouse was converted for use as a meeting house in 1691

STANSTED CHAPEL (W): Interior looking east

Watercolour by Mary Lewin, *c.* 1845, of a choir band in a West Sussex church. Note that the congregation has turned to face the band who are performing in the west gallery

BRIGHTON, ST. NICHOLAS (E): Watercolour of the interior by J. H. Scott prior to the restoration of 1853

BRIGHTON, St. MICHAEL (E): East end of south aisle. The reredos is Flemish, early 16th century and the altar frontal was designed by William Burges, *c.* 1861–2

Triptych, oil on panel, by Edward Burne-Jones. Painted for St. Paul's church, Brighton in 1861. Detail shows the Adoration of the Kings

CLAPHAM (W): The chancel after Gilbert Scott's restoration of 1873

Eight

WALL-PAINTINGS AND STAINED GLASS

BEFORE 1600

'PICTURES and ornaments in churches are the lessons and the scriptures of the laity . . . For what writing supplieth to him which can read, that doth a picture supply to him which is unlearned, and can only look. Because they who are uninstructed thus see what they ought to follow; and things are read though letters be unknown.' (William Durandus, d. 1296)

Images painted on walls and in windows in medieval churches had the central function of instructing as well as edifying the faithful. They could follow Christ's passion through a narrative series of pictures, seek the mediation of the saints similarly depicted on wall and in glass, take heed in the conduct of their daily lives of the moral lessons taught by themes such as the Seven Works of Mercy and the Seven Deadly Sins, and be reminded of the dreaded day of judgement with its rewards for the blessed and torments of the damned by the Doom painted on the wall over the chancel arch.

All of these themes appear in medieval wall-painting and stained glass in Sussex churches. Scenes from the life of Christ occur in the extensive murals at Cocking, Coombes, Hardham, West Chiltington (W), Preston and Southease (E). In stained glass there is an Annunciation of *c.* 1390–1400 at Poynings (E), and Crucifixions at Cowfold (W) and West Firle (E). Crucifixions also appear in wall-paintings at Amberley and Wisborough Green (W). Old Testament subjects are less common, the most notable being the early twelfth-century scenes of Adam and Eve in the chancel at Hardham (W); the Adam and Eve scene at Rotherfield (E) is much later in date, as also is the small figure of Moses in the tracery of the east window of the Oxenbridge chapel at Brede (E). Saints are represented frequently in Sussex. The Virgin appears in Nativity cycles at Hardham and West Chiltington and in her own right holding the child Christ in the Bishop's Chapel, Chichester (W). Another Virgin and Child is at Arundel (W). These are all wall-paintings and in stained glass the Coronation of the Virgin is to be seen at North Stoke (W), Hooe and Bexhill (E). The last also has figures of the apostles, who also appear in the glazing at Brede, Westham (E) and Poling (W) and on the chancel walls of Clayton, Coombes and Hardham (W). Amongst other saints of universal popularity throughout Western Christendom, St. Margaret is represented in glass at Battle (E) and wall-paintings at Binsted (W), and Preston (E); at Battle there is a cycle of scenes from her life. St. Christopher was a common subject in medieval murals as it was believed that those who looked on his image were safe from evil; he was usually depicted on the wall opposite to the main entrance to the church. A number of St. Christopher figures occur in Sussex, including Coombes, West Chiltington, Southease (E), Trotton and West Grinstead (W). A very early example of St. George is amongst the Romanesque frescoes at Hardham and there is a fifteenth-century St. Lawrence in the Bexhill glass. In the latter medium are the English saints at Alfriston (Alphege), Brede (Edward the Confessor) and Chalvington (Thomas Becket), all in East Sussex. The martyrdom of Becket in Canterbury Cathedral is depicted in an early fourteenth-century wall-painting at Preston (E).

During the fourteenth century moralising and didactic subjects began to appear in wall-paintings and stained glass. One of these is the image known as Christ of the Trades. The only Sussex example is a fifteenth-century mural at West Chiltington which has a bleeding figure of Christ surrounded by various implements, symbolising that Christ's passion is repeated because men commit the sin of working on Sundays. The Seven Deadly Sins and the Seven Works of Mercy occur in the late fourteenth-century wall-paintings at Arundel and Trotton (W). The latter are depicted on the west wall between Moses holding the tablets of law and below the figure of Christ in Majesty.

The Last Judgement or Doom is probably the best-known subject in English medieval mural painting and examples can be seen in Sussex dating from the late eleventh/early twelfth centuries onwards. The Clayton (E) cycle extends over the side walls of the nave; at Hardham scenes of Hell occur on the west wall. The most usual position for the Doom from the thirteenth century onwards in wall-painting was over the chancel arch, as at Ford (W), Patcham (E), All Saints at Hastings and

CLAYTON (E): Mural of Christ in Majesty flanked by angels over the chancel arch, *c.* 1080–1120

CHICHESTER CATHEDRAL (W): Vault decoration in Lady Chapel by Lambert Barnard, *c.* 1520–25

Rotherfield (E). In several examples St. Michael is shown weighing souls on the Day of Judgement: a particularly well-preserved example is at Rotherfield. Although popular attention tends to concentrate on the torments of the damned, medieval painters placed equal emphasis on the celestial Jerusalem which awaited the just. The Last Judgement also appeared in stained glass windows and there are the remains of Dooms in the glazing of Etchingham and Ticehurst (E), dating respectively from the late fourteenth and early fifteenth centuries.

Angels are represented in both media, but they were a particularly suitable subject to fill tracery lights in windows from the fourteenth century onwards. They occur holding censers at West Firle and Warbleton (E) and at Heyshott (W) they play musical instruments. The angels in the tracery of the east windows at Etchingham and Penhurst (E) bear shields of arms. Armorial bearings are more common in stained glass than wall-paintings, although the latter medium has produced the most impressive heraldic painting in Sussex, the recently uncovered Camoys shields and donors at Trotton.

Sussex is particularly rich in medieval wall-paintings and has several monuments which are of national importance. The paintings in five churches (Clayton, Coombes, Hardham, Plumpton and Westmeston – the last known only from copies) are the product of a single workshop active between *c.* 1080 and *c.* 1120. They have been associated with Lewes Priory although recently it has been convincingly argued by David Park that this connection has been over-emphasised. The paintings are amongst the earliest medieval murals to survive in England and are closely related in style both to contemporary Norman manuscripts and to indigenous Anglo-Saxon traditions. There are some dramatic compositions, notably the Atlas figure straining under the weight he is bearing on the chancel arch at Coombes, and the works are characterised by a distinctive 'bacon and egg' range of colours resulting from the employment of a very small range of locally available pigments. The remarkably complete series at Clayton and Hardham give a very good impression of the colourful interiors of even modest parish churches in the Romanesque period. The nave paintings at West Chiltington date from the second quarter of the thirteenth century and are also well-preserved. The narrative scenes, which are arranged in tiers under arcades with angels in the spandrels (an arrangement borrowed from contemporary sculpture), are no more than provincial work and cannot match the sophistication of the exquisite roundel depicting the Virgin and Child in the Bishop's Chapel, Chichester, of *c.* 1260. The later centuries did not produce in Sussex wall-paintings of the importance of the 'Lewes' group and Chichester, although the angel holding the soul in a napkin painted on a tomb at Winchelsea (E) in *c.* 1310–20 and the moralities at Arundel and Trotton which date from the end of the fourteenth century are of considerable quality. The Trotton west wall series is an early example of the International Gothic style in English art. The early Tudor period produced two non-figurative works which are of interest as they can be attributed to a painter named Lambert Barnard, who executed panel paintings for Bishop Sherborne in Chichester Cathedral and Amberley Castle. He was also responsible for the delicate flower, fruit and foliage patterns decorating a Lady Chapel vault in the cathedral and the chancel vaults at Boxgrove Priory. The former has Catherine of Aragon's device of a pomegranate and the latter includes shields of arms of Thomas West, Lord de la Warr, who was a close friend of Bishop Sherborne; both series probably date from the early 1520s. These vault paintings appear to be derived from vault decorations in

Continental churches, especially those in the Low Countries. Barnard's work is a reminder that not all medieval wall-painting was figurative and narrative. Several churches, including North Stoke, Slindon, West Hoathly (W), Beddingham and Rotherfield (E), reveal traces of purely decorative painting in the form of imitation ashlar masonry and trails of foliage.

Medieval stained glass in Sussex is the poor relation of wall-painting, a situation reflected by the paucity of literature on the subject. Only about fifty churches have remains of ancient glass (about twenty in West Sussex and thirty in East Sussex) and nowhere does it survive in significant quantities. For the most part the remains comprise a few fragments, mainly from tracery lights and dating from the fourteenth and fifteenth centuries. This state of affairs is at first sight surprising as Chiddingfold, one of the main centres for the manufacture of white window glass in the Middle Ages, is on the Surrey-Sussex border. The scanty remains also contrast with the riches to be found in the neighbouring county of Kent. Glass-making, however, was a craft distinct from that of glass-painting and so the proximity to Chiddingfold is no more than coincidental.

Stained glass in Sussex has suffered from iconoclasm, especially during the Reformation, as is evidenced by the churchwardens' accounts for St. Michael's at Lewes which record the deliberate defacing of two windows in 1548–9 (see above, p. 16). Notwithstanding losses through vandalism and neglect the impression persists that glass was never a major artistic medium in the area. The numerous

NEWICK (E): Watercolour by Charles Winston of an early 14th-century *Agnus Dei* in a chancel south window

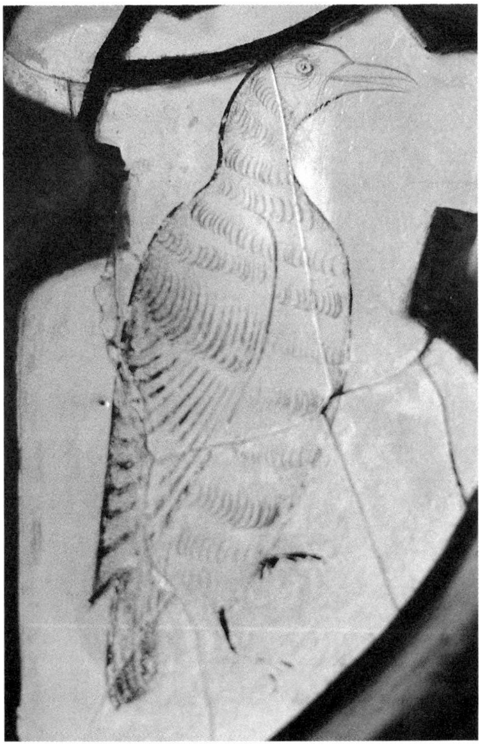

SALEHURST (E): Stained glass bird in a nave south window, *c.* 1400

churches built in the eleventh and twelfth centuries were better suited to mural decoration; their small and narrow window openings must have contained at best only a little coloured glass and probably the majority had no glass at all. At Poling (W) there is the remarkable survival of a wooden shutter from a window of this period; with its small opening to allow light to filter in through canvas, horn or even paper, it may have been the normal window filling in Norman churches. The lack of church building after the early thirteenth century also reduced the opportunities for glazing work and even when it occurs it seems for the most part to have been on a modest scale with non-representational quarry glass (diamond-shaped panels with naturalistic or stylised motifs) predominating over multi-coloured figural compositions.

The names of a few Sussex glass-painters are recorded. In 1240 John the glazier contracted with the dean and chapter of Chichester to keep the cathedral windows in good repair and make new ones (L. F. Salzman, *Building in England down to 1540*) and at the end of the Middle Ages John Harmon was employed in Lewes. Evidence of patronage is sparse and confined to the late Middle Ages. The only surviving donor figures are at Battle (E) and members of the Fitzalan family are recorded at Arundel (W), although they are now destroyed. Shields of arms of benefactors survive here and there, such as the De Brewse shields at Wiston (W) and those of the Pelham and Lewknor families at Warbleton (E); Wiston also has a quarry with the initials of Sir Richard Shirley (d. 1540). Local manorial lords appear to have been prominent among stained glass patrons. Sir William de Echyngham and the Poynings family probably included the glazing in the costs of the late fourteenth-century rebuilding of the churches at Etchingham (E) and Poynings (W). In 1496 Thomas Oxenbridge left 13s. 4d. to the parson of Brede 'towards the glassing of his chauncell' (*Sussex Rec. Soc.*, vol. XLI). The only clerical donor is represented by the east window of Chalvington which has an inscription to John Diliwyt, rector between 1388 and 1409.

No glass earlier in date than the thirteenth century survives in Sussex. Two lancet windows at Fletching (E), containing *grisaille* (white glass) painted with formalised plant leaves and stems, are of thirteenth-century date; so too are the *grisaille* fragments recently excavated at Battle and Bayham Abbey and published by Jill Kerr. The small Crucifixion at Cowfold and the two Coronation of the Virgin panels at North Stoke (W) perhaps date from the very end of the century. The best glass of the first half of the fourteenth century is the censing angels, head of Christ and Crucifixion in the south aisle east window at West Firle. A considerable amount of glass survives in East Sussex from the period *c.* 1350–1430, including Bexhill, Etchingham, Hooe, Poynings, Salehurst, Ticehurst, Warbleton and Westham. The only one of these of more than local significance is Salehurst, where in the south aisle are a series of beautifully drawn birds which are of a quality comparable with those in the well-known artists' sketchbook in the Pepysian Library at Magdalene College, Cambridge. The later glass in Sussex is unremarkable except for the early sixteenth-century fragments in the Oxenbridge chapel at Brede which reveal the infiltration of Renaissance motifs such as *putti.* Sussex is therefore an unrewarding county for English medieval stained glass, although before leaving the subject attention should be drawn to some fine pre-Reformation panels which have found their way into Sussex churches from elsewhere. Woolbeding (W) has early sixteenth-century Passion scenes of good Flemish workmanship which were made for the Chapel of the Holy Ghost in Basingstoke, Hampshire, and some fine French and German late medieval glass can be seen at Linch (W) and Frant (E).

R.M.

POST-REFORMATION UNTIL *c.* 1900

The 1547 Injunctions of Edward VI specified that 'there remain no memory of (idolatry and superstition) . . . in walls, glass-windows, or elsewhere within their churches . . .' This prohibition of religious imagery had a profound effect on the interiors of churches in Sussex and elsewhere. Figurative glass and mural-painting was largely replaced by painted religious texts required by the Canons of 1604 which codified Archbishop Matthew Parker's *Advertisements* of 1566 in stating that 'the Ten Commandments be set upon the east end of every church and chapel where the people may best see and read the same, and other chosen sentences written upon the walls of the said churches and chapels in places convenient'. In 1631 Thomas Henbage was given a licence from the Archbishop of Canterbury to view all the churches in the Diocese of Chichester and paint the Royal Arms, the Ten Commandments, 'and other holy sentences' in a prominent place in the nave or chancel (*Sussex Notes and Queries,* February 1929). Burton still has early seventeenth-century Commandments painted on the plaster tympanum above the Rood screen, and on the south wall is an extremely rare painted Royal Arms of Charles I, dated 1636. The text above reads: 'Obey them that have the rule over you'. The churchwardens' accounts for Billingshurst record the paying of a painter 'for striking out the King's Arms and setting up the States' (i.e. the Commonwealth) in 1653. In 1661 a painter was again paid for 'setting and painting the King's Arms' (West Sussex Record Office, PAR 21/9/1).

Painted Biblical texts continued to be the favoured form of wall decoration in the eighteenth and nineteenth centuries. In 1841 John Mason Neale and Benjamin Webb toured the churches of Sussex and noted texts at East Wittering, West Wittering, and Hunston (W); these no longer survive but examples can still be seen at Kingston Buci, Coombes (W), Arlington, Hamsey and Southease (E). Many must have disappeared when whitewash and plaster was removed by the nineteenth-century church restorers.

Wall-painting was revived to some extent in the nineteenth century, and texts continued to be produced, although usually confined to the chancel arch. Old photographs of the interiors of Angmering, Clapham, Nuthurst, Rustington (W) and Brede (E) show beautifully executed stencilled Decalogues and Creeds above and around the chancel arch (Hare Collection, Church House, Brighton, and P. M. Johnston Collection, Worthing Reference Library). At East Marden (W) the interior was stencilled by Holt of Chichester from designs by the diocesan architect Lacy W. Ridge (*Parish Record,* 1 November 1876–31 October 1877). Midhurst (W) had painted angels flanking the east window; these probably dated from Ridge's restoration of 1882. Above the north chancel chapel of Henfield (W) was a remarkable painting of the Decalogue, Creed, and Lord's Prayer surrounded by cherubs and trumpeting angels. The painting dated from 1897 and survived until the 1950s.

Twentieth-century churchmen seem to have had much the same attitude to nineteenth-century decoration as their Victorian counterparts had to the work of the eighteenth century. Much Victorian painted decoration presumably survives beneath layers of later paintwork. Harting (W) still has painted texts of about 1858 over the chancel arch and work of excellent quality can still be seen at Cuckfield (E) where Charles Eamer Kempe painted the roof in 1886, and at Bexhill (E) where the walls and ceiling of the chancel were painted by W. G. Rich in 1893. Clapham (W) and

Newick (E) still have overall decorative stencilling and painting in the chancel (see page 77) and St. Nicholas's, Brighton, has painting on the east and west walls designed by Somers Clarke and executed by the Kempe firm. At Findon (W) there is a painted tiled reredos, designed by William Morris in 1867.

Although chronologically outside the scope of this essay, the Bloomsbury Group wall-paintings at Berwick (E) commissioned by Bishop Bell of Chichester and executed between 1941–3 by Duncan Grant, Vanessa Bell, and Quentin Bell deserve a mention. Bishop Bell intended the paintings to follow in the tradition of medieval mural-painting in Sussex churches.

The small amount of ecclesiastical glass produced in the century following the Reformation was usually heraldic work painted in enamel colours, that is, colours made from crushed coloured glass bound in oil or gum, painted on the surface, and fired in a kiln. Although some encouragement was given to stained glass manufacture by Archbishop Laud, who promoted a revival of religious subject matter, the Civil War dealt a devastating blow to these tentative beginnings. It was not until the 1660s that stained glass was again produced on any scale by glass-painters such as Henry Gyles of York (1645–1709), but his work is not represented in Sussex.

The most important seventeenth-century glazing scheme in Sussex is at Stopham (W). The east window has armorial glass dated 1638 which was removed from Stopham Manor and the north aisle contains an early seventeenth-century window painted with figures of the Stopham family. The glass is signed by a Flemish glass-painter named Roelant and is particularly interesting as the style of the figures seems to be a conscious imitation of medieval work, and there is a limited use of pot metal (see below).

There was little call for stained glass in the eighteenth and early nineteenth centuries and Sussex possesses few examples. William Peckitt (1731–95) of York

BURTON (W): Painted royal arms on the south wall

STOPHAM (W): Watercolour by S. H. Grimm of the stained glass on the north side of the nave

painted the east window at Glynde (E) but this was destroyed in the 1890s. The church still has some armorial glass medallions signed by James Pearson (born 1750) and dated 1774. Stansted chapel (W) has an east window of about 1812 which is probably unique in a Christian place of worship as it is of wholly Jewish inspiration. The mission of the then owner of Stansted House, Lewis Way, was the conversion of the Jews and the window, probably painted by James Pearson, is decorated with Old Testament symbolism. The glass on the north side of the chapel is painted with armorials. Impressionistic descriptions of the glass appear in John Keats's poems *The Eve of St. Agnes* and *The Eve of St. Mark.* Keats was present at the consecration of the chapel in 1819.

William Collins (fl. 1801–1852) occupies a transitional position in the history of stained glass. He restored the medieval glass at Tewkesbury and had some knowledge of medieval glazing techniques, but much of his work was figurative painting in enamels. He painted the east window of Christ Church, Brighton (E), in about 1835 with a design based on cartoons by Reynolds. This is now in Bagborough, Somerset. Still *in situ* are the clerestory windows of St. Peter's, Brighton, glazed in 1834 (T. W. Horsfield, *History of Sussex,* 1835). Painted largely in enamels, the somewhat strident colours of blue, green, red, yellow and purple are typical of the time. The windows have the initials of the Wagner family and the words of the *Te Deum.* At the east end of Pagham (W) armorial glass by William Miller (1837) is combined with sixteenth-century Flemish glass.

By the beginning of the nineteenth century the Gothic Revival inspired an increasing interest in the technique and style of medieval glass. Manufacturers began to produce a rather thin pot metal (i.e. glass which is coloured in the molten state and therefore tinted through its substance) and the heraldic artist Thomas Willement (1786–1871) reintroduced the medieval mosaic principle, that is the making of windows from small pieces of pot metal cut to shape and leaded together. The figure painting was reduced to simple line drawing for features and drapery, and enamels were only used for shading and detailed work. Examples of Willement's work can be seen at Broadwater (W), where his east window was described by the *Ecclesiologist* in 1857 as 'deplorable', and Worth (E), where the south transept window of 1849 is painted in a Raphaelesque manner.

Much mid-nineteenth century stained glass was revivalistic in that it attempted to imitate medieval glass. However, the pot metal used differed from its medieval prototype in both colour and smoothness. William Wailes of Newcastle (1801–81) was probably the most successful manufacturer of glass of this type. Wailes worked with Pugin from 1842–5 and much of the firm's early glass was influenced by Pugin's knowledge of the medium. Wailes's work can be seen in the east window at St. Andrew's, Hove (E), and the east window at Burpham (W).

By 1865 James Powell and Sons of Whitefriars, London, had developed a type of pot metal glass similar to that used during the Middle Ages. The work had been initiated by Charles Winston (1814–1864), one of the first historians of stained glass who made some excellent water-colour copies of medieval glass in Sussex, including Newick (E). Winston realised that medieval glass contained streaks and bubbles and that its irregularities gave it variety and texture. This revival of densely coloured and textured pot metal paved the way for the developments in stained glass manufacture pioneered by major firms such as Morris and Company, Lavers and Barraud, Clayton and Bell, James Powell and Sons, and C. E. Kempe.

Morris glass is perhaps the best known today and Sussex is fortunate in possessing major examples of the company's work. The firm was founded in 1861 by William Morris under the title Morris, Marshall, Faulkner and Company, subsequently changed to Morris and Company in 1875. Dante Gabriel Rossetti, Edward Burne-Jones, Ford Madox Brown, and Philip Webb all produced designs for the company, although Burne-Jones was by far the most prolific artist. Morris glass often combines pictorial elements with stylised leafy decorative backgrounds. Colours are subtle and subdued and there is considerable use of white glass decorated with silver stain, that is silver nitrate applied to the surface of the glass which, when fired, turns yellow. The firm supplied the glass for St. Michael and All Angels, Brighton (E) in 1862, thus making it the earliest stained glass commission for Morris apart from All Saints, Selsey in Gloucestershire. The glass was designed by Morris, Webb, Madox Brown, Peter Paul Marshall, and Burne-Jones. Morris and Webb were in overall control of the design with Morris choosing the colours and acting in the rôle of master-glazier. The subject-matter of the glass was inspired by the dedication of the church and angels are very prominent. The west window has full-sized archangels and angels ringing bells, and the south aisle east window has an angel seated upon the empty tomb of Christ. The stained glass artist Selwyn Image (1849–1930) described the St. Michael's glass as 'the finest modern piece of stained glass that has ever been done . . . the magnificence of its design, the sense which it gave one of being in the presence of supernatural beings, the perfectness of its splendid colouring, and for everything that goes to make a fine stained glass window, this specimen seemed to be perfection'. It is a judgement that has stood the test of time.

BRIGHTON, St. MICHAEL (E): South wall, east chapel window designed by Burne-Jones for Morris and Company, 1862. The subject is the flight into Egypt

BRIGHTON, St. MICHAEL (E): Cartoon by William Morris for the Three Marys at the Sepulchre, 1862. The glass as executed is in the east window of the south aisle

Excellent Morris glass can also be seen at St. Wilfred's, Haywards Heath, Rotherfield, and Rottingdean (E). The east window at St. Wilfrid's was designed by Burne-Jones in 1867 but was destroyed in 1962; the glass in the south side of the chancel, the south aisle and the bapistry still survives. Morris, Madox Brown, and Burne-Jones all provided designs. The east window at Rotherfield, also by Burne-Jones, can be dated to 1874 on the basis of a sketch in the church. The theme of the window is the *Te Deum;* the praise of God by the heavenly host. The glass at Rottingdean illustrates the firm's late style. Designed by Burne-Jones in 1893, the glass shows the tendency towards greater pictorialism combined with deeper colour and lower luminosity. Burne-Jones's figures are calm and isolated from the world; as Sewter remarks, 'they look tired, anaemic and occasionally sexless'.

Many other stained glass manufacturers produced work of high quality. St. Mary's, Horsham (W) is a fascinating repository of Victorian glass, containing the work of William Wailes, Clayton and Bell, Heaton, Butler and Bayne, Michael O'Connor and Sons, and Charles Eamer Kempe. All these firms used medieval techniques as a starting point for innovative work, but C. E. Kempe (1837–1907) deserves especial mention, not only because he was born in Sussex, but also because he was one of the most prolific stained glass designers and examples of his work can be seen throughout the county. His best glass derives its inspiration not only from Morris but also from studies Kempe made of fifteenth-century English and North European glass, more especially that produced in Germany and France. He made extensive use of silver stain and his glass is characterised by intricate detail and muted colours. His later work can be repetitive and mannered but it does not justify A. C. Benson's contemptuous comment: 'window after window with the same simpering faces . . . wrapped up in carpets and staggering under the weight of jewelled chalices'. Kempe glass of the highest quality can be seen at St. Nicholas's, Brighton; the south and north aisle windows date from 1878 and illustrate the theme of the life and Passion of Christ. Ovingdean (E) has glass of about 1867–69 inspired by fourteenth-century French prototypes, while Cuckfield (E) has a Jesse window in the north aisle which dates from 1887; the figure work is by Edgar Carter, a Kempe pupil. The design shows the influence of German late fifteenth-century art. A superb collection of early Kempe glass can be seen at St. Andrew's, Worthing (W). The glass was originally commissioned for All Souls', Brighton, but was removed when the church was demolished in 1968. After 1876 Kempe often signed his glass with a shield bearing three wheatsheaves; this was sometimes combined with the monogram A.E.T. for the master glass-painter Alfred Edward Tombleson. By 1895 a single wheatsheaf was used. These motifs, derived from Kempe's coat of arms, help to identify his work.

D.B.

Nine

WOODWORK

THE MEDIEVAL PERIOD

ALTHOUGH much of Sussex contained heavily forested areas in the Middle Ages, the visitor looks in vain for screens and bench-ends of the elaboration and quality of the examples found in the richer regions of East Anglia and Devon and Cornwall.

Screens are the most common item of wooden pre-Reformation church furnishings to survive. Approximately twenty-five examples exist, the majority in East Sussex. Most are of Rood screens, dividing the chancel where the liturgy was enacted by the clergy, from the nave, as at Burton (W) and Fletching (E). Others, such as Eastbourne, Playden and Rodmell (E), act as parclose screens, separating chapels from the main body of the building. The earliest screens are the best, the finest being that between the chapel and the living quarters in St. Mary's

BIGNOR (W): Oak screen, early 14th century

ETCHINGHAM (E): Oak misericord, late 14th century (detail)

Hospital, Chichester (W). It dates from the last decade of the thirteenth century and is of eight bays, each with sub-divided lights under a crocketed gable. This is followed by the early fourteenth-century screen in the Bishop's Chapel, also in Chichester. This has oculi in the heads of the bays and is a more sophisticated version of the contemporary screens at Bignor, West Thorney (W) and Rodmell. Heavily restored early screens in West Sussex which may be of the same date as the St. Mary's Hospital example are at Findon and Old Shoreham. Most of the later church screens in the county are simple, rustic affairs like that at Burton (W) and Penhurst (E); the former retains its Rood loft and traces of painted decoration.

Seating for the laity, which was introduced into parish churches during the fifteenth and early sixteenth centuries, is unsophisticated. What little elaboration there is occurs on the bench ends. The most common type has straight tops, as at Hardham and Tortington (W); at Appledram, Kirdford, Slindon, Wisborough Green (W) and Buxted (E) the bench-ends terminate in roughly carved poppy-heads. The most rustic of all is the series at Didling (W) which defy accurate dating; their rough-hewn simplicity contributes much to the atmosphere of this remote, unrestored church.

Much more care was lavished on the stalls and hinged seats used by the clergy and placed in the chancel. The seats are known as misericords from the Latin word for pity, because when tipped up they provided support for their occupants during

RYE (E): Oak pulpit, early 16th century

ROTHERFIELD (E): Oak font cover, dated 1533

Oak chest from a West Sussex church, late 13th century

services. Their undersides permitted the medieval carver to give full vent to his imagination without being constrained by religious imagery. The best examples in Sussex occur in the corporate ecclesiastical foundations, such as the late fourteenth-century colleges at Arundel (W) and Etchingham (E). The latter's subjects include foxes dressed as clerics (a common medieval subject), fishes, and ladies clad in contemporary high fashion. St. Mary's Hospital in Chichester has no fewer than twenty-four, of the same date as the screen, and with some fine figures including a merman. This series seem to have been the source of inspiration for the thirty-eight misericords of *c.* 1320–30 in the cathedral. Amongst the lively carvings are dancing figures and a centaur beating a tambour. Although parish churches had fewer clergy and less prolonged services, misericords do occur here and there, as at Broadwater and West Tarring (W).

The increase in preaching which occurred in the late Middle Ages led to the construction of pulpits, of which the only wooden example in Sussex is at Rye (E). Of greater interest are four late medieval font covers, all in East Sussex. The earliest appears to be the cover at Battle (probably of the fifteenth century) and the others all date from the early sixteenth century. The Sedlescombe cover has linenfold carved panels and that at Ticehurst is embellished with Flamboyant tracery designs. The Rotherfield cover is of particular interest as it is dated 1533 and is mentioned in the churchwardens' accounts in 1532–5, when £3.10s.6d. was spent on it. The carvings on the cover are amongst the first instances of the use of Early Rennaissance motifs in Sussex.

Sussex also possesses some fine medieval church chests. Pride of place goes to the splendid piece at Climping (W) with its row of trefoil blank arcades flanked by delicately carved rose window designs. The chest dates from the end of the thirteenth century and is probably more-or-less contemporary with the chest at Buxted (E). Although this has similar carved motifs, the shallow sloping lid suggests that it may have been a container for relics rather than a repository for service books, vestments or plate.

R.M.

POST-REFORMATION UNTIL *c.* 1900

The seventeenth century was a rich period for church woodwork and Sussex has more to show from this period than has often been supposed. Much was lost in the nineteenth century when few churches escaped restoration (see pp. 70), but what survives is impressive enough.

The pulpit is often the most striking piece of woodwork in a church. Very few were made in the later sixteenth century as preaching was not encouraged because of Queen Elizabeth's fear of seditious teaching; the Injunctions of 1559 specify only four sermons a year. The 1569 Visitation of the Diocese of Chichester reported that 'many churches have no sermons, not one in seven years, and some not one in twelve years'. Bishop Richard Curteys attempted to increase the provision of preaching in the county during his episcopate (1570–82) and by 1577 it was reported that 'the pulpittes in most places sounde contynually with the voyce of learned and Godly Preachers'. After Curteys's death the bishops were lax in seeing that the obligation to preach quarterly was observed (R. B. Manning, *Religion and Society in Elizabethan Sussex,* 1969). No pulpits survive from this time; Worth (E) has a North German pulpit dated 1577 but it was only placed in the church in 1841. Seventeenth-century pulpits are well represented, however. The Canons of 1604 stated that every beneficed preacher was to preach every Sunday, and the churchwardens were to provide 'a comely and decent pulpit'.

BOTOLPHS (W): Early 17th-century pulpit

ROTHERFIELD (E): Pulpit

ASHBURNHAM (E): Three-sided altar-rail

J. M. Neale's *History of Pews* (1841) includes a list of dated Sussex pulpits: Kingston Buci (1608); East Dean (1621); Keymer and Crawley (1627); Climping (1633); Westbourne (1634); Pyecombe (1636); and Iford (1639). Of the pulpits on Neale's list those at Crawley, East Dean (actually dated 1623), Kingston Buci (W), and Pyecombe (E) survive. St. Anne's, Lewes (E), has a pulpit inscribed 'Habar Springat Gentleman made this pulpit in the yeare of our Lord 1620', and Bury (W) has an example dated 1628; it is decorated with patterns burned into the surface with a hot poker. Botolphs (W), Buxted, Penhurst, and Wilmington (E) have notable undated early seventeenth-century pulpits; that at Wilmington has a tester or sounding board decorated with an openwork obelisk, and the pulpit at Penhurst is combined with a reader's desk to form a two-decker. The parson read the service from the reading desk and ascended to the pulpit for the sermon.

The finest pulpit in Sussex is at Rotherfield (E). The tester has obelisks and strap carving and the back panel has magnificently carved eagles. The pulpit was made in the 1630s by Francis Gunby of Leeds for the Chapel of the Archbishops of York at Bishopthorpe. It was brought to Rotherfield in 1896. A virtually identical pulpit, also by Gunby, is at St. John's church, Leeds. It has the same Antwerp mannerist ornament as the Rotherfield example.

Seventeenth-century altar rails can be seen in many churches. They were occasionally installed during Elizabeth's reign but the main impetus to provide them derived from the reforms instituted by Archbishop Laud in 1634 when it was ordered that the altar should be at the east end of the chancel with 'a fit and decent rail, made from sound and good timber of the best sort'. This was to stop profanation by dogs, then commonly admitted into church, and also prevent the altar table from being moved into the chancel or nave, a device common after 1559. Laud intended that the rails should run from north to south of the sanctuary and that communion should be received at the altar rails, but some rails were made on three or four sides so that communicants could kneel round the altar. At a series of Visitations of the Archdeaconry of Lewes (1638–41) it was stated that the altar table should be railed in 'to keep off dogs and to free it from other pollutions'; in 1635 Laud's Vicar-General,

LURGASHALL (W): Chest

Sir Nathaniel Brent, suggested that churchwardens should copy the rails in the church of St. Thomas in the Cliffe, Lewes (cited in A. Fletcher, *Sussex 1600–1660: A County Community in Peace and War,* 1980). But many parishes refused to follow the Injunctions and in 1641 Parliament ordered the removal of altar rails. After the Restoration they were again installed; Kirdford (W) has a fine set dating from the later seventeenth century. Four-sided altar rails are extremely rare and none is known to survive in Sussex but a scarce three-sided altar rail given in 1638 by the splendidly named Thankful Frewen survives at Northiam (E). The panelling behind the altar and the altar table are from the same benefactor. Poynings and Ashburnham (E) also have three-sided rails; the former may be early seventeenth century, while the latter date from the 1680s.

The best ensemble of seventeenth-century woodwork in Sussex is at Ashburnham. This comprises a pulpit, gallery, cut-down box pews, font cover, and altar rails (see page 55). The altar table is probably late sixteenth century. Sussex possesses some good late sixteenth and early seventeenth-century altar tables; one of the finest, of about 1610, is at Etchingham (E), and there are others at Botolphs and Hardham (W). At the end of the reign of Edward VI some churches had communion tables while others still had stone altars. The Elizabethan Injunctions of 1559 sought to impose uniformity of practice, the main aim being that 'the Sacrament be duly and reverently ministered'. In place of the stone altar every church was to have a decently made 'holy table'. Matthew Parker's *Advertisements* of 1556 repeated the Injunctions in enjoining that each parish should 'provide a decent table, standing on a frame for the Communion Table'. By the early seventeenth century most parishes possessed one.

Box pews originally developed from low benches by heightening the backs and the ends; often privately owned or rented, few survived the church restorers. Neale's *History of Pews* lists dated examples at St. Pancras, Kingston (1608),

Storrington (1626) and Climping (1634). None of these survives though an oak panel dated 1633 on the west wall of the north transept at Climping (W) probably came from a dismembered pew. Good examples of early seventeenth-century pewing still exist at Twineham, Poynings (E), and Kingston Buci (E), although in the last they are cut down. Twineham, West Grinstead (W) and Shermanbury (W) have pews inscribed in early nineteenth-century lettering with the owner's name or farm. Kingston Buci also has an extremely rare seventeenth-century singing desk; another example used to exist at Bobbing in Kent.

Many churches possess a seventeenth-century chest. These were generally for the storage of parish records, plate, or occasionally vestments; that at Lurgashall (W) deserves mention as it is inscribed with the churchwardens' names and is dated 1667.

Eighteenth and early nineteenth-century pews and galleries were almost inevitably destroyed by the Victorian church restorers. What little survives can be summarily dealt with. Galleries were once common; they provided extra accommodation for the congregation, the choir, or the village choir band. Many faculty petitions survive which often give the names of the carpenters. At Salehurst (E) John Cole and John Walker built a gallery in 1702 and at Albourne (E) Joseph Wood and John Gilham built a west gallery in 1723. These no longer exist but Ninfield and Worth (E) still have seventeenth-century west galleries, and eighteenth and early nineteenth-century galleries can be seen at Singleton (W), Brightling (E), St. John's, Chichester (W), and Holy Cross, Uckfield (E).

CHICHESTER, St. JOHN (W): The three-decker pulpit

There are few surviving eighteenth-century box pews. East Guldeford (E) has late eighteenth or early nineteenth-century box pews made of deal and Parham (W) has a set dating from the 1820s which includes a squire's and parson's pew. Of finer quality are those at Warminghurst (W) which date from the 1770s. Indeed, Warminghurst is the eighteenth-century equivalent of Ashburnham as far as woodwork is concerned. But the most striking of all pews in the county is at Warbleton (E) where, in the north aisle, is the galleried manorial pew of the Roberts family for which a faculty was given on 5 April 1722. It is approached by a staircase and is in the form of a miniature room.

Three-decker pulpits developed out of the earlier two-decker variety. The parish clerk read the responses (usually a straightforward 'Amen' after prayers) from the lower deck while the parson read the service from the second stage and, donning a black preaching gown, delivered the sermon from the pulpit. The best surviving example in Sussex is in St. John's church, Chichester (W). Dating from about 1813 and made of American birch, the pulpit was originally designed so that the three elements were in front of each other but at a later date it was arranged on a north–south axis.

The radical re-ordering of churches that took place in the nineteenth century often lead to the replacement of old woodwork by mass-produced items chosen from ecclesiastical furnishers' catalogues. The Ecclesiologists often recommended suitable models for copying. J. M. Neale in *A Few Words to Church Builders* (1841) suggested that the screens at St. Nicholas's, Brighton, Ovingdean, Fletching (E), and Old Shoreham (W) were all worthy of 'study and imitation'. Occasionally, as at Appledram (W), the seating was copied from a surviving medieval bench. In general, however, local characteristics were often ignored in favour of a preconceived 'ideal'. In a long article entitled 'open seats' in the *Ecclesiologist* (November 1842), the Society suggested that the hated pews should be replaced with oak benches of uniform height secured with wooden pegs. They should not be 'carved with incorrect or scanty detail' or be 'of ludicrous and fanciful design'. The open seats at Steeple Aston and Hasely, Oxfordshire, lithographed by the Oxford Architectural Society, were recommended as models. Victorian wooden pulpits are in general undistinguished; the most interesting is at Whatlington (E) where the pulpit is supported by winged angels representing Faith, Hope and Charity. It was exhibited at the Great Exhibition in 1851, and is thought to be French or Belgian.

However, the major church architects did take a personal interest in the design of church furniture. The *Ecclesiologist* reported in 1856 that R. C. Carpenter had supplied nave seating at Bodiam (E) copied from seats of his own design at St. Mary Magdalene, Munster Square, London, built in 1849–52. William Butterfield designed the pulpit at West Lavington (W) in 1850, and probably the nave seating at All Saints, Hastings (E, 1869–70) and St. Mary's, Battle (E, 1866–69). G. E. Street closely supervised the detail of all his churches and he probably designed the seating at St. Saviour's, Eastbourne (E, 1865–72). William Burges designed the walnut choir stalls at St. Michael and All Angels, Brighton (E) in 1868. Examples could easily be multiplied but the church with the best surviving nineteenth-century woodwork is St. Martin's, Brighton (E), where all the major fittings were designed by Somers Clarke between 1872 and 1875.

D.B.

Ten

TOMBS, MONUMENTS AND CHURCHYARDS

TOMBS AND MONUMENTS BEFORE 1600

SUSSEX is rich in medieval and Tudor sepulchral monuments. The great and the good are paraded in their trappings of office and include all the men and women of substance in East and West Sussex: nobles, prelates, knights and high-born ladies. The not-so-great are also well-represented on tombs: merchants, craftsmen, yeomen and parish priests, all portrayed appropriate to their calling in life. A wide range of types of monument is found and the materials used include limestone, marble, alabaster, wood, brass and iron. The makers of the Sussex tombs largely remain anonymous. A carver named Flynton was responsible for the impressive wall-monument to Richard Covert (d. 1579) at Slaugham (E) and the Netherlandish sculptor Gerard Johnson, who was resident in Southwark, made the elaborate tombs of Sir Edwin Gage (d. 1569) and John Gage (d. 1598) at West Firle (E). The designs for both monuments survive, together with the correspondence between Johnson and John Gage, as a result of which modifications taking into account Gage's comments were made to the designs, especially for the brasses representing his two wives.

A few records survive of the cost of late medieval monuments in Sussex. The grave-stone of William Wedden, vicar of Bodiam (E) cost 26s.8d. in 1373–4 and in 1500 John Dudeley left ten marks to pay for his and his wife's shields of arms and an inscription to be incorporated in their existing tomb at Arundel (W). Elaborate monuments cost considerably more. Sir Anthony Browne bequeathed £20 'aboute fynnishing of my tombe at Battel [Battle] if I chaunce not to fynshe the same in my lifetime' (*Sussex Rec. Soc.*, vol. XLI). Covert's monument at Slaugham cost £30. To give an idea of comparative values, in 1303 a well-to-do peasant paid £20 per year rent for lands in Surrey (J. Coales (ed.), *The Earliest English Brasses,* London, 1987).

Tombs were often placed in the chancel near to the main altar or, in the nave, adjacent to subsidiary altars, where the proximity of the Blessed Sacrament and the celebration of Masses could be efficacious for the soul of the deceased. The location to the north of the high altar of some of the early Tudor wall-monuments which proliferate throughout Sussex suggests that they combined the functions of tomb and Easter Sepulchre, upon which the Blessed Sacrament representing Christ's body was displayed during the Easter liturgy. This function is made explicit in the will of Thomas Fiennes, Lord Dacre (1531): 'My body to be buried in the parishe church of

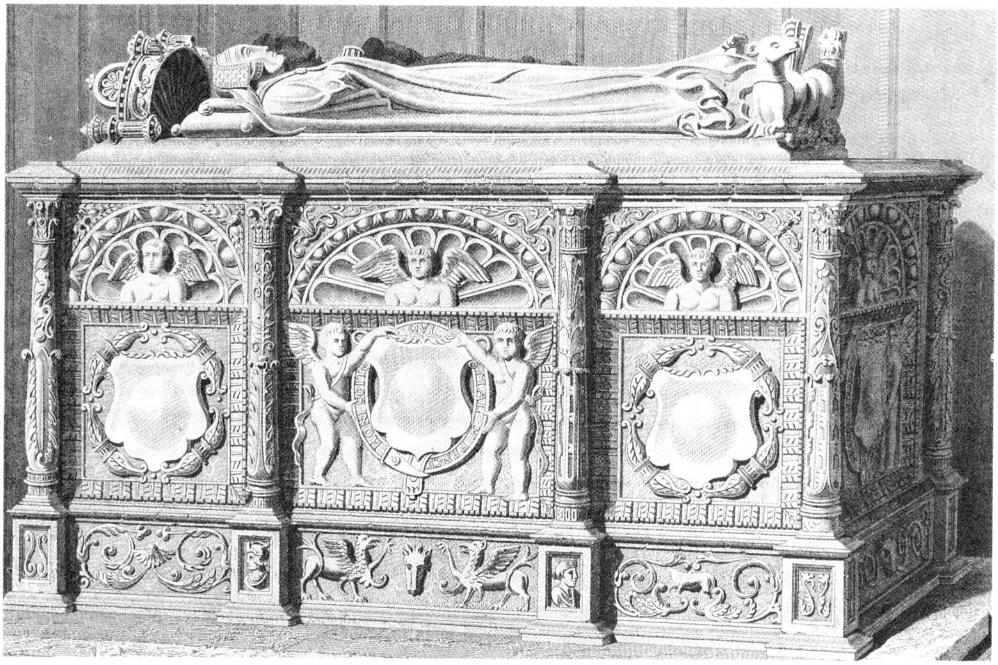

BATTLE (E): Lithograph of 1826 after a drawing by Blore of the alabaster tomb of Sir Anthony Browne (d. 1548) and his wife

Hersemounceux [Herstmonceux (E)] in the northside of the High Awter there, where the sepulcre used to be made; And one tombe there to be made and ordeyned convenient for the making and setting of the said Sepulcre' (*Sussex Rec. Soc.*, vol. XLII). Many tombs, such as the twelfth-century carved monument at Bishopstone (E), and the early sixteenth-century slab to John Collins at Burwash (E) (the earliest known tomb made by the Sussex iron industry) were designed to be set in the floor. From the fourteenth century onwards both brasses and stone recumbent effigies were often raised on chests. Such tombs took up floor space and the introduction of wooden seating for the laity must have contributed to the popularity of wall-monuments in the fifteenth and sixteenth centuries. The costliest memorials were independent chapels in their own right, enclosed within free-standing architectural structures in which Masses for the deceased were said and sung. The most elaborate of these 'chantry tombs' are those of the ninth and tenth Earls of Arundel at Arundel (W) and the grandiose De la Warr monuments at Boxgrove and Broadwater (W).

Recent conservation of the tomb of the ninth Earl of Arundel and his wife has revealed the exceptional quality of the polychrome (painting and gilding) applied to the stone effigies of the Earl and Countess (*Jnl. Church Monuments Soc.*, vol. 1, Pt. 2). Many stone and alabaster monuments were originally painted and gilded; one of the fine early fourteenth-century gabled tombs at Winchelsea (E) has the remains of a mural depicting an angel holding the soul of the deceased in a napkin. Such rare survivors should always be preserved, just as the deplorable modern fashion for recolouring monuments (notably the Dacre tomb at Herstmonceux and Sir Anthony Browne's tomb-chest at Battle (E)) must be avoided.

Down to the late thirteenth century sepulchral monuments consisted of relief-carved or incised slabs and coffin lids, the design often comprising a cross.

SOUTHOVER (LEWES, E): Black marble tomb slab of Gundrada, co-founder of Lewes Priory, *c.* 1145

Recumbent effigies began to appear from the second half of the thirteenth century, and some good examples exist from the period *c.* 1300–1350 in Chichester Cathedral, Ifield (W) and Winchelsea (E). Monumental brasses occur from the beginning of the fourteenth century, the vast majority dating from the fifteenth and first half of the sixteenth centuries. Sussex rates tenth in the number of surviving brasses in county surveys and the indents of many lost brasses have been recorded. In addition to brasses of knights and ladies of gentle birth and clergy there are some interesting individual memorials, such as that of Peter Denot (*c.* 1440) at Fletching (E), whose trade is represented by a pair of gloves, and an incised slab to a brewer at Playden (E). Other uncommon memorials include a carved slab in Chichester Cathedral commemorating a heart burial, possibly of Lady Joan de Vere (d. 1293). At Arundel the tomb of John, seventh Earl of Arundel, who was killed at the Battle of Beauvais in 1435, is commemorated by two effigies. The upper one is clad in full panoply of war resting on a tomb-chest with open arcading through which can be seen a grim cadaver in a shroud, a reminder of how death comes to high and low-born alike; this 'memento mori' theme occurs on a number of monuments in England during the fifteenth century. Sometimes descendants commissioned brasses to their parents and ancestors, as at Stopham (W), where the brasses of John Barthelot (d. 1426) and John Barthelot (d. 1453) were both engraved in *c.* 1470.

The finest sepulchral monuments in Sussex are of national importance and are by the leading craftsmen of their day. The Tournai marble tombstone of Gundrada, co-founder of Lewes Priory now in Southover church (E), was carved in *c.* 1145 by a sculptor who seems to have been in the service of Henry of Blois, Abbot of Glastonbury and Bishop of Winchester, one of the leading patrons of the arts in the twelfth century. The brass at Trotton (W) to Margaret de Braose, wife of Ralph de Camoys, dates from *c.* 1310 and lays claim to be the earliest surviving life-size figural brass in England. It was executed by a London workshop which was responsible for most of the major brasses in the period *c.* 1305–*c.* 1335 (J. Coales (ed.), *The Earliest English Brasses*). The best of the later Sussex monumental brasses are also probably to be attributed to metropolitan rather than local craftsmen, notably the impressive memorial of Thomas Nelond (d. 1433), Prior of Lewes, at Cowfold (W).

The numerous early Tudor wall-monuments are for the most part probably of local workmanship, although the design is by no means peculiar to Sussex. The basic formula is of a marble or stone recess containing a tomb-chest and with a back panel for brasses or carvings of the deceased and his/her family, together with a *Pietà*,

Resurrected Christ or other religious image; this is flanked by solid side walls which are linked by curved pieces with a flat arch or lintel. Classicising details and motifs such as *putti* appear on some of the tombs executed in the middle years of the sixteenth century, but as with other Sussex sepulchral monuments of the late 1520s onwards, such as the De la Warr tombs at Boxgrove and Broadwater (W), the Browne monument at Battle (E) and the tomb of Sir Goddard Oxenbridge (d. 1537) at Brede (E), these are far from being fully-fledged Renaissance-style works of art; rather it is a case of some novel details incorporated into what is still a medieval idiom. By the 1570s the last traces of the Middle Ages had disappeared from tombs. The Covert monument carved by Flynton at Slaugham (E) with its fluted columns and fine proportions is reminiscent of the restrained classicism characteristic of works of the 1550s found in less conservative regions. More typical of tomb design in the last quarter of the sixteenth and early seventeenth centuries are a series of ostentatious monuments, chiefly in coloured alabaster, and whose source of inspiration lay in the Low Countries from where the leading carvers like Gerard Johnson came to England as Protestant refugees. The figure of the first Viscount Montague (d. 1592) is shown kneeling above his two recumbent wives on the incomplete monument at Easebourne (W), a pose that was introduced for effigies in the late sixteenth and early seventeenth centuries. The same pose occurs at Friston (E), Harting and Wiston (W). Another manifestation of the taste for depicting the deceased as if still alive can be seen on the grandiose Jefferay tomb at Chiddingly (E), erected in 1612. Here the elaborate effigy of Sir John Jefferay reclines on his elbow above the recumbent figure of his first wife. The other effigies of this tomb, representing their daughter and her husband Sir Edward Montague, are shown as standing figures, a unique motif in English monuments of the pre-Civil War period. This grandiose *tableau vivant* exudes a self-confident and even secular air by no means untypical of Elizabethan and Jacobean tombs.

R.M.

MONUMENTS AFTER 1600

At the beginning of the seventeenth century the traditional Elizabethan form of monument was still represented in Sussex. The form was usually that of a recumbent life-size effigy on a table tomb with kneeling children beneath, set against an architectural background as in the monument to Sir Thomas Caryll (d. 1616) and his wife at Shipley (W). By mid-century a new simpler style of hanging wall monument began to appear, comprising a bust set within an oval recess. Examples are the monuments to Sir William Springett (d. 1643) at Ringmer (E), John Nutt (d. 1656) at Berwick (E) or a bust set with a scallop surround as at Arundel (W) (d. 1633).

The most outstanding monuments of this period are to be found at Ashburnham and Withyham (E). In the latter stands the revolutionary monument to the young Thomas Sackville (1677) by Caius Gabriel Cibber. In an attempt to convey real emotion the grieving mother and father kneel by their dying son who reclines on a tomb chest clasping a skull. At Ashburnham a monument by John Bushnell dates from 1675 and although less spontaneous in expression it is as sharp a break from the past as Cibber's. In front of antique draperies the distraught husband William Ashburnham kneels behind his reclining wife who, resigned to death, leans on one arm whilst a cherub anoints her with a crown. Both these monuments break with tradition in their treatment of grief and their attempt to display real emotion. The contrast with the formality of earlier memorials is evident at Ashburnham where the adjacent monument to John Ashburnham and his two wives dates from 1671 and although only four years earlier than Bushnell's work, the two memorials are totally different in conception. The former is solidly traditional, a recumbent effigy in armour lying between his two wives, one of whom is depicted in her shroud. One other example of Bushnell's work has recently been restored to view at Mid-Lavant (W). The pock-marked life-sized effigy of Dame Margaret May was originally erected in 1676, but was walled up under the floor during the nineteenth-century restoration of the church.

Examples of baroque cartouches can be found at Warminghurst (W) and Lurgashall (W), while florid drapery, chubby cherubs and a Latin inscription combine on the wall tablet to William Parker at Willingdon (W, 1727). Allegorical figures appear, most notably at Cuckfield (E) where Thomas Adye designed the female figure of Truth perching on the edge of a sarcophagus in front of an obelisk grasping a mirror in her right hand and, assisted by a putto, holding a portrait medallion of Charles Sergison (d. 1732) in her left.

By the early eighteenth century a more restrained classicism appears in church monuments. There are several fine portrait busts like that of Sir William Morley (d. 1728) at Boxgrove (W). At Racton (W) the bust of Sir Charles Nicholl (d. 1733) is set in an elaborate architectural frame. The undated bust of Sara Cook at Goring (W) is equally impressive and at Warbleton (E) Rysbrack's monument to Sir John Loade (1740) is an exceptional piece although the effect is diminished by the intrusion of a nineteenth-century organ chamber. Later examples in the same tradition are Rouw's bust of 'Mad Jack' Fuller (d. 1834) at Brightling (E) and a pair of busts of *c.* 1840 at Donnington (W).

The typical eighteenth-century symbolism of urns (signifying not the ashes of

ASHBURNHAM (E): Monument to William Ashburnham (d. 1675) and his wife, the Countess of Marlborough by John Bushnell

WITHYHAM (E): Monument to Thomas Sackville (d. 1677) by C. G. Cibber. The deceased reclines grasping a skull while his distraught parents kneel on cushions on either side of his tomb

cremation but an antiquarian interest in classical antiquity) and grieving females clad in flowing robes are found throughout the county. At West Grinstead (W) Rysbrack represented William Powlett (d. 1746) and his wife in Roman dress standing either side of an urn, the husband with his legs nonchalantly crossed. Souls are shown ascending to heaven. The monument at Petworth (W) to the Revd. John Wickins (d. 1783) has a child angel sitting on a cloud and pointing to an inscribed open book. This was a design employed by the sculptor, John Flaxman, on a number of monuments throughout the country.

By the middle years of the eighteenth century sentimentality was increasingly evident in the design of monuments but restrained classicism can still be found in Flaxman's monument to Sir William Burrell (d. 1796) at West Grinstead (W). The simple design consists of an urn on top of a sarcophagus. Undoubtedly one of the best eighteenth-century monuments in Sussex is that to Mary, Countess of Derby (d. 1752), at Boxgrove (W). This has an impressive sarcophagus with a carved relief showing the duchess seated beneath a tree offering relief to the poor and directing them to a refuge behind her. Her memorial mirrored her life as she had endowed both almshouses for a dozen aged women and a school for twelve children. Another noteworthy memorial is the monument to Anthony, Earl of Newburgh (d. 1814) in Slindon Roman Catholic church (W). It is one of only three examples in England of the work of the Danish sculptor, Bertel Thorwaldsen and the figures are carved with feeling.

By the end of the eighteenth century sentimentality is rife, exemplified by three monuments at Withyham (E). Joseph Nollekens' monument to John Frederick, Duke of Dorset, is signed and dated 1802 and has three putti hanging a garland over an urn bearing a portrait of the deceased whilst in the same church Flaxman's monument to the Fourth Duke of Dorset (d. 1815) represents his grieving mother in Greek costume resting her head on an altar with an urn on it. Above her there is a fine portrait medallion of the deceased Duke in contemporary costume. The third Withyham memorial is Chantrey's design for the tomb of Arabella, Duchess of Dorset, completed in 1831 at a cost of £829. This depicts her two bereft daughters, both classically attired, kneeling before a draped urn.

A death bed tableau appears at Herstmonceux (E) where the memorial to Georgina Hare Naylor (d. 1806) reveals the deceased lying resigned to death with figures of her sister(?), a young child and an angel in attendance. There are numerous simple tablets with no figural sculpture but a narrative relief detailing the deceased's good deeds and intended to act as an incentive to the onlooker to live a good life. The memorial at Felpham (W) to William Hayley includes an obituary thirty lines long.

By the early years of the nineteenth century, the quality of workmanship had visibly declined and the diversity of church monuments faded as benefactors were encouraged to provide money to renew the church fabric, through new organs, fittings and stained glass rather than through grand family monuments. The occasional pieces of quality therefore tend to stand out like the Baptism of Christ by J. E. Carew (1835) in the Roman Catholic church of St. John the Baptist, Brighton (E). Unfortunately, all too often all that is left is oppressive sentimentality as in the monument to Earl de la Warr (1869) at Withyham (E), where a young woman casts a wreath upon the waters.

Cast iron tomb slabs are an important rarity that are found only in the Weald and in the Welsh Marches. About one hundred slabs have been identified from the Weald

ASHBURNHAM (E): Monument to John Ashburnham (d. 1671) who lies in armour between his two wives

in some thirty different churches, of which eighteen are in Sussex. Designed to lie on top of a grave these thick slabs of cast iron with embossed letters, measure approximately six feet by two feet. Most date from the seventeenth century through to the mid-eighteenth century. The earliest example is in Burwash Church (E). It commemorates John Collins, an iron master and dates from *c.* 1537. The earliest dated example is at East Grinstead (E) and bears the date 1570. The slabs were produced by casting in a bed of sand using letter moulds pressed into the sand. Mistakes often occurred, with the letters N and S appearing back-to-front. Frequent errors in spacing between words and inappropriate breaks in words split between lines also suggest that the casters were illiterate.

Non-conformist monuments are rare but it is worth mentioning the wooden monument boards which adorn the walls of the former Rehobeth Chapel at Pell Green, Wadhurst (E).

Evidence for two other associated funereal customs survive in Sussex churches. During the sixteenth and seventeenth centuries the custom of displaying funerary armour arose. Examples still survive at Racton (W) and Fletching (E) amongst other churches. The armour was carried in the funeral procession before being displayed in the church. Genuine armour was not generally used for this purpose. However, the surviving helm from Broadwater church (W), which was preserved by the architect William Burges who found it lying loose and heavily damaged in the church in 1879, is an Italian jousting helm of *c.* 1520. It is now in the Tower of London Armouries. This tradition was later continued in the inclusion of sculptured symbols of rank or weapons as trophies atop a memorial tablet as on the monument to Sir Henry Hollis Bradford at Edburton (W).

From the early seventeenth century the custom developed of carrying an armorial token of mourning in the funeral procession which was then displayed on the deceased's house for some months. Painted on board or canvas these hatchments were finally hung in the church. 114 hatchments survive in the county, less than one third of the number to be found in neighbouring Kent. The earliest surviving example dates from 1710 at Chiddingly (E), the latest from 1975 at Northiam (E). Good examples can be found in many churches including Boxgrove (W), Ashburnham and Glynde (E). Before the Victorian restorations many more survived judging from the studies of Sir William Burrell and the Reverend William Hayley.

J.R.

CHURCHYARDS

The churchyards surrounding an old church probably contain a thousand years of burials. It is no accident that churchyards are often raised above their surrounding land due to the displaced earth and layers of successive interments. Few of these burials were likely to have been marked by any form of commemorative headstone before the seventeenth century. The poorer members of society were buried wrapped simply in a shroud tied hand and foot and lowered straight into the ground from the parish bier. A bier dated 1697 still survives in Bury church (W) and an elaborate Victorian example, all frills and ebonised wood, is preserved at Ticehurst (E). Coffin stools, on which the coffin would rest, can be seen at Beddingham (E) and in the General Baptist chapel at Billingshurst (W). Certificates dating from the years between 1667 and 1814, when burial in a woollen shroud was compulsory, survive amongst the parish documents.

Many of the first grave markers were probably made of wood and have long since perished. Nineteenth-century examples can be found in a sadly neglected condition; one was even discovered by the author on a churchyard bonfire. Consisting of two posts joined by a board recording details of the deceased, these markers are called dead boards or leaping boards. Cheap and easy to produce in a county with little good freestone, they are a regular feature of many eighteenth and nineteenth-century illustrations of the county's churches. The earliest still surviving dates from 1658 and is preserved at Sidlesham (W); it is lettered on two sides. Nineteenth-century examples are more frequent as at Twineham or Cuckfield (E), and they continued to be produced into this century: the Cade Street Chapel at Heathfield (E) has a dead board dating from the 1960s. The design of dead boards was later copied in stone with two stone supports supporting a wooden, stone or iron board. Examples can be found at East Grinstead (E, 1703) and Billingshurst (W, 1734) as well as at Ardingly, Balcombe, Maresfield, Horsted Keynes and Westfield (E). The stonemasons May and Parsons of Lewes charged £5 in 1800 for one of these stone leaping boards. There are also cast-iron examples; a dozen examples alone survive from St. Anne's, Lewes (E), dating from between 1828 and 1887.

The earliest stone grave markers were at the head and the foot, the former inscribed with details of the deceased, the latter with an epitaph. Originally head and footstone faced outwards from the body so that they could be read without trampling on the grave. It was only in the nineteenth century that the practice of turning the headstones to face the grave was adopted. Seventeenth and early eighteenth-century headstones are smaller, made from thicker pieces of stone and use simple and plain forms of lettering. As the eighteenth century progressed the stones became slimmer and larger in size in answer to the pressure to provide more details of the deceased. The epitaphs grew longer and were now placed under the inscription rather than on the footstone. The larger slabs provided more opportunity for the carver to display his artistic abilities, either in rich symbolism or in skilful examples of fine lettering.

The finest headstones occurred in the eighteenth century, when the concern about mortality and the re-emergence of classical symbolism led to a wealth of powerful images. A strong emphasis was placed upon mortality with crudely carved skulls at Brede, Salehurst and Ewhurst (E).

At Cowfold (W) Father Time stands on top of skulls and bones holding an empty hour-glass, and Wartling (E) has a headstone with Father Time stabbing the deceased with a trident. At Ringmer (E) Death lies in a shroud stabbed by his own dart. The symbolism is fairly clear: the winged hour-glass to remind mankind of how time flies and Death is usually personified as a skeleton. One of the best examples of such eighteenth-century symbolism is seen at Warbleton (E) on the stone commemorating Charles Cook (d. 1767). Cook is shown under a fallen tree, by which means he reputedly met his death; overhead Christ is shown wreathed in clouds suspending a pair of scales. On either side winged cherubs descend blowing trumpets and the fallen tree is flanked by Father Time wielding a scythe and an hour-glass resting on a skull.

Westbourne churchyard (W) has several interesting stones including several images of open coffins revealing skeletons in addition to the more usual hour-glasses, skeletons and trumpets such as can be found at Old Shoreham (W) and elsewhere. Westbourne and many other places have examples of the eighteenth-century taste for winged cherubs, many of which may have been gaudily painted. Other popular

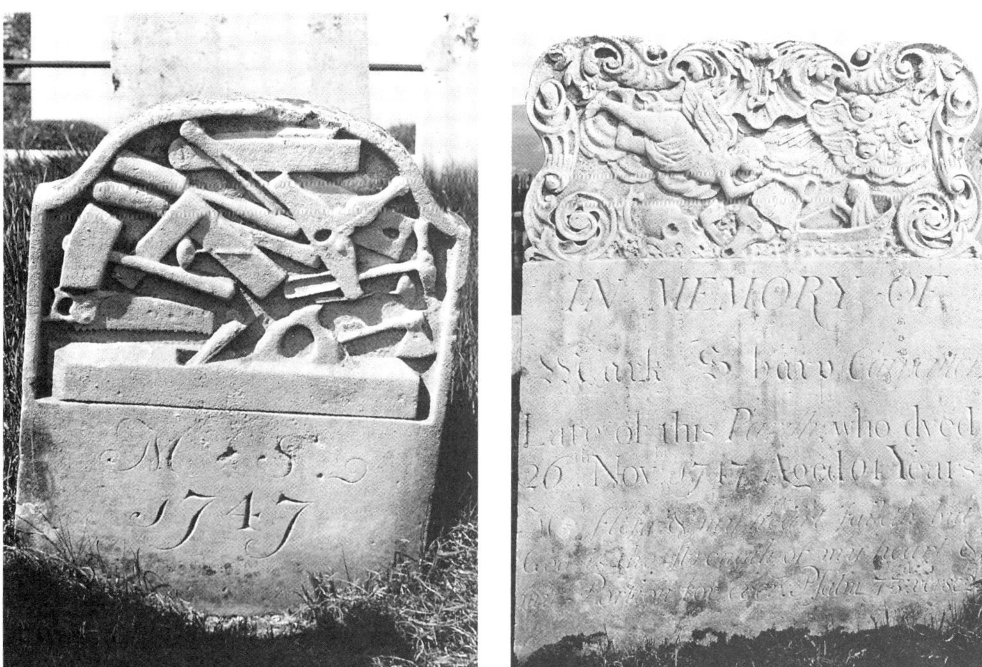

LEWES, ST. JOHN (E): The head and footstones of Mark Sharp (d. 1747). Note the representation of the Last Judgement on the former and his carpenter's tools on the latter

themes include a representation of the Resurrection at Rotherfield (E, dated 1778) and general resurrections at Cowfold (W, 1798) and Newhaven (E, 1764). The Last Judgement is represented on the stone to Richard Valler at East Dean (W, 1776) and that to Elizabeth Penfold at Broadwater (W, 1793). The symbols of Faith, Hope and Charity also occur, Hope symbolised by an anchor at Pulborough (W, 1763), Charity by a heart at Cuckfield (E, 1764) and Faith by a cross, as at Wadhurst (E, 1789). By this date crosses are rarely seen. They were regarded as popish ornamentation and are therefore rare before the mid-nineteenth century, when they found favour as a result of Tractarian influence. A number of interesting or amusing tombstones are worthy of note. At Sidlesham and Westbourne farmers are represented by ploughs. The footstone to the carpenter, Mark Sharp, in St. John's, Lewes (E), displays a variety of his working tools including a saw, jack plane, axe, mallet, square, bevel, gouger, augers and compasses. At Newhaven (E) the brewer Thomas Tipper has a representation of the Newhaven bridge as well as a witty rhyme carved on his stone. Ship's master Richard Barrow is depicted at Bosham (W). He died in 1759, drowning in an accident from his sloop, *The Two Brothers.* The survival of so many examples of eighteenth-century tombstones is partly due to the closure of overcrowded churchyards to further burials at the end of the eighteenth and early nineteenth centuries. Increasingly towns required additional burial grounds and cemeteries. In Brighton (E) the new parochial burial ground situated opposite St. Nicholas' church opened in 1840 and eleven years later the Extra-Mural Cemetery received its first burial.

Classical symbolism can also be seen in the terracotta oval plaques produced by Jonathan Harmer of Heathfield (1762–1849). A stonemason, he emigrated to America but returned in 1800 and designed a dozen inexpensive terracotta plaques intended for insertion into headstones and monuments. They are easily recognisable and are usually clearly marked with his name. The designs cover a variety of subjects including Charity represented as a seated female figure suckling three children, and a basket of fruit and flowers, both of which originally cost 8s. Other alternatives include an ornamental vase, an urn or a winged cherub, the latter sometimes shown with a crown and rays. Harmer terracottas still survive in at least seventeen Sussex churchyards and burial grounds in the locality of Heathfield, the best selections being at Mayfield, Herstmonceux and in Heathfield (E) itself, including those of the Cade Street Chapel. They were cast in both the local red clay and an imported pale coloured clay. The casts continued to be used for tombstones after Harmer's death in 1849. The plaques were intended to be inset into headstones but in some cases they appear to have been added as an after-thought. At Heathfield a plaque depicting a basket of flowers has been inserted in place of the originally inscribed stone which simply read 'Sacred'. Harmer plaques also appear on monuments inside churches, notably those to the Reverend George Gilbert (1827) in Cade Street Chapel and to members of the Luck family at Wadhurst (E, 1817). A number of the plaques are now preserved in the collections of the Sussex Archaeological Society and Brighton Museum. The only plaque cast in iron is now preserved inside Wartling church and is in the form of a basket of fruit and flowers. Originally it was one of a pair which surmounted either upright of a stone 'bed-end' form of leaping board in the churchyard. This was a unique Sussex example of the use of an iron framework to support inset stone slabs although Remnant quotes two known instances in neighbouring Kent.

Harmer terracottas were a cheaper form of adorning a monument available to the moderately well-off. The various monuments composed of Mrs. Eleanor Coade's 'artificial' stone were popular for similar reasons. Coade stone, which was in reality a kiln-fired stoneware, was principally manufactured between 1769 and 1843 and Sussex is fortunate in having several fine examples. The monument to Sarah Goring (d. 1798) in Wiston church (W) and the churchyard monument to the actress Anna Maria Crouch (d. 1805) at St. Nicholas, Brighton (E), are two excellent examples. There are further examples in West Sussex at Ifield, Old Shoreham and West Tarring.

During the second half of the nineteenth century cheap grave markers in the form of cast iron tablets and crosses became popular. At their most rudimentary the inscriptions were painted, but for greater permanence embossed lettering was available (although in the latter case once cast additional names could not be added). The designs include a variety of types of cross as well as others in clear imitation of stone tablets. One at Wisborough Green (W) is capped by a pediment surmounted by a rather charming owl with outstretched wings and at Southease (E) the more usual symbolism of a winged hour-glass is employed. There are single flat castings, but at Burwash (E) there are examples dating from near the turn of the century with a three-dimensional tablet including a separate cast inset for the inscription. Cast iron grave markers can still be seen in a number of churchyards. Thirteen survive at Wisborough Green (W) and twenty can be seen at Cocking (W), the latter produced by the Guildford firm of Filmer and Mason. A simple cross like that to Luke Blunder (1891) cost about 10s. and its embossed inscription would have cost about 2d. per letter.

NINFIELD (E): Tombstone of Ann Blackman (d. 1761). Note the winged devil, hour-glass, scythe and skull

NEWHAVEN (E): Gravestone of the local brewer Thomas Tipper (d. 1785) depicting the Newhaven Bridge

Some unusual churchyard memorials exist in Sussex. At Twineham (E) part of the churchyard was used as a Quaker burial ground between 1694 and 1732. This rare accommodation between the Established church and Dissent came about because the vicar's daughter married a Quaker. The Quakers agreed to pay 1s. rent for the plot, but to allay their sensibilities over supporting the 'steeple-house' the parish then paid them 1s. 6d. for the right to use the mown grass. At Westham (E) a communal grave from an outbreak of plague in 1666 is marked in the churchyard. Most spectacularly of all the churchyard at Brightling (E) is dominated by the pyramid mausoleum of John Fuller erected in 1810 some twenty years before its intended recipient's death. Known as 'Mad Jack' by his contemporaries, legend had it that Fuller was interred in his pyramid seated and dressed for dinner, faced by a full meal and bottle of claret; in reality the body lies recumbent under a floor slab. The legend, like his reputation for eccentricity, does not do justice to an intelligent and energetic patron of the arts and sciences.

As can be seen from the contemporary catalogues of funerary sculpture, the nineteenth century saw the loss of the individualistic quality of eighteenth century tombstones. This was the result of the introduction of mass-production techniques and the use of imported foreign white marbles which were (and still are) out of sympathy with the natural hues of the older stones and of the church itself. Increasingly grave plots came to be regarded as private property, emphasised by the appearance of railings, fences and kerbs surrounding them. Entwined boughs, broken columns, anchors and other memorials of little originality came to fill the burial grounds and cemeteries. The very survival of such symbols shows the failure of the Camden Society and its supporters whose rejection of the pagan symbolism, non-Christian associations and sheer individualism of the eighteenth century was never universally adopted. In the words of the *Ecclesiologist* the churchyards were 'disfigured by misshapen head stones, displaying emblems of heathen annihilation and rhymes of extravagant eulogy . . . every effort should be made to prevent the intrusion of "headstones", "footstones", "breastones", "tablet boards" and the like . . . and those at present existing, with their hour-glasses, weeping willows, death's heads, cherubims, scythes and inscription of "afflictions sore" would . . . soon moulder away'.

In his *Tract Upon Tombstones* published in 1843 the Reverend F. E. Paget was vehement in his opposition to the painted cherubs so common on Georgian tombstones. 'Certainly if tawdryness of colour can attract, then these look smart enough when they come out of the stone-mason's yard, but let a few months pass, and what a change takes place! The summer's sun has faded the red of the cheeks, and the damps of the autumn have covered, perhaps one half of the face with mouldy green, so that the remains of its former brilliancy only make this ugly representation still more hideous'. Yet the adverse effects of the Victorians on our churchyards can hardly be any worse than the evils of our own generation. The churchyard today can provide a major maintenance problem, but can that be an excuse for the clearance of headstones leaving open mown areas surrounded by walls lined by headstones, sometimes placed face-to-face abutting one another thereby rendering the inscription unreadable? Such is the case at Singleton (W), while at Stoughton (W) the tombstones have been relaid as paving.

J.R.

Eleven

CHURCH PLATE AND METALWORK

THE MIDDLE AGES

FOR a county which proved resistant to the Reformation for so long, the surviving medieval church plate of Sussex is surprisingly sparse – although nowhere in England does it exist in any quantity. The principal survivals are of the vessels used in the sacrament of the Mass: the chalice and the paten. Fewer than a dozen English medieval chalices exist throughout East and West Sussex, not all of which survive in their original form. These remnants are a far cry from the riches possessed by Sussex churches during the Middle Ages. Surviving wills and inventories show that on the eve of the Reformation parish churches were well-endowed with plate. An inventory of the church goods at Rotherfield (E) in 1509 includes five silver chalices and patens, a pyx (the container for the consecrated wafer or Host), a chrismatory (vessel for the holy oil), eight pewter cruets, three sacring bells (for ringing at the elevation of the Host during Mass), a gilt-bronze processional cross, a gilt-bronze censer and frankincense holder and six candlesticks (*Sussex Arch. Colls.*, vol. XLI).

The earliest, and finest, surviving church plate in Sussex is associated variously with the diocesan mother church and a monastic foundation; all were found in coffins, a common burial custom for clergy and those in monastic orders in the Middle Ages. In 1840 a copper-gilt and *champlevé* enamelled chalice with Christ blessing and three angels on the foot was found in a coffin on the site of the Benedictine nunnery at Rusper (W). The chalice was probably made in *c.* 1200 by a craftsman from Limoges in France, a famous centre for *champlevé* enamelling in the twelfth and thirteenth centuries. Enamelled copper chalices from Limoges may have been quite common in the Middle Ages, but this is the only known example to survive. The shallow hemispherical bowl, stem with knot and rounded foot conform to the standard chalice design used in western Europe during the late twelfth and thirteenth centuries. Three chalices found in bishops' tombs at Chichester have the same shape as Rusper. One is of lead or pewter and the other two are silver and partly-gilded. The base-metal example and one of the silver cups are of twelfth-century date. The foot of the third chalice is more elaborate and is embossed with two rows of downward radiating trefoil-shaped lobes; this dates from the thirteenth century. All three of the Chichester chalices are accompanied by their patens for the consecrated bread. The two silver patens both represent the standard medieval types, one with the central part sunk as a multifoiled depression and the other with circular and quatrefoil depressions. Each has an engraved design in the centre, one with the hand of God *(Manus Dei)* and the other the lamb *(Agnus Dei),* which are motifs found on patens throughout the Middle Ages. The Chichester silver chalices and patens are amongst the finest examples of English church plate to survive.

During the Middle Ages it was considered that only precious metals such as gold and silver should be used for the most sacred liturgical vessels. In the late twelfth and thirteenth centuries English bishops issued instructions that even parish churches should have silver chalices and patens. Sometimes exceptions were made for Limoges chalices like the Rusper example, and base-metal plate also occurs, such as the thirteenth-century pewter chalice and paten from East Dean (E) (regrettably stolen) and the Chichester mortuary chalice and paten mentioned above. However, the Rotherfield and other churchwardens' accounts show that by the early sixteenth century most parish churches had silver chalices and patens.

Apart from Chichester, no silver chalices and patens earlier than the fifteenth century survive in Sussex, by which time the round shape of the foot of the cup had been superseded by a hexagonal form. This seems to have been introduced as the result of a change in liturgical custom whereby the chalice was laid on its side to drain after Mass; the new shape of the foot prevented the chalice from rolling. A chalice of the typical late medieval design is owned by the Roman Catholic church at West Grinstead (W). It dates from *c.* 1500 and is a rare example of a chalice in three sections which can be screwed together. It was almost certainly used by a priest for saying Mass on his travels or while administering to the sick and elderly in their houses. One face of the foot has a cast figure of Christ on the Cross, which either in

CHICHESTER CATHEDRAL (W): Silver-gilt chalice found in a bishop's tomb, *c.* 1225–50

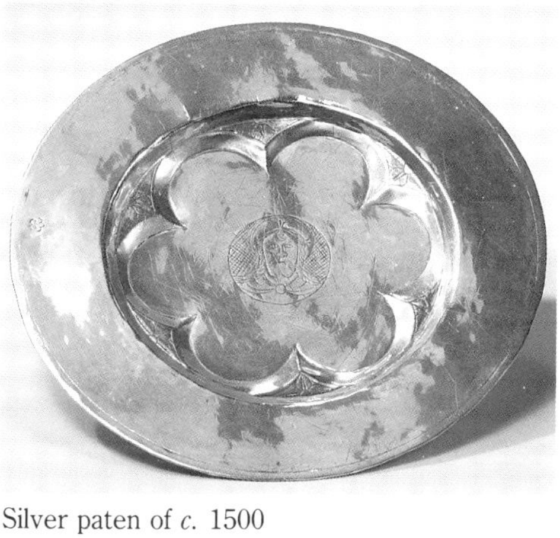

Silver paten of *c.* 1500

this form or engraved is the most common subject represented on English later medieval chalices. The only other intact late medieval chalice in Sussex is also in the possession of the Roman Catholic Church, at Arundel Castle. The remaining examples, at Piddinghoe, Southease, and Telscombe, all in the rural deanery of Lewes, and Tarring Neville (E) were converted during the Reformation to communion cups (see also below, p. 122). Their medieval origin is betrayed by the hexagonal feet with traces of the original Crucifixion on one face. All except Telscombe have their patens, similarly adapted in Elizabeth I's reign. Those at Southease and Piddinghoe are engraved with the Vernicle (the impression of Christ's face made on His shroud), as also is the unaltered paten at Donnington (W). Other patens exist at Arundel Castle and Whatlington (E).

The only other surviving piece of metalwork used in church services in Sussex prior to the Reformation is the upper section of a Limoges enamel censer found in the churchyard at Barnham (W). A Limoges enamel book-cover which may have

Limoges *champlevé* enamelled book-cover depicting the Crucifixion, early 13th century. Found in the churchyard at Rottingdean (E)

Bronze door-knocker from Rye church, 12th–13th century

SHIPLEY (W): Limoges copper and *champlevé* enamelled casket, early 13th century (Present whereabouts unknown)

decorated the Gospels or Epistles used during services was also discovered at Rottingdean (E) in 1770. The most impressive medieval metalwork artefact in the possession of a Sussex parish tragically has been stolen. This is the casket from Shipley (W), which is embellished with Limoges enamels depicting the Crucifixion and various saints. It dates from the early thirteenth century in common with the book and censer-cover mentioned above. It is not known how this casket came into the possession of Shipley, a church built by the Knights Templars.

There are some other non-liturgical metalwork artefacts of pre-Reformation date in Sussex. Matrices used for wax seals on documents are known from Chichester Cathedral (a very fine early thirteenth-century silver example engraved with a church design, now in the British Museum) and a bronze matrix belonging to a priest named Thomas de Climping found at Amberley (W). Amongst miscellaneous objects is a complicated lock from Graffham (W) (present whereabouts unknown) with heads of a king and a bishop and a bronze door-knocker from Rye (E) now in Hastings Museum. On a larger scale are the more than one hundred medieval church bells in Sussex churches. The oldest may date from the early twelfth century (Hardham, W) and amongst others cast before 1300 are bells at Findon (W) and Southease (E). The treble bell at Ford (W) bears the name of the London founder Robert Ridre (d. 1386) and other London makers, including William Burford, Richard Hille (d. 1440) and his widow Joanna, variously cast bells at Clayton, Fairlight, Hollington, Westfield (E), Sidlesham and East Preston (W). Casting was carried out in Sussex in earlier times. Amongst the late eleventh-century tenants of Battle Abbey (E) was one 'Aedric who cast the bells' and traces of a bell mould probably dating from early in the twelfth century have been found at Chichester. What must have been the most lavishly bedecked item of medieval metalwork in Sussex was the shrine of St. Richard (Bishop Richard de Wych, d. 1255, canonised 1263) at Chichester. This was destroyed in 1538, but it is possible that the remains of the wrought-iron grilles from the cathedral now in the Victoria and Albert Museum originally formed part of the shrine enclosure (*Age of Chivalry* exhib. cat., Royal Academy, 1987, No. 364). The iron grille separating the nave and the Fitzalan Chapel in the parish church of Arundel is another rare survival; it dates from after 1380. Also rare are the lead fonts at Pyecombe (E, twelfth century), Edburton (W, probably early thirteenth century) and Parham (W, bearing the arms of Sir Andrew Peverel, Knight of the Shire in 1351).

A few items of foreign medieval metalwork found their way into Sussex in more recent times. St. Michael's church in Brighton and Westbourne (W) possess late medieval copper-gilt Italian chalices. The former also owns a fifteenth-century processional cross, as does St. Paul's in West Street, Brighton. The best piece is the high altar Crucifix in the chapel of Lancing College (E) which dates from *c.* 1490 and comes from Toledo in Spain.

R.M.

THE REFORMATION TO THE NINETEENTH CENTURY

In 1569 a Visitation of the Diocese of Chichester by the Archbishop of Canterbury's Commissaries reported on the slow progress of the Reformation in Sussex: 'In many places they keep yet their chalices looking for to have mass again, when they were commanded to turn them into Communion cups after one fashion keeping still weight for weight that the parish might not be charged with buying of one altogether new; and yet they have so charged their parishes, to keep their chalices, hoping for a day for the use of the same'. (Victoria County History, *Sussex,* vol. 2)

The spoliation of medieval plate belonging to the parish churches began in Sussex, as elsewhere, with the Privy Council directive of 3rd March, 1551, which ordered the seizure of parish plate; only one 'cuppe or chalis' was to be left. In 1553 the instructions were repeated; small parish churches were allowed one chalice and cathedrals and town churches could have two. Finally, in about 1560, Matthew Parker, Archbishop of Canterbury, decided that chalices must be converted into communion cups, probably because the chalices were secretly used to celebrate mass in private houses. In the Diocese of Chichester the instruction must have been given in about 1568, judging from the surviving number of communion cups of that date. Chalices were either remodelled as communion cups or melted down and sold, the money being used to provide a new cup. The churchwardens' accounts for Rotherfield (*Sussex Arch. Colls.,* vol. XLI) show the process in action at parish level. In 1509 the church had five chalices and four patens; by 1558 there was but one silver chalice and a bronze pyx. By 1571 the chalice had been replaced by a communion cup.

What replaced the medieval chalice? In 1548 it was ordered that the people should be given communion in both kinds (i.e. consecrated wine and bread). It is possible that new and larger cups became necessary as the old chalices were designed for use only by the priest. A more probable reason for the change, however, was the Protestant dislike of the presence of the Crucifix and other religious images on chalices. The new cups were not invariably of greater capacity than the chalices they replaced. Only eighteen communion cups survive from the reign of Edward VI (1547–1553) and half of these were made for London parishes. Most parishes continued to use the chalice, probably supplemented by an extra flagon of communion wine. It is curious in view of the strength of Catholicism in Battle (E) that the church possesses one of the rare Edwardian cups. Hallmarked London, 1552 and with the maker's mark of a stalked daisy, it is the earliest post-Reformation cup in Sussex. The silver from two medieval chalices was usually required to make one communion cup, but the Battle example appears to have been beaten out of one chalice. Its inspiration is purely secular; a beaker-shaped bowl is mounted upon a spool-shaped stem supported on a circular foot. The cup signals a radical break with the past; the emphasis was to be on communion as a fellowship meal rather than an offering made by the priest on behalf of the laity.

Chalices continued to be used during the reign of the Catholic Queen Mary (1553–1558) but with the accession of Elizabeth communion cups became compulsory. Piddinghoe, Southease, Telscombe, and Tarring Neville (E), all churches in the Ouse valley, possess communion cups which have been made from pre-

Communion cup, 1552. The earliest post-Reformation cup in Sussex

Flagon, 1665. Maker's mark S with crown above

Chalice and paten, 1849. Maker's mark of John Hardman & Company, Birmingham. Designed by A. W. N. Pugin

Reformation chalices (see above p. 119). At Telscombe and Tarring Neville the medieval origins of the communion cups can only be faintly discerned.

The typical Elizabethan communion cup has a beaker-shaped bowl, spool-shaped stem, and a stepped and moulded base. The accompanying paten-cover is slightly domed and has a small foot. The communion cup from Preston (E) may be taken as a representative example and the cup from Itchenor (W), probably made locally in 1568, appears to be one of several in the diocese made by the same maker; it has a conical bowl with zig-zag strap decoration. Many cups have a paten-cover of rather later date as there was some doubt as to whether the medieval patens had to be removed or adapted. The Royal Injunctions of 1559 ordered the use of wafer bread but the bishops often insisted on the Prayer Book rubric which stated that in order to avoid superstition (i.e. any lingering belief in the Real Presence) the bread should be such as is 'eaten at the Table wyth other meates'. In practice this often meant sliced wheat bread which was too large for the Elizabethan patens. Household bread gradually replaced the wafer and patens became larger; by the 1630s a salver-paten or bowl had developed. Bishop Richard Montague's Chichester Diocesan Visitation Articles of 1636 asked: 'Have you a plate or patten, faire and deepe, of the same material (silver) for the bread' (quoted in C. Oman, *English Church Plate 597–1830,* 1957).

The conversion of the medieval chalice into the Elizabethan communion cup created a pattern which was to last, with minor variations, for more than a century. As the cup had often to be replenished with wine, flagons, known as 'pots' until the 1640s, were required. These were expensive items for a parish to purchase, a fact recognised by Bishop Montague's Visitation which noted that Cocking, Parham, and Wiggenholt (W) had flagons which were 'like an ale house quart pot'; at Wisborough Green (W) the flagon was 'but a glasse bottle wherein they fetch the wine from the tavern' (quoted in A. Fletcher, *Sussex 1600–1660: A County Community in Peace and War,* 1980). Many parishes never managed to acquire a silver flagon; pewter, or, later, Sheffield Plate, was often all they could afford.

Archbishop Laud's concern to revive certain forms of pre-Reformation ritual is often cited as the reason for the return to medieval shapes in some seventeenth-century plate. However, Lancelot Andrewes (1555–1626), successively Bishop of Chichester, Ely and Winchester, was much more important in this respect. He was interested in late medieval art and he encouraged the acquisition of complete services of communion plate rather than single items. By the 1630s the shape of some communion cups was inspired by pre-Reformation chalices. The Civil War largely put an end to such experiments but after the Restoration some High Churchmen commissioned plate based on medieval forms. Ashburnham (E) possesses a remarkable silver-gilt set of communion plate made between 1665 and 1668. Following High Church practice the flagons are surmounted by an orb and a cross, and one of the communion cups, dated 1665, is based on the shape of a medieval chalice.

In the eighteenth and early nineteenth centuries communion cups and their accompanying flagons and salvers generally reflected secular shapes. The form of sacramental vessels was influenced not by the Church, but by tradition and taste. Eighteenth-century plate was usually very conservative, but Glynde (E) possesses a magnificent silver-gilt flagon made by Thomas Whipham and Charles Wright in 1765. The flagon is embossed with grapes, vine leaves, and ears of corn and the shape is derived from contemporary Rococo silver.

In the 1840s the freedom of silversmiths to follow secular taste in the design of altar plate was challenged by Pugin and the Cambridge Camden Society (see p. 69). In 1838 John Hardman of Birmingham established a business as a 'medieval metalworker' in association with Pugin. Although Pugin advocated medieval manufacturing methods, much of Hardman's church plate used industrial techniques such as electro-gilding and plating. Withyham (E) has a chalice, paten and flagon designed by Pugin and made by J. H. Hardman and Company in 1849. The chalice is based on two medieval models: a chalice of 1527 at Trinity College, Oxford, and a chalice of about 1510 at Leominster, Hereford. The purchaser was the incumbent, the Reverend R. W. Sackville-West, 7th Earl de la Warr. Because Pugin was a Roman Catholic, Hardman and Company was tainted with Popery and the acquisition of plate from the Company sometimes occasioned controversy. In 1845 E. E. Estcourt, a Cirencester curate, ordered a Hardman chalice but asked the firm to 'be so good as to prevent any card or paper being placed in the packing case which may lead to the discovery of its coming from your well known manufactory – or even from Birmingham' (C. Blair and S. Bury, 'Metalwork' in *Change and Decay: The Future of Our Churches,* 1977).

Pugin unofficially advised the Camden Society on its campaign to reform church plate although his rôle was deliberately underplayed. In October 1842 William Butterfield suggested in a letter to the *Ecclesiologist* that the Camden Society should engage a goldsmith to manufacture chalices 'of the ancient form' not only because goldsmiths were 'running perfectly wild' in their plate designs, but also because the long deep cups in general use were difficult to drain properly. Butterfield suggested that the chalices at Trinity College and Corpus Christi College, Oxford, should be used as models. In its reply the Society recommended that chalices should have a shallow circular bowl on a stem with a knot and 'a base generally octangular'. The revival of medieval chalices implied a new reverence for the Eucharistic elements and the Society was often accused of Popery. It is easy to see why critics such as Francis

Close, Vicar of Cheltenham, believed that reviving a chalice in its original form was either 'an empty pageant' or smacked of a belief in the Real Presence. Nevertheless, the Society's fulminations against current designs in church plate struck a chord with churchmen already intent on freeing their churches of post-Reformation 'barbarisms'. In April 1843 the *Ecclesiologist* wrote that modern chalices were 'meagre and tasteless' and flagons were 'in no respect different from a coffee pot' except for an engraved Sacred Monogram. To remedy the situation William Butterfield (1814–1900) was appointed to supply designs for church plate and other furnishings for the approval of the Committee. John Keith and Son of London became the Society's official manufacturer. Between 1844–47 Butterfield's designs were published in *Instrumenta Ecclesiastica* and vast quantities of plate in the medieval manner were produced. St. Mary Magdalene, West Lavington (W), has a silver-gilt chalice made in 1849. It was almost certainly designed by Butterfield, the architect of the church.

G. E. Street (1824–81) was also a favoured designer of the Ecclesiologists. He contributed designs to the second series of *Instrumenta Ecclesiastica* (1850–56) and in 1857 he became superintendent of the Society's plate scheme. St. Paul's, Brighton (E), has a chalice designed by Street in 1868 and made by Hardman and Company. The foot has finely executed niello roundels of the Evangelists, the Agnus Dei, and a floriated cross.

Chalice, 1864, from a Brighton church. Maker's mark of John Hardman & Company, Birmingham. Designed by William Burges

By the end of the century virtually every parish church had at least one Gothic Revival chalice. As with other church furnishings, the best plate was designed by architects of the calibre of Pugin, Street, Burges, and Butterfield. William Burges (1827–81) succeeded Street as superintendent of the Ecclesiological Society's plate in 1864 and Keith was replaced as manufacturer by Barkentin and Krall of London. St. Michael's, Brighton, possesses two silver chalices, a brass alms dish, and a silver flagon designed by Burges. One of the chalices, made by Hardman and Company in 1862, is decorated with semi-precious stones and the foot is engraved with representations of the Four Rivers of Paradise. The inscription around the foot is taken from a 'Hymn for the dedication of a church', dating from 700–800 AD. The chalice is partly based on Byzantine examples, but it owes more to Burges's formidable learning and ability to invoke romantically his own dream of the Middle Ages. The other chalice, also by Hardman, was made in 1864. It is studded with gemstones given by pious members of the congregation and the foot has niello panels of Christ and the Archangels Gabriel, Michael, and Raphael. St. Paul's, Brighton, also has a chalice probably designed by Burges and made by Hardman in 1874. It was commissioned as a memorial to the Reverend John Purchas (1823–72), an *avant-garde* ritualist who was tried at the Court of Arches for offences against the Prayer Book rubrics. The 'Purchas Chalice' is set with semi-precious stones and has an arcaded base adapted from a thirteenth-century chalice at Rheims. All these chalices exemplify Burges's dictum (*Ecclesiologist,* August 1858) that 'nothing can be too precious or too good for a chalice'.

Occasionally designers sought to experiment with more unorthodox forms. The chalice at St. Bartholomew's, Brighton, designed by Henry Wilson in about 1898, is parcel-gilt and is decorated with ivory and enamel. The knot is in the form of intertwined monsters and the stem is cased in ivory carved to represent a vine.

Altar plate is usually the most distinguished metalwork in a church, but a brief mention should be made of some of the other metal furnishings of the post-medieval period. Sussex had a flourishing iron industry in the seventeenth century and Wadhurst (E) has no less than thirty cast iron tomb slabs dating from 1617–1799; those in the chancel are decorated with shields and initials. Ashburnham (E) has wrought iron screens made locally in about 1665. Brass chandeliers are fairly well represented. The classic form, with detachable S-shaped branches emerging from a central globe and baluster was imported from the Low Countries in large quantities in the sixteenth and seventeenth centuries. By the late seventeenth century they were being imitated in England primarily for use in churches. As they were very expensive they were usually the gift of a benefactor. Northiam (E) has a chandelier dated 1727, the gift of the Frewen family, and Mayfield (E) two dated 1737 and 1773. Other examples exist at Burpham (W) and elsewhere. Of the large number of Victorian brass lecterns in the county, two deserve especial mention: William Butterfield's lectern at St. Patrick's, Hove, designed in 1867 in the form of an eagle sitting on a globe with a figure of St. Patrick in a niche on the central stem between two Celtic round towers, and John Hardman Powell's extraordinary lectern at St. Paul's, Brighton. J. H. Powell (1827–95) was a pupil of Pugin and became chief designer to John Hardman and Company in 1852. The angels which support the lectern are designed to illustrate St. John's vision of the Apocalypse.

D.B.

Twelve

SUSSEX CHURCH MUSIC AFTER THE REFORMATION

"THERE is perhaps no part of religious worship that is so pleasing and attractive as that of singing." So wrote the Sussex historian and minister of Westgate Chapel, Lewes, the Reverend Thomas Walker Horsfield.

The Reformation caused a re-definition of the rôle and practice of church music. The Protestant reformers were against the use of the organ and viewed choral music with suspicion regarding it as a form of papist ritual. They favoured simple unharmonised music such as that described by Thomas Cranmer in a letter to Henry VIII in 1544: 'the song that should be made thereunto would not be full of notes, but as near as may be, for every syllable a note'. The official position, opposing any form of complexity in church music, was forthrightly expressed in 1583 in the *Second Book of Homilies:* 'piping, singing, chanting and playing upon the organs' were things 'which displeased God so sore and filthily defiled his holy house'. Six years later, however, the Royal Injunctions allowed that 'in the beginning, or in the end of common prayers, either at morning or evening, there may be sung a hymn, or such like song, to the praise of Almighty God, in the best sort of melody and music that may be conveniently devised, having respect that the Sentence of the hymn may be understanded and perceived'.

The Book of Common Prayer Noted was issued by John Marbeck soon after the 1549 Prayer Book was published and, as the title suggests, it put the services of the Prayer Book to music. In practice Marbeck created a simplified version of Catholic plainsong but followed the principle of one note for each syllable. Since it was never re-issued or up-dated in line with the prayer book its influence was clearly limited. The psalms were more acceptable to the reformers than elaborate choral works as the former were the word of God. In 1549 Thomas Sternhold and John Hopkins translated forty-four psalms into English rhyming verse and seven years later during Queen Mary's reign, whilst in exile in Geneva, they published *One and fiftie Psalms of David in Englishe metre.* In 1562 they, in association with John Day, issued *The Whole Book of Psalmes collected into English metre.* These were relatively simple tunes easily learnt and able to be sung in unison since they followed regular verse patterns. Such metrical psalms dominated parochial church music until the revival of the hymn which occurred in Anglican worship in the nineteenth century.

By the middle of the seventeenth century, and presumably as a result of

Detail of an etching by Smith of Mr. Penniket, 1859. Penniket is shown playing in Woodmancote Church to a less than enthusiastic audience

widespread illiteracy, the practice of 'lining-out' the psalm had been established whereby the parish clerk would read out each line in advance of the congregation singing it. The result must have been to create a rather ponderous and droning effect with a slow tempo, but such was the practice recommended by the *Directory of Public Worship,* issued to replace the *Book of Common Prayer* in 1644 and in force until 1660. Where 'many in the congregation cannot read, it is convenient that the minister, or some fit person appointed by him and the other ruling officers, do read the psalm, line by line, before the singing thereof'.

Organs were known in medieval churches but found themselves in increasing disfavour throughout the sixteenth century culminating in their prohibition under the 1644 Directory. Nevertheless references in churchwardens' accounts suggest that they were still in use in a number of Sussex churches. In 1570 West Tarring spent 10s. on 'orgayne pypes' and there are references to an organ at Buxted. Many organs were not replaced after the Civil War because of the cost of the instrument itself, the need to pay a trained organist and its perceived Papist associations. By 1677, however, when John Playford issued *The Whole Book of Psalms* he used notation to assist the organist 'since so many of our churches are lately furnished with Organs'. The changes were assisted by the formation in 1698 of The Society for the Promotion of Christian Knowledge, one of whose aims was to enhance the music and singing in parish churches. In 1696 *A New Version of the Psalms of David* were published by Nahum Tate and Nicholas Brady. The eighteenth century witnessed a revival in choral singing in urban parish churches. This was greatly assisted from the seventeenth century onwards by the re-appearance of the organ, financed by wealthy local families and tradesmen, combined with the formation of choirs of charity school children, as was the case in Chichester, for example.

By the early eighteenth century singing in many churches was choir-led. As organs were expensive many churches began to use local musicians and choir bands grew up to accompany the services. Vic Gammon has traced the emergence of these groups in Sussex. These choirs often sang from galleries erected at the west end of the church to accommodate them, so that when they performed the congregation would stand, turn and literally 'face the music', as can be seen in the mid-nineteenth century painting by Mary Lewin of Ifield church (E). This practice was facilitated by the widespread use of box pews whose seats often faced in several directions and not simply towards the chancel. The spread of west galleries in Sussex can be traced through faculty licenses. In the first half of the eighteenth century, seventeen were issued as against five between 1750–1800. West galleries were installed at Bolney in 1670, East Hoathly in 1747 and Northiam (E) in 1785. Most of these were torn out by the Victorian restorers although an example dating from 1610 survives at Worth (E). The intention was clearly summed up by the churchwardens at Mayfield in 1731 who claimed that they were 'desirous to promote the singing of Psalms in the said church to the honour of Almighty God in the most decent orderly manner, and do judge that a gallery, to be built in the west end of the parish church, will be convenient to answer to that end'. Before the erection of these singing galleries it seems likely that pews were set aside for the singers. An entry dated 1615 in the register of All Saints, Lewes, refers to a burial on the north side of the chancel 'under [the] singing mens pewe'. At Selsey a front pew was employed with a singing desk attached.

It is difficult to trace the appearance of voluntary choirs. Groups may have emerged during the seventeenth century but as they became more ambitious in their repertoire the next logical step was the introduction of instruments. Initially probably only a pitch-pipe with a bassoon supplied the base; later there were violins, clarinets and flutes. It is significant that the Mayfield faculty already quoted and the 1699 rules for the Cuckfield choir both refer to 'singers'. This was the first stage in the formation of choir bands, prior to the introduction of instruments.

Churchwardens' accounts reveal instruments being repaired, as for example at Ticehurst in the late eighteenth century where 7s.6d. is spent on a 'pich pipe' whilst further expenditure is incurred in 1771 'mending the Bassoon'. In 1802 payment is authorised to 'Mr. Peckham at Lewes for 8 reeds for the Chuch Musick'. Mayfield in 1775 purchased 'one bassoon and one book of Instruction and one reed case'.

In Sussex we have to thank Canon K. H. Macdermott, who earlier this century preserved so much physical and oral evidence regarding the Sussex choir bands. Many of the musical instruments and music books he saved from Sussex churches are preserved amongst the collections of the Sussex Archaeological Society. The members of the choir bands were enthusiastic practitioners of their craft, performing at secular events as well as church services. Such enthusiasm could manifest itself in embarrassing ways, as at West Tarring where the musicians' leader, Henry Pelling, was in the habit of excitedly striking the gallery with his baton while crying out 'Well done my lads' after a particularly good rendering of an anthem. They were self-taught musicians who regularly practised. The rules of the Hollington choir insisted on weekly two-hour practice on pain of a 3d. fine. The better bands would often visit neighbouring local communities to perform. There are many examples of dynasties of bandsmen who provided several generations of performers for their parish church. Such were the Arnold family who were represented in the Bosham church band for

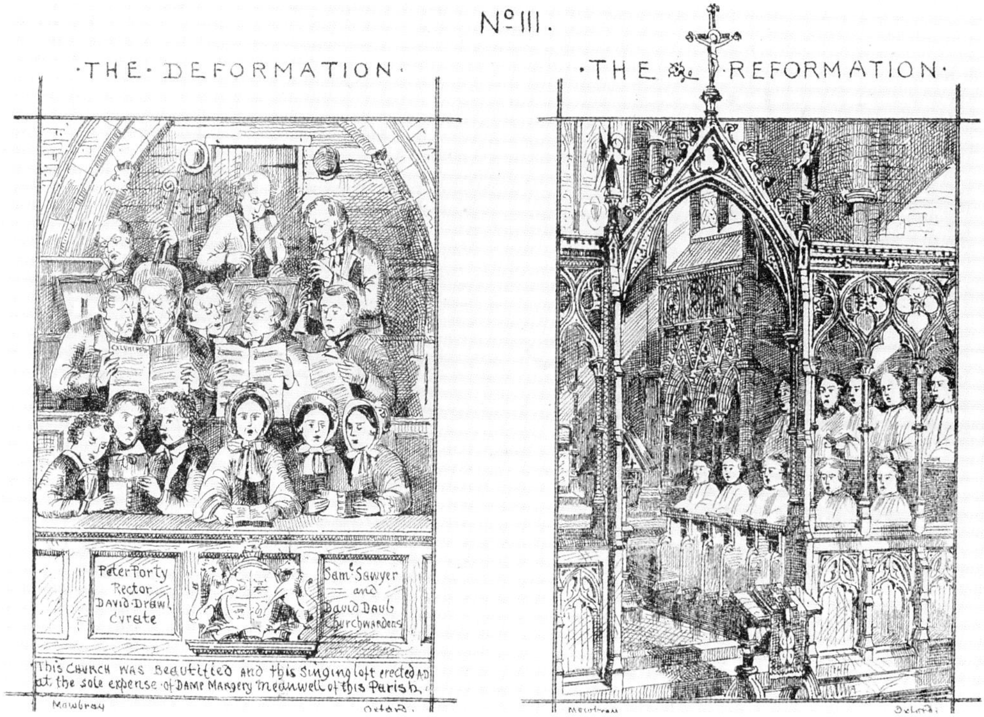

THE SINGERS: Lithograph by A. R. Mowbray from *The Deformation and the Reformation,* 1873

over ninety years or the Ashbys at Wadhurst, the Cootes at Clymping or the Ransomes at Sidlesham.

Much of the evidence of these choir bands collected by Canon Macdermott is anecdotal, providing the impression of uneducated agricultural labourers performing with great enthusiasm but limited skill. One contemporary description will give the flavour of many: 'our choir got a little out of sorts; there's old Jaemes Comber, he's been at it sixty year or more, he should know what singing is, and he would get on pretty well if Joe Jenkins didn't keep a boffling of him and his clarinet, and then there's Master Mitchell he does do his uttermost, but when there's anything that wants to goo very high, then his cough comes'. Many of these contemporary descriptions come from hostile witnesses, principally clergy, looking to abolish the choir bands. In 1750 Dr. Burton described the situation at Shermanbury (W): 'The more shrill-toned they maybe, the more valued they are, and in Church they sing Psalms, by preference, not set to the old and simple tune, but as if in tragic chorus . . . but yet there is something offensive to my ear when they bellow to excess and bleat out some goatish noises with all their might'. Such sentiments could be multiplied for the eighteenth and nineteenth centuries but reform awaited the re-institution of a resident clergy with the backing of Tractarian ideology. The mid-nineteenth century choir at Willingdon were described as 'a lot of young men who sang, or bawled, unaccompanied'. This is almost certainly a grossly exaggerated picture. Vic Gammon has shown that the musicians were not incompetent yokels but 'independently minded rural labourers and artisans who held themselves and their music in high esteem'. Certainly they did not always approve of the congregation joining in with their singing. The rules for the Cuckfield singers dating from 1699 instructed that the singers should occasionally disperse themselves amongst the congregation to assist them to sing. In *Under the Greenwood Tree,* Thomas Hardy gives a realistic description of one of these choirs where one of the characters observes 'Tis the gallery have got to sing, all the world knows . . . Why soul's, what's the use o'the ancients spending scores of punds to build galleries if people down in the lowest depths of the church sing like that at a moment's notice'. The same attitude obviously still existed in 1854 when rule eleven of the Hollington Choir forbade them from objecting to others joining in the singing in church.

Gammon has identified the occupations of sixty-seven Sussex church musicians and has shown them to be essentially artisan tradesmen with a sprinkling of agricultural labourers. They were predominantly men who had some leisure time for the necessary practices and performances and who could afford the cost of the instruments. Although there are examples, already quoted, of church funds being spent on musical instruments these seem to be the exception. However, there are a few examples of home-made instruments like the fiddle made and played by James Nye in 1863 and now preserved in the collections of the Sussex Archaeological Society or the copper cello formerly used at Bosham. The commitment of the members of the choir bands should not be under-estimated. The son of one Lindfield musician refused to take up an instrument as he feared it would lead to the ruin of the family farm if he spent as much time at music as had his father.

Often the choir band relied upon an enthusiastic individual for its impetus, as at Lurgarshall (W) where four violins led by George Sadler accompanied the singing. The Sunday after Sadler's death in 1838 the band broke down and was 'niver no sense arterwards'. Often the leading figure also occupied the office of parish clerk, a post which traditionally had led the responses in church services, as for example Thomas Cox of Ditchling, John Unstead of Waldron and John Wells of Lindfield, of whom a silhouette survives showing him performing on a bassoon. Michael Turner, a shoemaker from Warnham (1796–1855) was another instance. Turner played the violin in the Warnham band which operated from the Rood loft until it was removed in 1847. He, like many of the musicians, dressed smartly for his performances; he wore a white smock, red handkerchief, tie and breeches and a beaver hat on Sundays. At Brightling in 1820, John Fuller presented the male members of the choir with white smocks, buckskin breeches and yellow stockings and the females with red cloaks. Another well-known Sussex church musician was Old Penniket who led the bands at Amberley, Henfield and Woodmancote (W) and who played the clarinet and trombone. He is depicted in a humorous print performing in Woodmancote church in 1850, where part of the congregation is depicted asleep although he is playing the anthem 'Awake thou that sleepest'.

Not every parish church had a choir band. Many churches coped with unaccompanied singing using perhaps a single wooden pitch-pipe to set the note for the singers. A survey of Seaford rural deanery in 1853 found that ten out of seventeen churches had no musical instruments while of those that did one possessed only a pitch-pipe and two others a single flute. A similar survey in 1861 found nine churches using both Tate and Brady's psalms and a hymnal, five using the newly published *Hymns, Ancient and Modern,* one using a local hymnal and nine others replied that they chanted canticles. Arlington and Blatchington responded that they undertook 'no singing of either psalms or canticles'. Nevertheless Gammon argued that there is evidence for the existence of choirs or bands in over half the rural parishes of Sussex. Macdermott identified over 340 instruments in more than one hundred Sussex churches with twenty-four different types of instrument in use. These included the flute, clarinet, bassoon and the violin through to the less common, oboe and horn. Amongst the more unusual instruments were the banjo at Brightling, the concertina at Balcombe, the serpent at Upper Beeding and a drum at Nuthurst. One of the rarest is the vamphorn from Ashurst which is made of tin and painted green with yellow lettering reading 'Praise Him upon ye Strings and Pipe, 1770, Palmer fecit'. It probably provided a droning accompaniment to the choir.

Much of the music of these bands has been lost as it was rarely written down. There are, however, a number of manuscript books which have survived, including one produced by the Collins family of Waldron which runs to over fifty pages and several connected with the Welch family of Bosham, each written for a different part, e.g. bass, tenor, etc. The books often include secular as well as religious tunes emphasising the bands were not just church bands. In addition, Macdermott managed to identify forty-five different examples of printed hymnals and psalmodies, a dozen of which were by Sussex men. *A Collection of Psalms and Hymns sung at the Parish Church of Brighthelmston* by Nathaniel Cooke, the organist of St. Nicholas, Brighton, included 93 tunes, 78 by Cooke himself. This ran to three editions and was in use in several Sussex churches. Another collection, sung at Selsey, was published in 1842. It was apparently compiled by a local schoolmaster, W. Bramwell, who encouraged

RUDGWICK (W): Depicting the first peal of the newly re-cast bells on the 27 July 1770. Painted on plaster, the panel was recovered from the wall of The King's Head, Rudgwick

LEWES, St. ANNE (E): The surpliced choir, *c.* 1880

the congregation to earnestly 'unite the efforts of their voices (however feeble and however uncultivated) to swell the loud and rich note of praise to God'.

In the eighteenth century a cheap form of organ was available for church use. The barrel organ required no skill to play, merely the stamina to turn the handle and 'grind out' the tune. They included only a limited number of tunes, perhaps as many as ten, but were nevertheless installed in at least sixty Sussex churches, particularly in those where there is little evidence of previous musical activity. Hartfield possessed a barrel by 1726 and Salehurst (E) purchased one in 1836 and the Brighton churchwardens' accounts include payments 'for grinding out the music'. One of the largest examples was installed in Brightling (E) church in 1820 where it occupies the west gallery. A barrel organ was offered to Cuckfield (E) in 1838 in order to enhance the services and with the demise of their band the former clarinet and viol player, Joseph Anscombe, was employed as organ grinder. This was only a short-lived experiment since within four years a manual organ was installed.

These organs posed a real threat to the parish choir bands as did the reforming ideas of the Tractarian Movement with its desire to revive the singing of simple plainsong by the congregation, leaving the more complex anthems to the surpliced choirs that were now to be installed in 'restored' chancels rather than west galleries (see page 130). At first the new choir was often unaccompanied since during the 1840s the Camden Society did not favour organs, claiming (wrongly) that they had no medieval precedent. Early experience of organs was not encouraging, for like their predecessors in the choir bands, many an organist was carried away with his own performance. The *Ecclesiologist* commented in 1849 that too few organists saw the organ 'as a mere subsidiary and unessential appendage to the Divine offices' (James Nye had identified a similar problem in the love of church music: 'I cannot help being carried away with the sound instead of the substance'). By 1850 the *Ecclesiologist* had shifted its position and favoured the replacement of metrical psalms, the introduction of surpliced choirs and advocated congregational singing of 'ancient' hymns translated from Latin or Greek and accompanied by an organ. Increasingly the organ came to be seen as the perfect accompaniment and organ chambers were often installed in the chancel, frequently to the detriment of the architecture. The restored 'medieval' chancel with its choir stalls was now to be occupied not only by priests but by the reformed and surpliced choir firmly under the control of the parish priest. The attitude of the ecclesiologists is summed up in an illustration in A. R. Mowbray, *The Deformation and the Reformation* (1873), which contrasts the newly restored chancel with its orderly surpliced choir with the choir band performing in a west gallery fronted with the royal arms and an inscription, 'This church was Beautified and this singing loft erected A.D. . . . at the sole expense of Dame Margery Meanwell of this Parish. Peter Porty Rector, David Drawl Curate, Sam'l Sawyer and David Daub Churchwardens'. In the preface to a collection of Selsey hymns and psalms published in 1842 and already referred to it was claimed that organs were now 'within the range of economy (however limited) of every parish'. Battle (E) had an organ by 1837, and Glynde (E) in 1856. The Tractarian adoption of hymns was rather more surprising in view of the strong association of hymn singing with Non-Conformity which dated from the Wesley brothers use of the hymn in the 1740s. In the eyes of many people the hymn book was as associated with Non-Conformity as the Prayer Book was with the established church. But this was not true of all dissenting denominations. Groups like the Quakers rejected hymn singing and the General Baptists were hostile to their application for many years. They preferred the psalms as the direct Word of God as against modern hymns which were seen as the interpretation of individuals. In 1694 the Independent Congregationalists produced a *Collection of Divine Hymns* and the dissenting tradition of hymn writers included Isaac Watts and the Wesley brothers. To a Non-Conformist hymns were an easily learnt and memorable summary of belief. By contrast the Anglicans were slower to accept hymns. Nevertheless the greatest Anglican hymnologist lived in Sussex. John Mason Neale (1818–1866) was rector of Crawley (E) and later Warden of Sackville College, East Grinstead (E). He was responsible for such well-known hymns as 'Jerusalem the Golden' and 'O Happy Band of Pilgrims'.

Such reforms inevitably led to conflict between reforming vicars and the established parish-band. Criticism of the choir bands occurred throughout the eighteenth century, but it was only with the reappearance of an enthusiastic and increasingly resident clergy in the early nineteenth century that action was taken which often led to confrontation. James Nye's spiritual diary describes the appearance of just such a young curate at East Chiltington (E) in 1853–4: 'the first thing our new Parson did was to try to rule the singing'. As a consequence Nye, an ardent singer, left the church and began attending the Non-Conformist chapel. The concern of the reformers may have had less to do with musical standards than with the behaviour of the musicians and the lack of control and authority which the incumbent could exert over them. There were similar attempts to reform the church bell ringers. These too were regarded as an independent and disruptive group who often behaved more like a social club than with the decorum expected of church bell ringers. They did not necessarily remain for the service and expected to be paid for their services (unlike the musicians). Twineham (E) still preserves a communal drinking jug decorated with bell ringing rhymes.

As far as it can be ascertained, the musicians appear to have been popular people. Their funerals were elaborate and well attended affairs. A well-known musician like Michael Turner could expect to receive assistance from admirers in his old age and in his case they also subscribed to his tombstone in Warnham churchyard (W). Nevertheless the reforming ideals of the Tractarian clergy triumphed over sentiment. The process of the disbandment of the choir bands can be followed in many Sussex parishes. The west galleries were removed from church after church:

Bishopstone (E) in 1848, Funtington in 1859, Billingshurst in 1866, Poling in 1874, Aldingbourne (W) in 1890 and so on. The musicians were replaced by organs and harmoniums. At Bosham (W) the six-to-eight instrument band was replaced by a harmonium, Berwick (E) had a harmonium installed in 1862 and Ifield (E) a barrel organ replaced the band in 1850. At Stanmer the restoration of the church saw the village band give way to a small organ given by Lord Pelham's sisters. However, the band continued in operation for another quarter of a century, performing in cottages and carol singing until 'most of the old men having died our band disbanded'. By the final quarter of the nineteenth century the choir bands were a rarity and their demise involved a personal cost as evidenced by the poem quoted in the Ashurst magazine of 1847 which refers to a former singer who 'felt too old to learn to sing again'. Nathaniel Blaker's description of a mid-nineteenth century service taking place in Edburton church reveals the church band at their best. 'The service was performed by the Parson and Clerk, each reading a verse alternately in the psalms, and the Clerk saing "Amen" at the end of the prayers; the congregation, many of whom could not read, not joining in the responses. The hymns were sung by a choir, consisting of eight or ten men of the village, who sat in a pew with a desk in the centre, and were accompanied by a bass viol, flute, and "all kinds of music". They took great pleasure in their performance, and frequently met at each other's houses for practice'.

J.R.

LULLAM, THE DWARF ORGAN BLOWER: Lithograph by W. H. Hunt, *c.* 1840–3. He operated the organ bellows at St. Clement, Hastings (E)

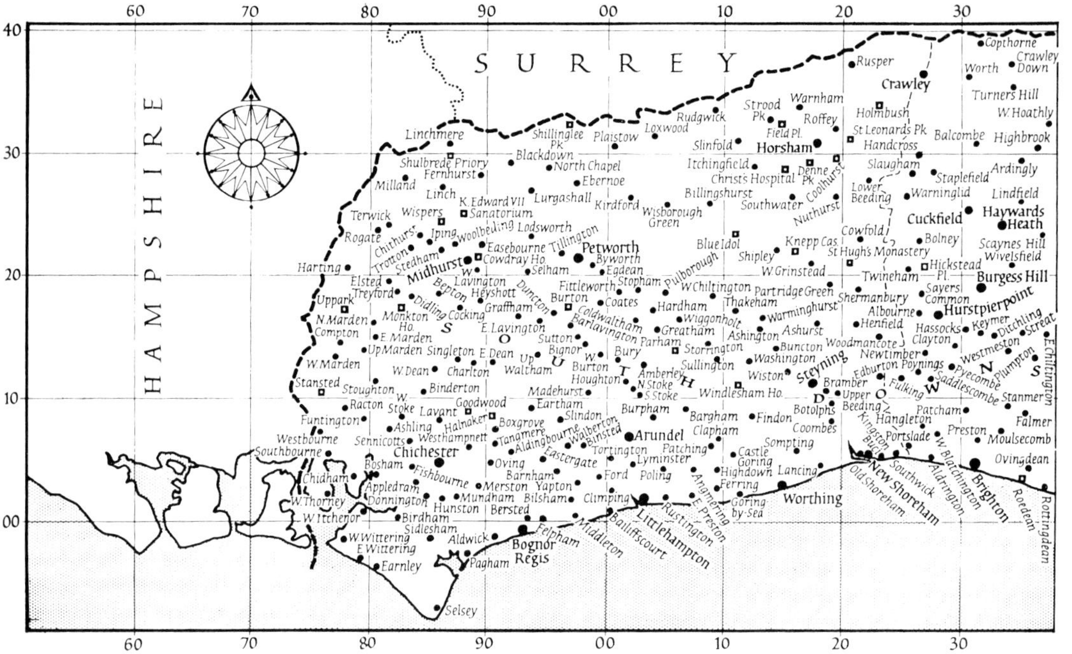
SURREY
HAMPSHIRE
Copthorne
Crawley Down
Worth
Rusper
Crawley
Turners Hill
W. Hoathly
Warnham
Strood Pk
Holmbush
Roffey
Field Pl.
Rudgwick
Loxwood
St Leonards Pk
Balcombe
Highbrook
Linchmere
Shillinglee Pk
Plaistow
Slinfold
Horsham
Handcross
Blackdown
Shulbrede Priory
North Chapel
Itchingfield
Denne Pk
Slaughter
Ardingly
Fernhurst
Ebernoe
Christ's Hospital
Staplefield
Milland
Coolhurst
Lower Beeding
Lindfield
Linch
K. Edward VII Sanatorium
Lurgashall
Billingshurst
Warninglid
Terwick
Wispers
Kirdford
Wisborough Green
Southwater
Nuthurst
Cuckfield
Haywards Heath
Rogate
Chithurst
Iping
Woolbeding
Lodsworth
Cowfold
Bolney
Tillington
Blue Idol
Knepp Cas
Scaynes Hill
Trotton
Stedham
Easebourne
Petworth
St Hugh's Monastery
Wivelsfield
Cowdray Ho.
Byworth
Shipley
Harting
Midhurst
W. Lavington
Selham
Egdean
Pulborough
W. Grinstead
Hickstead
Twineham
Pl.
Burgess Hill
Elsted
Stopham
Fittleworth
W. Chiltington
Partridge Green
Sayers Common
Treyford
Bepton
Heyshott
Duncton
Uppark
Burton
Thakeham
Shermanbury
Graffham
Coates
Hardham
Warminghurst
Albourne
Hurstpierpoint
Didling
Coldwaltham
N. Marden
Monkton Ho.
Cocking
Wiggonholt
Henfield
Keymer
Ditchling
Streat
Barlavington
E. Lavington
Greatham
Hassocks
Compton
E. Marden
Sutton
Parham
Ashington
Ashurst
Woodmancote
Clayton
E. Chiltington
Westmeston
Up Marden
Singleton
E. Dean
Bignor
Bury
Storrington
Buncton
W. Marden
Newtimber
Up Waltham
W. Burton
Washington
Sullington
Poynings
Plumpton
W. Dean
Charlton
Steyning
Edburton
Pyecombe
Houghton
Amberley
Wiston
Stansted
Binderton
N. Stoke
Bramber
Saddlescombe
Stoughton
Madehurst
Fulking
W. Stoke
S. Stoke
Windlesham Ho.
Upper Beeding
Racton
Goodwood
Eartham
Burpham
Botolphs
Stanmer
Lavant
Slindon
Bargham
Findon
Hangleton
Funtington
Patcham
Falmer
Ashling
Halnaker
Boxgrove
Coombes
Clapham
Kingston Buci
Portslade
Preston
Moulsecomb
Westbourne
Sennicotts
Westhampnett
Tangmere
Binsted
Walberton
Arundel
Patching
Sompting
Aldingbourne
Southbourne
Chichester
Tortington
Castle Goring
Lancing
W. Blatchington
Ovingdean
Eastergate
Lyminster
Highdown
Southwick
Bosham
Oving
Fishbourne
Barnham
Ford
Poling
New Shoreham
Aldrington
Brighton
Chidham
Apuldram
Merston
Yapton
Angmering
Ferring
Old Shoreham
Roedean
W. Thorney
Donnington
Mundham
Bilsham
Climping
Goring-by-Sea
Worthing
Rottingdean
Hunston
Bersted
Rustington
E. Preston
W. Itchenor
Birdham
Littlehampton
Sidlesham
Felpham
Aldwick
Bailiffscourt
W. Wittering
E. Wittering
Middleton
Bognor Regis
Earnley
Pagham
Selsey
S O U T H   D O W N S

KENT
Holtye Common
Hammerwood
Blackham
East Grinstead
Hartfield
Groombridge
Forest Row
Withyham
Eridge
Frant
Bayham Abbey
Kidbrooke Park
Colemans Hatch
Mark Cross
Crowborough
Wadhurst
Ticehurst
Flimwell
Miles
0
10
Horsted Keynes
Tidebrook
Nutley
Herrons Ghyll
Rotherfield
Mayfield
Stonegate
Hurst Green
Danehill
Fairwarp
High Hurstwood
Bodiam
Maresfield
Burwash
Etchingham
Northiam
Iden
Hadlow Down
Salehurst
Ewhurst
Peasmarsh
Sheffield Pk
Fletching
Buxted
Cross-in-Hand
Burwash Common
Robertsbridge
Beckley
Possingworth
E. Guldeford
Newick
Uckfield
Framfield
Heathfield
Mountfield
Playden
Rye
Chailey
Little Horsted
Waldron
Brightling
Netherfield
Brede
Udimore
Rye Harbour
Isfield
Horam
Dallington
Whatlington
Camber Cas
Camber
Warbleton
Sedlescombe
Winchelsea
Spithurst
Halland
E. Hoathly
Penhurst
Battle
Icklesham
Barcombe
Chiddingly
Ashburnham
Catsfield
Westfield
Guestling
Hamsey
Ringmer
Laughton
Baldslow
Pett
Glyndebourne
Hellingly
Ninfield
Ore
Offham
Ripe
Upper Dicker
Michelham Priory
Herstmonceux
Crowhurst
Hollington
Fairlight
Lewes
S. Malling
Chalvington
Glynde
Hailsham
Hooe
Hastings
Kingston
Beddingham
Arlington
Wartling
Iford
W. Firle
Selmeston
Bexhill
Rodmell
Alciston
Berwick
Polegate
Stone Cross
Pevensey
Southease
Tarring Neville
Telscombe
Piddinghoe
Wilmington
Folkington
Westham
Alfriston
Lullington
Denton
Saltdean
Bishopstone
Litlington
Willingdon
Langney
Jevington
E. Blatchington
Peacehaven
Newhaven
Westdean
Seaford
Eastdean
Eastbourne
Friston
Beachy Head
SUSSEX

SUSSEX CHURCHES AND CHAPELS SUGGESTED ITINERARIES

The following is a selection of some of the most interesting places of worship to visit, which for convenience have been grouped by location. The itineraries should be accomplished within a day, although delays may be caused by the need to locate the key for locked churches, an all too frequent occurrence necessitated by thefts. Many of the churches are mentioned in the essays in this book, but the selection remains a personal one and the compilers are aware that they run the risk of offending parishioners and visitors alike by the omission of favourite places of worship. Some noteworthy buildings in the north of the county, such as Worth and the attractive Quaker meeting-house at Ifield, have not been included as they do not easily fit into an itinerary. These are 'musts' for any church-lover; similarly churches other than those listed in the itineraries will often repay a visit. I. Nairn and N. Pevsner, *The Buildings of England Sussex,* Penguin Books, 1973, and relevant Ordnance Survey maps are essential equipment for the church-visitor. For convenience the numbers printed next to the place-name refer to the grid-lines on the maps, which are reproduced by kind permission of Penguin Books Limited.

DB, RM, JR

ITINERARY A

1. **BATTLE** (a) **St. Mary** (7010)

A large, basically 12th-century, church. Worth a visit for the early 14th-century wall-paintings of the life of St. Margaret in the nave and the Early Renaissance tomb of Sir Anthony Browne (d. 1548), Master of the King's Horse, and his wife. Remains of 15th-century glass in poor condition in the nave north aisle. Good Perpendicular font cover.

(b) **Abbey** (7010)

Remains of the Benedictine monastery founded on the site of the Battle of Hastings. Little survives of the church apart from the undercroft of the east end, rebuilt in the early 14th century in imitation of Henry III's Westminster Abbey.

2. **HASTINGS** (a) **St. Clement** (8000)

Perpendicular, probably rebuilt after the French sack of the town in 1377. In a wall case are remains of an oak screen. Fine octagonal font carved with Passion instruments. The poet and painter D. G. Rossetti married Elizabeth Siddall here. At east end of south aisle are painted panels of Moses and Aaron by Roger Mortimer. On the basis of a churchwarden's account these can be dated to 1755. They originally formed part of an altarpiece in All Saints', Hastings. Good benefaction board to Archibald Hutcheson dated 1721.

(b) **All Saints** (8000)

Another Perpendicular church – it is called new in a will of 1436. The most notable feature is the Doom painted over the chancel arch. Good cork model of the church prior to restoration in 1870 and painted belfry rules dated 1756.

(c) **St. Mary sub Castro** (8000)

Built 1824–28 as a proprietary chapel by Joseph Kay for the Earl of Chichester. The noble exterior has an Ionic portico and the interior has a D-shaped galleried auditorium which resembles a theatre rather than a church. The building was designed to form the visual climax of Pelham Crescent. It is no longer used as a church.

HASTINGS, ALL SAINTS (E): Lithograph showing the pre-restoration exterior

3. **WINCHELSEA** (a) **St. Thomas** (9010)

A noble church, even without its transepts and nave (the latter may never have been finished). The chancel with its flanking chapels was built in the early 14th century on a grand scale. Good Decorated tracery windows and the interior embellished with marble shafts to the piers and richly carved sedilia and piscina. Fine canopied tombs with effigies in the north and south chapels. The monument supposed to commemorate Gervaise de Alard (d. 1310) features in Millais' painting *L'Enfant du Régiment,* and Pugin depicted it in *Contrasts* (1836).

(b) **Franciscan Friary** (9010)

One of the few remaining Franciscan churches (see also Chichester). Only the ruined chancel with its polygonal apse survives.

---

4. **RYE** **St. Mary** (9020)

An impressive town church in an attractive hill town. The interior includes fine examples of Commandment boards and Royal Arms as well as a mahogany holy table *c.* 1740. There is also glass by Kempe and Morris and Company. Externally the clock on the north transept with painted quarter boys dates from *c.* 1760 but the mechanism is older, probably 16th-century.

---

5. **EAST GULDEFORD** **St. Mary** (9020)

Simple rectangular brick church consecrated in 1505. Lovely interior with early 16th-century box pews, two-decker pulpit, Commandment boards and Royal Arms of George IV. The east, north and south walls of the sanctuary are painted with a late 19th-century frieze of angels carrying musical instruments. In location and atmosphere this building belongs with the Romney Marsh group of Kent churches.

---

6. **NORTHIAM** **St. Mary** (8020)

The church has one of the four pre-Victorian stone spires in Sussex. Interior largely Early English, but the east end was rebuilt in 1837, and in 1846 Sydney Smirke added the stark Turner mausoleum. The church has a particularly good set of fittings: the three-sided altar-rail, altar table, and panelling date from 1638–40; there is a brass chandelier given by C. Frewen in 1727; and there are two early 16th-century brasses.

---

7. **BREDE** **St. George** (8010)

Externally Perpendicular but internally has south aisle of *c.* 1200 and north aisle of a century later. Bequests for the new chancel and its glazing occur in 1493 and 1496 and the chancel south chapel probably dates from a little later. This chapel served as the Oxenbridge family mausoleum and contains a respond with an Oxenbridge shield of arms and supporters, the brasses of Robert Oxenbridge (d. 1482) and his wife and the fine tomb of Sir Goddard Oxenbridge (d. 1537). Sir Goddard was, according to local tradition, a cannibal giant whose habit it was to devour a baby every night. There are fragments of 15th and early 16th-century glass, a poor box dated 1687 and a fine carved Virgin and Child by Clare Sheridan, a former owner of Brede Place.

ITINERARY B

1. HERSTMONCEUX **All Saints** (6010)

Quite a large church situated near the castle and with a splendid vista towards the Downs. The building is mainly of the late 12th and early 13th centuries but with the chancel and north chapel added in brick (no doubt from the same kilns as the castle) in the 15th century. Fine unrestored exterior with picturesque mid-19th century dormer windows. Good brass to Sir William Ffiennes (d. 1402); the Norman–French inscription offers 120 days' pardon for sins for those who say an *Ave* and *Paternoster* for the benefit of his soul. There is a large 'Easter Sepulchre' monument to Thomas, Lord Dacre (d. 1533) and his son, using earlier effigies to the Hoo family removed from Battle Abbey, but regrettably repainted. Good 'Gothick' pews and, in the chancel, the Commandment boards from the former main altar. In churchyard two tomb-chests and seven headstones with Harmer terracottas.

2. ASHBURNHAM **St. Peter** (6010)

One of the most interesting churches in Sussex. Apart from the 15th-century tower the building dates from 1665–67 and is in a 'Gothic Survival' style. The interior contains a perfect set of Stuart fittings which include the pulpit, west gallery, cut-down box pews, marble font and cover, locally made wrought iron railings and three-sided altar rail. The former reredos, now on the the south wall, is perhaps the finest in the county. Dated 1676, it has painted figures of Moses and Aaron flanking the Commandments. The frame is contemporary. In the north chapel are two monuments to the Ashburnham family; John, 1671, and William, 1675. The contrast in style between the two is marked: the earlier is still Jacobean in feeling, while the latter is full-blown Roman Baroque. The church formerly contained the shirt and silk drawers reputedly worn by Charles I at his execution. Until as late as 1828 it is said the relics were touched by those suffering from scrofula or the King's Evil.

3. PENHURST **St. Michael** (6010)

Almost untouched church isolated with the adjacent Court Farmhouse in the Ashburnham Estate area. Mainly Perpendicular and particularly worth a visit for the medieval chancel screen, Jacobean pulpit and reader's desk, box pews and nave panelling. 15th-century stained glass canopies and angels in the east window and fragments in other windows. Lovingly cared for.

4. BRIGHTLING **St. Thomas** (6020)

The churchyard has stunning views over the vale. The church is dominated by a massive pyramid mausoleum built in 1810 by 'Mad Jack' Fuller. A fine bust of him by Henry Rouw survives inside the church. The 13th-century nave and tower (of Tillgate stone) was remodelled in the 14th century with the addition of a north aisle and chancel. The south porch is an early example of 'Gothick' Revival dated 1749. Internally an 18th-century west gallery still contains a substantial barrel organ donated by courtesy of 'Mad Jack'. The nave retains its original waggon roof and the church has the tortoise stove which provided the only form of heating before the Victorian restorers introduced ducted heating.

5. **SALEHURST** **St. Mary** (7020)

Worth a visit for the exquisite scenes of birds, including a hawk and a peacock, in several windows in the nave south aisle. They date from *c.* 1400 and are the most memorable pieces of medieval stained glass in Sussex. The font has a 13th-century base with four salamanders; these were said to be impervious to fire and were emblematic of the Sacrament of Baptism which enabled a good man to pass through the fires of temptation unhurt. Several 17th and 18th-century cast iron tomb-slabs. One of the most attractive and atmospheric churchyards in Sussex.

---

6. **ETCHINGHAM** **The Assumption and St. Nicholas** (7020)

A grand church built by Sir William de Echyngham (d. 1389), whose fine brass is in the chancel, together with some other good brasses. The chancel is longer than the nave because the former was collegiate and still contains stalls and misericords. Some good window tracery and fragments of late 14th-century stained glass in the east and several nave windows. The chancel is laid with Minton tiles copied from surviving medieval originals. In south aisle good Jacobean altar-table.

---

7. **TICEHURST** **St. Mary** (6030)

Mainly 14th-century church with some contemporary glass in a nave north aisle window and, in a chancel north window, the remains of an interesting 15th-century Doom. Brass of a knight and his two wives. Good early 16th-century font cover, Victorian bier in North aisle, and interesting copy of a pew-plan at the west end.

---

8. **WARBLETON** **St. Mary** (6010)

The interior is dominated by the squire's pew of 1722 which rises on stilts in the north aisle and includes a separate enclosure for the family's servants. The church consists of a 13th-century chancel and nave to which a Perpendicular tower and north aisle chapel and porch were added. The fittings include an attractive Victorian painted reredos probably by Heaton, Butler and Bayne and an unusual octagonal relief hatchment dated 1813. Good brass to William Prestwych (d. 1436) and an outstanding Rysbrack bust to Sir John Lade (1740). In the churchyard the site of the house of one of the Sussex Martyrs, Richard Woodman, is marked. Opposite the lych gate the row of cottages was the original parochial workhouse.

ITINERARY C

---

1. **NEWICK** **St. Mary** (4020)

Worth visiting to see the excellent restoration by John Oldrid Scott who, in 1886–7, lengthened the nave and rebuilt the chancel. The latter is sumptuously decorated with stencilling, tiles and a gesso frieze. The reredos is painted in a style reminiscent of Burne-Jones. At the top of the windows in the south wall of the chancel are two 14th-century medallions depicting the Agnus Dei.

2. CHIDDINGLY (5010)

A sandstone church with one of the few stone spires in Sussex. Worth visiting for the Jefferay monument for which the south transept was built. It was erected in 1612 to commemorate Sir John Jefferay (d. 1571) who is depicted reclining on one elbow above an effigy of his second wife. Standing on either side are his only daughter and her husband, Sir Edward Montague. The very naïve Royal Arms may have been painted by the 19th-century antiquarian Mark Anthony Lower. Externally the churchyard fence was formerly maintained by individual landowners. There is one Harmer terracotta plaque. Substantial remains of Chiddingly Place, the home of the Jefferays can be seen further down the road from the church.

---

3. ROTHERFIELD **St. Denys** (5030)

Large mainly 13th-century church with Perpendicular west tower, porch and many windows. Medieval wall-paintings include the Doom, St. Thomas, Adam and Eve; the font has a wooden cover dated 1533 and other woodwork includes two Perpendicular screens and the canopied pulpit made in the early 17th century by Francis Gunby of Leeds for the Chapel of the Archbishops of York and Bishopsthorpe. Box pews in the nave are tiered at the west end. Excellent east window glass designed by Burne-Jones and executed by William Morris & Co.

---

4. FRANT **St. Alban** (5030)

Built 1819–22 by John Montier of Tunbridge Wells. The church is remarkable as the aisle glazing bars and the piers are all of cast iron, a material that was to be condemned by the Victorians. The north and south windows contain bought-in pieces of 15th and early 16th-century Continental glass. The ceiling of the nave was prettily stencilled in 1861.

FRANT (E): Watercolour by George de Paris, 1894

5. **WITHYHAM** **St. Michael** (4030)

Late 17th-century church with fine Sackville monuments by Cibber, Nollekens, Flaxman, Chantrey and Tyler. Also an Italian 14th-century polyptych with 15th-century predella and three 14th-century Italian paintings of the life of Christ; these were purchased in Italy by William Young Ottley. The church also has a local iron tomb-slab to William Alfrey (d. 1610).

ITINERARY D

1. **EASTBOURNE** **All Souls** (6090)

An extraordinary church built in 1882 by A. P. Strong but reminiscent of the small group of Victorian Italian Romanesque churches built in the 1840s. The detached campanile is 83 feet high.

2. **JEVINGTON** **St. Andrew** (5000)

Worth a visit for the Saxon west tower and the stone sculpture of Christ incorporating interlace of the Urnes style, which shows that Viking influence continued into the late 11th or even 12th centuries. It was found under the floor of the tower in 1785. The Urnes style derives its name from Urnes church, Norway; it is characterised by four-legged animals in combat with snake-like creatures interlaced with foliage tendrils.

3. **BISHOPSTONE** **St. Andrew** (4000)

An ancient church, possibly the oldest in Sussex. The south porch was originally the porticus of a Saxon building of which parts of the nave also survive; the date could be as early as the 8th century, although the 10th is more likely. The Normans added the west tower, south doorway, north aisle, chancel and sanctuary. The church possesses an impressive Romanesque coffin-lid carved with a cross, *Agnus Dei* and two birds all within three roundels; it was discovered when the church was restored in 1885. Supposedly Saxon sundial inscribed EADRIC over the porch.

4. **NEWHAVEN** **St. Michael** (4000)

Prominently situated on a hill as dedications to St. Michael frequently are, the church has been much altered over the centuries. At the core is a Norman central tower and aspidal chancel. The rest of the visible church dates from the 1854 restoration by Habershon. The graveyard contains a stone to a local brewer Thomas Tipper that includes a witty rhyme to the potency of his ale and a representation of the Newhaven bridge. There is also an obelisk recording the loss of HMS *Brazen* off Newhaven in 1800. Only one of the crew of 104 survived and 75 bodies were recovered and buried here.

5. **SOUTHEASE** (4000)

Attractively situated on a rise above the village green and little touched by restoration. Mainly of Norman date, the church has lost its original chancel and aisles. The round tower is one of three in Sussex. Faded wall-paintings include a 13th-century Passion cycle and 17th-century Biblical texts. Elizabethan communion table, Jacobean altar-rails and pulpit. The modern pews harmonise with the remaining Jacobean box-pews.

---

6. **HAMSEY** **St. Peter** (4010)

Another church spared by the restorers and set in an isolated position on a hill above a loop in the Ouse. Norman nave and chancel with late 14th-century east window and Perpendicular tower. Ancient seating, Royal Arms of George II and a standard recessed wall monument to Edward Markwick (d. 1538); in his will dated 1534 Markwick left directions that the Easter Sepulchre was to be placed on his tomb.

---

7. **LEWES** (a) **Jireh Chapel** (4010)

An important unspoiled 19th-century chapel interior, Jireh has a galleried interior, central pulpit entered from above and a railed communion enclosure surrounding the clerk's desk. The walls are lined with chapel hatpegs, the pews are pitch pine and a ground floor vestry is separated from the body of the chapel by shutters. Built in 1805 it was enlarged in 1826. For economy the builders used mathematical tiles in imitation of brick. Adjacent is the burial place of William Huntington S.S. (Sinner Saved). To the north of the chapel is a Sunday school erected in 1874.

BISHOPSTONE (E): Late 19th century watercolour by G. de Paris, showing the church from the south-west

(b) **Westgate Chapel** (4010)

Dating from 1700 the chapel is set back behind the Bull Inn and entered from the High Street. The interior has been re-ordered on several occasions.

(c) **St. John the Baptist, Southover** (4010)

Originally the *hospitium* or Guest House of Lewes Priory and adjoining the ruins of the great Cluniac monastery. Worth a visit for the Tournai marble tomb slab of Gundrada, co-founder of the Priory, carved in *c.* 1145. The slab is housed in a neo-Norman chapel built in 1847.

---

8. **GLYNDE** **St. Mary** (4000)

The finest 18th-century church in Sussex and the only one built in a classical style. Built 1763–5 and designed by Sir Thomas Robinson, the church contains its original box pews, pulpit, west gallery and altar rail. The east window by Kempe has been unfairly criticised; its neo-Renaissance motifs accord with the style of the church. The splendid brass gasolier, probably by Hardman of Birmingham, is also noteworthy. The church is superbly sited adjacent to Glynde Place.

---

9. **WEST FIRLE** **St. Peter** (4000)

A large church at the foot of the Downs near Firle Place. Some good early 14th-century glass in the east window of the south aisle, but the chief glories of the church are the late 16th-century family monuments in brass and alabaster made by Gerard Johnson, the designs for which are at Firle Place.

---

10. **BERWICK** (5000)

The church is worth visiting primarily for the Bloomsbury Group wall-paintings commissioned by Bishop Bell of Chichester between 1942–3. Duncan Grant painted the Christ in Glory over the chancel arch; beneath, to the left, are figures of a sailor, soldier and airman, and on the right are portraits of Bishop Bell and the Rector of Berwick. Also by Grant is the Calvary on the west wall. Vanessa Bell painted the Annunciation and Nativity in the nave, and her son, Quentin Bell, painted the east side of the chancel arch and the altarpiece.

---

11. **ARLINGTON** **St. Pancras** (5000)

Almost untouched exterior and quite sensitive late Victorian restoration of the interior. The nave is late Saxon, the chancel and north chapel Norman. 13th-century north aisle and tower. Traces of medieval wall-paintings and Biblical texts on the nave walls. Good king-post roofs and fine early 14th-century head-stops to the east window and one of the arches to the north chapel. Screen made at Mayfield in 1890–96. Medieval storage jar and funeral bier. The Queen Anne pulpit was re-carved to Charles Powell's designs during the Victorian restoration as was the altar-table. The interesting 15th-century churchwardens' accounts are now in the British Library.

ITINERARY E

1. BRIGHTON (a) **St. Nicholas** (3000)

Although the church was maimed by R. C. Carpenter's savage restoration of 1853–4, there is still much of interest inside. The oldest object is the 12th-century font, carved with scenes of the Last Supper, the Baptism of Christ, and the Life of St. Nicholas. The screen is heavily restored but is basically 15th century. Also worthy of note is the excellent stained glass by Kempe, the extraordinary Wellington memorial designed by R. C. Carpenter in the form of an Eleanor Cross, and the colourful wall decoration by Kempe to Somers Clarke's designs. Outside the south east chapel is a statue of St. Nicholas by Ninian Comper. The churchyard contains some good 18th-century headstones.

(b) **St. Peter** (3000)

Designed by Charles Barry 1824–28 the church is one of the best examples in England of a Regency Commissioners' Gothic church. The spacious interior contains Kempe glass and, in the clerestory, rare Regency glass by William Collins. The nave vaulting is made of plaster. The church originally had galleries on three sides and high box pews.

(c) **St. Martin** (3000)

A big red-brick church designed by Somers Clarke in 1872–75. The interior is extraordinarily powerful and contains the best 19th-century fittings in Sussex; most of these were designed by the architect.

BRIGHTON, St. PETER (E): Lithograph

(d) **St. Michael and All Angels** (3000)

Two churches in one. The first church was designed by G. F. Bodley and built 1860–2; this is now the south aisle to William Burges's cathedral-like addition executed in 1893 after the architect's death. The interior is breathtaking and contains outstanding works of art. The old church has Morris glass of 1862; the west window is particularly fine. There is also an early 16th-century Flemish reredos, a superb pulpit by Bodley and stained glass in the east and west windows of the nave designed by H. W. Lonsdale. The finest Victorian church in Sussex.

(e) **St. Paul** (3000)

Designed by R. C. Carpenter 1846–8. One of the first churches in Sussex to be built on Tractarian principles. Interior contains Pugin stained glass, good wall-painting in the chancel (by Bodley) and an extraordinary lectern, designed by J. H. Powell to illustrate themes from the Apocalypse. The rood-screen is by Carpenter.

(f) **St. Bartholomew** (3000)

The cathedral of Brighton Anglo-Catholicism. Built 1872–4 to the designs of Edmund Scott for Father Wagner. The interior is unique and breathtaking; the massively high brick walls are admirably set off by the opulent furnishings designed by Henry Wilson between 1895–1908. John Betjeman once imagined the clergy entering on elephants.

---

2. **HOVE** **All Saints** (3000)

The new parish church of Hove, designed on a cathedral scale by J. L. Pearson. Work started in 1889 but was not completed until 1924. Interior contains fittings designed by Pearson and his son. Much of the stained glass is by Clayton and Bell.

3. **PRESTON** **St. Peter** (3000)

Good example of a 13th-century Sussex church. The tower is picturesquely situated in the gardens of Preston Manor. The interior contains early 14th-century wall-paintings of the Nativity, Last Supper, murder of Becket and St. Michael weighing souls. More were visible before a fire in 1906. The nave was over-restored by James Woodman in 1872. The chancel was restored by Ewan Christian in 1878; the extremely attractive decorative stencilling and choir stalls, one of which is carved with a Red Indian's head, are presumably by him. There is good stained glass in the nave, probably by Lavers, Barraud and Westlake; in the chancel armorial glass of excellent quality commemorates the marriage alliances of the Stanford and Macdonald families.

ITINERARY F

---

1. **NEW SHOREHAM** **St. Mary de Haura** (2000)

Although lacking its nave this is still one of the grandest parish churches in Sussex. The transepts date from *c.* 1130, and the splendid vaulted choir is an excellent example of Transitional work of the late 12th and early 13th centuries. Three-storey elevation with clustered shafts to the columns, elaborate arch mouldings and carved capitals.

---

2. **OLD SHOREHAM** **St. Nicholas** (2000)

Less sophisticated and more heavily restored than New Shoreham. A cruciform church with traces of Saxon work in the unaisled nave. Transepts and central tower of *c.* 1125–50, with the crossing arches embellished with chevron and billet carving. The very restored chancel screen dates from *c.* 1300. The restoration of the church in 1841 was undertaken by John Mason Neale and the Camden Society on behalf of the patron, Magdalen College, Oxford. It was one of the first churches to be restored under the auspices of the Society.

---

3. **COOMBES** (1000)

Next to a farmyard and one of the loveliest interiors in Sussex. Remains of Romanesque wall-paintings by the same workshop as Clayton and Hardham, partly over-painted by post-medieval texts. The flint church is unaisled and mainly of late Saxon and Norman date.

---

4. **BOTOLPHS** **St. Botolph** (1000)

Small attractive church which shows evidence of economic decline in a blocked 13th-century north arcade and signs of house platforms opposite the church. The fittings are not outstanding but include a Jacobean pulpit.

---

5. **STEYNING** **St. Andrew** (1010)

Grandiose late Romanesque nave of *c.* 1170 with round piers and richly ornamented arches. The early 12th-century carved capitals on the south aisle arch at the east end are worth a look. There is also an excellent Queen Anne Royal Arms dated 1703, and, behind the altar, fine 16th-century wooden panelling, originally in the vicarage. The chancel was rebuilt by G. M. Hills in 1863.

---

6. **POYNINGS** **Holy Trinity** (2010)

A large aisleless cruciform church below the Downs built at the end of the 14th century from a bequest in the will of Michael, Lord Poynings (d. 1369). Early Perpendicular window tracery and fragments of medieval stained glass include an Annunciation in the north transept. Medieval screen and Jacobean pulpit, three-sided altar rails and two family pews.

---

7. **CLAYTON** **St. John the Baptist** (2010)

Saxo-Norman overlap church with impressive chancel arch. Famous for the excellent series of Romanesque murals in the nave by the Coombes–Hardham workshop. The principal subject matter is the Last Judgement. The murals were discovered in 1893; further discoveries were made by P. M. Johnston in 1917–19. Brass to Richard Iden, 1523, depicting him in vestments holding the chalice and wafer.

ITINERARY G

1. **SOMPTING** — **St. Mary** (1000)

In a fine position on the southern slope of the Downs and separated from the village and urban sprawl of Worthing by the A27. Well-known for its west tower, the lower stage of which is Saxon while the upper stages, which appear to be late 11th century, end in a 'Rhenish helm' spire which dates from the early 14th century. The *Ecclesiologist* described the church in 1857 as: 'a relic, solitary, destitute of history, and till lately undeciphered, of that long and vigorous civilisation . . . of which the monumental knowledge is so faint and flickering, compared with what we (know) of the . . . constructions of Sennacherib or Rameses'. The rest of the church was rebuilt at the end of the 12th century.

2. **CLAPHAM** — **St. Mary** (0000)

A small village church excellently restored by Gilbert Scott 1873–4. The chancel contains a tiled reredos painted with Pre-Raphaelite angels against a vine leaf background; the north and south walls have unfortunately been largely painted over. The pulpit and lectern are incorporated in a low alabaster screen. Good 16th-century brasses in the chancel.

3. **ANGMERING** — **St. Margaret** (0000)

Worth visiting to see the extraordinary 'restoration' by S. S. Teulon in 1855. Apart from the tower the church was virtually rebuilt. The nave has beautifully carved capitals and winged angels by Forsyth. Fittings by Teulon include the alabaster pulpit decorated with angels and inset with mosaic and the oak prayer desk. The frenetically carved sanctuary chair is also probably by Teulon. It came from Ecclesden Manor. Outside the church the school and vestry hall are by the same architect.

4. **POLING** — **St. Nicholas** (0000)

A modest church with Saxo-Norman nave and Perpendicular chancel. Interesting fittings include part of an 11th or 12th-century wooden window shutter, a poor box which may be of medieval origin, part of the original screen with its Rood-beam and a good brass to Walter Dury (vicar 1442/3–1499).

5. **BURPHAM** — **St. Mary** (0000)

Beautifully situated at the end of a drive up the Arun valley, Burpham has stunning views of Arundel over the river. The church is noted for the early 13th-century vaulted stone chancel. Medieval fittings include a piscina and double aumbrey and some 15th-century bench-ends. Sympathetically restored by T. G. Jackson in 1869 the church includes 17th-century altar rails and some German glass roundels of the same date in the chancel. In the churchyard a tombstone commemorating Benjamin Brewster, a jockey who died in 1785, includes a relief of a racehorse.

ITINERARY H

1. **NORTH STOKE** (0010)

An unrestored gem in a tiny hamlet near the Arun. Cruciform, with Norman nave, early 13th-century chancel and transepts of *c.* 1290. Bare whitewashed interior enlivened by carved corbels, a little decorative wall-painting and two Coronation of the Virgin stained glass panels of *c.* 1290–1300.

2. **ARUNDEL** (a) **St. Nicholas** (0000)

Large cruciform church rebuilt after 1380 by the Earls of Arundel. The Fitzalan Chapel, Lady Chapel and the Mausoleum of the 14th Duke of Norfolk at the east end are the private property of the Duke of Norfolk and separated from the nave. The latter contains a Perpendicular stone pulpit, but the church is chiefly famous for the fine series of sepulchral monuments to the Earls of Arundel and Dukes of Norfolk dating from the early 15th to the 20th centuries. On north wall are 14th-century wall-paintings of the Seven Deadly Sins and the Seven Works of Mercy.

(b) **St. Philip Neri** (0000)

Dominating the Arundel skyline, the Catholic cathedral was designed in the French Gothic style by J. A. Hansom and Son (the former better known as the inventor of the Patent Safety Cab) and built between 1870 and 1873. Internally the size is impressive although the details are unremarkable with the exception of some good 19th-century glass by Hardman. The north transept contains the shrine of St. Philip Howard. The church was paid for by the 15th Duke of Norfolk, who had a strong devotion to St. Philip Neri.

---

3. **TORTINGTON** **St. Thomas** (0000)

Redundant Norman flint church with attractive wooden bell-turret and fine south doorway and chancel arch, the last with beakhead decoration. Jacobean pulpit and 18th-century hatchments. Now in the care of the Redundant Churches Fund.

---

4. **FORD** **St. Andrew** (9000)

Simple two-cell Norman church without aisles enclosed in its graveyard in flat fields north of the seaside sprawl. The peaceful ensemble is unfortunately marred by an adjacent caravan park. Unrestored exterior with white-painted wooden bell-turret and brick porch dated 1637 with Dutch gable. Interior with plain plastered walls, Norman chancel arch and traces of 15th-century murals, including a Doom.

---

5. **CLIMPING** **St. Mary** (0000)

Chiefly notable as one of the finest 13th-century churches in Sussex. The tower has late Norman carving of unusual liveliness. The interior is nobly proportioned and contains one of the two medieval stone pulpits in Sussex and one of the finest

13th-century chests in England. Some of the benches incorporate 15th-century woodwork. In the north transept are allegorical paintings (1925–6) by Heywood Harty. One picture shows Christ preaching to a group of villagers in typical Arun scenery.

---

6. **YAPTON** **St. Mary** (9000)

The largely unrestored exterior has a roof with 17th-century dormers similar to those which adorned many churches before Victorian restoration. Interior chiefly notable for the very fine 12th-century capitals of the arcades. The east window was designed by the architect and antiquarian P. M. Johnston in 1905; it replaced a simple 18th-century window.

---

7. **SLINDON** **St. Mary** (9000)

Unrecognisable as a medieval church from the outside thanks to T. G. Jackson's 'restoration' in 1866. Inside his chancel has merit and the nave retains medieval features, notably the late 12th-century scalloped capitals and traces of ashlar wall-painting in the south aisle. A few 'poppy-head' medieval benches in the south aisle and the only wooden effigy in Sussex, a figure in 16th-century armour probably representing Sir Anthony St. Leger (d. 1539). Ancient north door.

ITINERARY I

---

1. **BOXGROVE** **St. Mary and St. Blaise** (9000)

The most impressive survivor of the former monastic churches of Sussex. Few traces of the 12th-century nave remain, but the chancel of *c.* 1220 is intact. The two-storey elevation with lancet windows, marble shafts and rib vaults is closely related to the design of the Chichester Cathedral retrochoir. The delicate vault paintings were commissioned in the early 1520s from Lambert Barnard by Thomas, Lord de la Warr (d. 1526), whose splendidly elaborate chantry chapel incorporates Renaissance ornamental motifs. Curiously, Thomas is not buried in his chapel; when he died in 1526 he was buried at Broadwater, where his tomb may still be seen. Good hatchment in the north transept commemorating Lord Robert Spencer, 1831, and a monument to Mary, Countess of Derby (d. 1752) depicting her giving alms to the poor.

---

2. **CHICHESTER** (a) **Cathedral** (8000)

The mother-church of the diocese and, fittingly, the largest and most distinguished medieval edifice in Sussex. It was begun by Bishop Ralph de Luffa after 1091 and dedicated in 1108 and although the elevation and east end were altered after a fire in 1187 the church is still basically a Romanesque building. Amongst the wealth of fittings and furnishings are two famous reliefs depicting Christ coming to the House of Mary of Bethany and the Raising of Lazarus which probably belonged to a choir screen and may date from as early as 1108. There are a fine series of tombs including a wall-monument to John Cawley, one of the Regicides (d. 1666), choir stalls with misericords of *c.* 1320–30 and large panel paintings and vault decoration executed in the early 16th century by Lambert Barnard.

(b) **Providence Chapel** (8000)

Built in 1809, the plain exterior hides a simple yet noble interior. Small and compact and with its fittings still intact, a visit to Providence is a moving experience. The pulpit dominates the chapel and is entered from the minister's vestry which is located in the adjoining minister's house. Above the entrance a single gallery overlooks the pulpit and railed communion area.

(c) **St. John** (8000)

A superb example of an auditory church, St. John's was designed by James Elmes and built of white brick in 1812–13. The focal point of the galleried interior is the three-decker pulpit which towers over the nave and masks the small railed sanctuary. The four-sided gallery is supported on iron columns. The survival of this typical Georgian low-church interior from the enthusiasts of the Camden Society is surprising.

(d) **Cawley's Almshouses** (8000)

A block of almshouses dated 1625 which includes a simple chapel.

BOXGROVE (W): Chantry of Thomas, Lord de la Warr (d. 1526), and his wife

(e) **Greyfriars** (8000)

The chancel of the former Franciscan church built after 1269 and probably completed by 1282. Simple and austere, with a fine five-lancet east window and good bar tracery side windows.

(f) **St. Mary's Hospital** (8000)

Fascinating survival of a medieval hospital in which the hall, still occupied by self-contained living quarters for elderly ladies, terminates in a chapel. Similar arrangements can be seen in medieval hospitals at Beaune and Tonnerre in Burgundy and Lübeck, Germany. The building dates from *c.* 1290–1300, together with the fine screen between the chapel and the hall and the twenty-four stalls with their lively misericords.

---

3. **WEST WITTERING** **St. Peter and St. Paul** (7090)

An unattractive exterior following a harsh 1875 restoration but the interior retains a fine pair of recessed Tudor wall monuments in the north wall of the chancel. One was erected by William Earnley to commemorate his first wife, while the second records Earnley himself and was provided by his second wife. The first and larger monument includes a defaced relief of the Resurrection, the second an Annunciation and a rare lily-crucifix.

---

4. **BOSHAM** **Holy Trinity** (8000)

Church made famous by its idealised depiction in the Bayeux Tapestry, but only the lower part of the tower certainly dates from before 1066. The tall and elaborately moulded chancel arch is an example of the Saxo-Norman overlap, and the chancel and the nave were rebuilt on an impressive scale and with good detailing in the early 13th century. Unplastered rubble walls, vaulted crypt below the south aisle adjacent to an early 14th-century tomb recess with three excellent head-stops. Some medieval 'poppy-head' benches at the west end of the south aisle.

---

5. **SENNICOTTS** **St. Mary** (8000)

Built in a rustic 'Gothick' style, the light and airy interior still retains its box pews. Beautifully situated in a park.

---

6. **RACTON** (7000)

Simple church consisting only of a nave and chancel divided by a tympanum surmounted by a Royal Arms. The airy interior retains a brick floor and oil lamps (now converted to electricity). Worth visiting for three fine monuments, two of which are to the Gounter family. The earliest, of about 1520, is of the same type as the de la Warr chantry at Boxgrove.

---

7. **STANSTED CHAPEL** (7010)

Built in the grounds of Stansted House, the brick chapel was constructed in 1812–15 out of parts of the original late 15th-century house. The Regency 'Gothick' details of the interior are delightful; the stained glass is of particular interest as descriptions of it feature in John Keats's *Eve of St. Agnes* and *Eve of St. Mark*.

---

8. **STOUGHTON** **St. Mary** (8010)

Late 11th-century cruciform church attractively set on a hillside above the village. Plastered flint exterior with tower added to the south transept in the 14th century. Monumental chancel arch and, in the nave which is lit by converted oil lamps, some good pewing, Commandment boards and an interesting small brass to James Smyth (d. 1565), which still uses the Catholic invocation of prayers for the soul of the deceased.

---

9. **SIDLESHAM** **St. Mary** (8090)

A large church despite the loss of its chancel. The transept and aisled nave of the same date and similar noble proportions and rubble construction as Bosham. The church largely escaped 'tidying-up' by the Victorians and has retained its 19th-century dormer windows and aisle windows, one of which is dated 1596. Some good 17th and 18th-century gravestones in the churchyard. Preserved inside the church is the oldest surviving wooden deadboard in Sussex, dated 1658.

ITINERARY J

---

1. **TWINEHAM** **St. Peter** (2020)

An isolated Tudor brick building consisting of a nave, chancel, timbered south porch and squat western tower with broach spire. The interior retains a western gallery and a good 17th-century pew. Part of the churchyard was used as a Quaker burial ground between 1694 and 1732 and is still marked out today.

---

2. **SHERMANBURY** **St. Giles** (2010)

Secluded in a parkland setting, the church is adjacent to Shermanbury Place. An aisleless church, whose medieval walls remain, it was remodelled in 1710 and 1885. The interior contains pews inscribed with the names of local farms, a timber chancel arch and a fine example of a painted Royal Arms of Queen Anne. Some Kempe glass survives at the east end and there is an organ in the west gallery, which is entered from outside.

---

3. **WEST GRINSTEAD** **St. George** (1020)

Another parkland setting, the stone built exterior is rather heavy and uninspiring with a solid 13th-century tower. The highlight of the grim exterior is the 15th-century north porch. The interior has benches marked with the names of the owners' farms, an intriguing monochrome Royal Arms of George IV and a good example of Kempe glass in the east window. A monument by Rysbrack has William Powlett and his wife (1746) clad in Roman costume flanking an urn. There is also a signed monument to Sir William Burrell by Flaxman.

4. **WARMINGHURST** **Holy Sepulchre** (1010)

Beautifully situated in the Weald with only a farm for company, this 13th-century church is constructed of a blend of stone, brick, shingles and tile-hanging. The moving interior is the finest example in Sussex of how many churches must have looked before the Victorian restorers. The largely 18th-century fittings include a pulpit and clerk's desk, box pews and a screen with the tympanum painted with the Royal Arms of Queen Anne. The altar rails and table are late 17th century. On the west wall is a wrought iron font crane for raising the font cover. There are three 18th-century funeral hatchments and, in the chancel, a good 16th-century brass to the Shelley family; the details of the costume are of great interest.

---

5. **SHIPLEY** **St. Mary** (1020)

Large sandstone church with square-ended chancel, central tower and originally unaisled nave. Its monumental scale and austere decoration can be explained by the fact that it was built in the 1130s for the Knights Templars.

---

6. **COOLHAM** **Blue Idol Friends' Meeting House** (1020)

Part of a timber framed 16th-century farmhouse was converted in 1691 to create a meeting place. The simple interior with gallery and minister's stand is very moving. Associated with the meeting house are two small burial grounds.

---

7. **BILLINGSHURST** **General Baptist Chapel** (0020)

This small brick built chapel dates from 1754 and lies within its own burial ground

WEST GRINSTEAD (W): Nave north porch, 15th century

which is set back from the main street. A brick extension to provide a baptistry and vestries was added to the west in 1825 and rebuilt in 1886. This led to a reorganisation of the internal fittings so that the pulpit is now against the south wall where it would originally have faced the main entrance. A northern gallery was added in the 18th century and this includes two pews inscribed 'James Knight 1788'. Over the entrance is an impressive clock by Inkpen of Horsham, 1756.

---

8. **WISBOROUGH GREEN** **Zoar Chapel** (0020)

An attractive village of Wealden cottages around a green. The chapel, built in 1753, is like a small cottage. Nearby is a small and secluded burial ground. The chapel is named from the Hebrew for 'room' since God had seen fit to find a room for the congregation.

---

9. **HORSHAM** **General Baptist Church** (1030)

Subsumed in modern Horsham, the chapel was built in 1721; a porch was added in 1727 with a baptistry and vestries following in 1772. Most of the internal fittings were lost in a 19th-century re-ordering and our own century has seen the removal of the burial ground.

---

10. **WEST CHILTINGTON** **St. Mary** (0010)

Unspoilt exterior with yellow plastering and only lightly touched interior. The latter provides one of the best impressions of how a Sussex village church looked in the Middle Ages, chiefly because so much wall-painting survives. The murals at the east end of the south aisle are of 12th-century date and in the main body of the nave most of the 13th-century narrative scenes of the life of Christ are preserved. In a window splay is the only example in Sussex of a Christ of the Trades. Other features include a medieval marble altar-slab, Jacobean pulpit and communion table, a 'Breeches' Bible of 1611 and an interesting brass inscription in the chancel to Robert Johnson, parson (d. 1611). The church itself is a modest two-cell structure dating from the 12th century.

ITINERARY K

---

1. **BUNCTON** **All Saints** (1010)

Approached through a ravine, the church has an unrestored Norman interior. Exterior has an arcade on the north chancel wall decorated with mouldings and a kind of formalised beakhead.

---

2. **PARHAM** **St. Peter** (0010)

A splendid example of an estate church situated in the grounds of Parham Park. Structurally of 1545, the interior is as complete an example as could be wished of an 1820s 'Gothick' remodelling. Fittings include a two-decker pulpit, box pews, vicar's pew, and squire's pew complete with fireplace. The rare lead font is 14th century.

3. **HARDHAM** **St. Botolph** (0010)

Another church with a well-preserved series of wall-paintings, which in this case are the main surviving works by the Coombes–Clayton artists, active in the period *c.* 1080–*c.* 1120. The Hardham cycle includes scenes of Adam and Eve, the Nativity and early life of Christ, the apostles and Hell; also of St. George.

---

4. **GREATHAM** (0010)

One of the most appealing churches in Sussex. Diminutive single-cell ironstone building next to the manor house. The church is Saxo-Norman overlap with 13th-century windows. Inside the fittings, comprising dark-stained two-decker pulpit and box pews, are all early 19th-century except for the 17th-century communion rails. The only lighting is by oil-lamps.

---

5. **BURTON** (9010)

An estate church in the grounds of Burton Park. This vies with Warminghurst as the finest unrestored interior in the county. Structurally Norman, the church is memorable for its Perpendicular screen with a plaster tympanum painted with the Commandments in about 1636, a painted Royal Arms of the same date, and a series of 16th-century monuments to the Goring family. In the splay of the north window is a wall-painting reputed to be St. Uncumber, a bearded lady who was crucified upside down. Also known as St. Wilgefortis, this saint was popular with wives praying for separation from their husbands.

---

6. **UP WALTHAM** **St. Mary the Virgin** (9010)

A tiny charming unrestored Downland church. Essentially of 12th and 13th century, it is one of only four in Sussex with an apsidal end.

PARHAM (W): Squire's pew

ITINERARY L

1. SELHAM **St. James** (9020)

An 11th-century church in a beautiful location east of Midhurst. The Norman chancel arch is supported on capitals which hark back to Saxon times; one is vigorously carved with interlace and foliage, and the other has a superb monster's head. The stained glass windows contain shields commemorating the supposed Plantaganet lineage of the children of the Rev. Robert Blackburn, Rector of Selham from 1842–99. A letter of 1889 records that when the Rector was asked about the windows 'he drew himself up to his full height, and replied in deep solemn tones "They are the arms of my children's ancestors".'

2. WEST LAVINGTON **St. Mary Magdalen** (8020)

Built in 1850, this is the only church in Sussex designed by William Butterfield. The interior contains good stained glass by Hardman, almost certainly to Butterfield's designs; the glass is in an early 14th-century style. The oversized naturalistic corbels of the chancel arch are also noteworthy. The church was built for Henry Manning, Archdeacon of Chichester, but he went over to Rome before he could hold services in it.

3. WOOLBEDING **All Hallows** (8020)

Beautifully situated adjacent to Woolbeding Hall, the nave walls of the church have prominent Saxon pilaster strips. Interior chiefly notable for the good Gothic Revival furnishings in the chancel and the 16th-century Continental stained glass in the nave.

GREATHAM (W): Interior looking east

4. CHITHURST (8020)

Chithurst stands on a raised mound in a remote and attractive setting. Built in the 11th-century there have been few alterations, the most notable being the addition of larger 13th-century windows. The church was carefully restored by P. M. Johnston in 1913.

---

5. TROTTON **St. George** (8020)

Spacious Decorated church notable for its extensive wall-paintings of the late 14th and early 15th-centuries. On the west wall are the Seven Deadly Sins and Seven Works of Mercy and the side wall murals include shields of arms and donor figures of the Camoys family. The latter are represented on two magnificent brasses, one of Margaret, Lady Camoys (d. 1310) and the second of Thomas, Lord Camoys (d. 1419) and his wife.

---

6. MILLAND **St. Luke and the Old Church** (8020)

The churches make a telling contrast with each other. St. Luke's was built in 1880 in a Decorated Style when the old church had become too small; it has an extremely prominent west tower. The old church survives behind St. Luke's; it is difficult to date but is probably 16th century. The derelict interior has a moving simplicity.

UP MARDEN (W): Interior looking east

7. THE MARDENS

(a) **St. Michael, Up Marden** (7010)

One of the most atmospheric churches in Sussex situated in the beautiful countryside of the South Downs. The structure is 13th century but what is memorable is the unrestored interior: whitewashed walls, clear glass, brick floors, benches, and ceiled roof. The church is still lit by candles. The triangular chancel arch is a 16th-century addition.

(b) **St. Mary, North Marden** (8010)

A tiny Norman church consisting only of nave and apse. The 18th-century altarpiece consisting of the Creed, Decalogue and Lord's Prayer is now in the nave. The interior preserves its rustic simplicity and is still candlelit.

8. DIDLING

St. Andrew (8010)

A small 13th-century church standing under the Downs. The gentle restoration of 1878 (after the church had been struck by lightning) respected the integrity of the building. Interior remarkable for the medieval benches in the nave, good Jacobean altar rails, and a 12th-century tub font.

SELECT BIBLIOGRAPHY

Some bibliographical references are given in abbreviated form in the text, e.g. P. Ferriday, 1964. Full details are given in this bibliography. Periodical references in the text have been abbreviated as follows: Sussex Arch. Colls. (Sussex Archaeological Collections); Sussex Rec. Soc. (Sussex Record Society); Proc. Battle Conf. (Proceedings of the Battle Conference in Anglo-Norman Studies). E and W placed after churches refers to their location in either East or West Sussex.

GENERAL WORKS

Betjeman, J. (ed.), *Collins Pocket Guide to English Parish Churches,* London, 1968.
Brandon, P., *The Sussex Landscape,* London, 1974.
Cox, J. C., *English Church Fittings, Furniture, and Accessories,* London, 1923.
Cox, J. C., and Harvey, A., *English Church Furniture,* London, 1907.
Harrison, F., *Notes on Sussex Churches,* 3rd ed., Hove, 1911.
Johnston, P. M., 'Ecclesiastical Architecture', in Victoria County History, *Sussex,* vol. 2, London, 1907, pp. 327–379.
Nairn, I., and Pevsner, N., *The Buildings of England, Sussex,* Harmondsworth, 1965.
Randall, G., *Church Furnishing and Decoration,* London, 1980.
Salzmann, L. F., 'Ecclesiastical History', in Victoria County History, *Sussex,* vol. 2, London, 1907, pp. 1–44.
Sussex Historic Churches Trust, *Sussex Churches,* 1984.

SUSSEX CHURCHES AND THE REFORMATION

Kitch, M. J., 'The Reformation in Sussex', *Studies in Sussex Church History,* ed. M. J. Kitch, London, 1981, pp. 77–98.
McCann, T. J., 'The Clergy and the Elizabethan Settlement in the Diocese of Chichester', *idem,* pp. 99–123.
Manning, R. B., *Religion and Society in Elizabethan Sussex,* Leicester, 1969.

ROMAN CATHOLICISM IN SUSSEX

Caplan, N., 'The Sussex Catholics *c.* 1660–1800', *Sussex Archaeological Collections,* vol. CXVI (1979), pp. 19–29.
Elleray, D. R., *The Victorian Churches of Sussex,* Chichester, 1981.
Fletcher, A., *Sussex 1600–1660: A County Community in Peace and War,* London, 1980.
Hernaman, I., *West Grinstead and our Sussex Forefathers,* London, 1924.
Little, B., *Catholic Churches since 1623,* London, 1966.
McCann, T. J., 'West Grinstead, A Centre for Catholicism in Sussex 1671–1814', *Sussex Archaeological Collections,* vol. CXXIV (1986), pp. 193–212.

THE CHURCH AND THE COMMUNITY FROM THE MEDIEVAL PERIOD TO THE EIGHTEENTH CENTURY

Bettey, J. H., *Church and Parish, A Guide for Local Historians,* London, 1987.
Cox, J. C., *Churchwardens' Accounts,* London, 1913.
Johnstone, H. (ed.), 'Churchwardens' Presentments', *Sussex Record Society,* vols. XLIX and L, 1947–1949.
Mayhew, G., *Tudor Rye,* Falmer, 1987.
Tate, W. E., *The Parish Chest,* Chichester, 1983.
Vaisey, D. (ed.), *The Diary of Thomas Turner 1754–1765,* Oxford, 1984.

SUSSEX NON-CONFORMITY

Brent, C. E., 'Rural Employment and Population in Sussex between 1550 and 1640', *Sussex Archaeological Collections,* vol. CXIV (1976), pp. 27–48 and vol. CXVI (1979), pp. 41–55.
Caplan, N., 'An Outline of the Origins and Development of Non-Conformity in Sussex 1603–1803', unpublished MS, 1961, in library of Sussex Archaeological Society.
Caplan, N., 'Sussex Religious Dissent *c.* 1830', *Sussex Archaeological Collections,* vol. CXX (1982), pp. 193–203.
Caplan, N., 'The Methodist Revival in Sussex', *Sussex Notes and Queries,* vol. XVI.
Caplan, N., 'The Lean Years of Sussex Non-Conformity', *Transactions of the Congregational Historical Society,* vol. XIX.
Caplan, N., 'The Numerical Strength of Non-Conformity in Sussex 1669–1676', *Transactions of the Unitarian Historical Society,* vol. 22, no. 1 (1963).
Chambers, R. F., *The Strict Baptist Chapels of England: Sussex,* Thornton Heath, 1954.
Connell, J. H., *The Story of an Old Meeting House,* Lewes, 1916.
Cooper, J. H., 'A Religious Census of Sussex in 1676', *Sussex Archaeological Collections,* vol. XLV (1937), pp. 142–148.
Everitt, A. M., *The Patterns of Rural Dissent,* Leicester, 1972.
Fletcher, A., *Sussex 1600–1660: A County Community in Peace and War,* London, 1980.
Hague, G., *The Unitarian Heritage,* Sheffield, 1986.
Homan, R., 'The Society of Dependents', *Sussex Archaeological Collections,* vol. CXIX (1981), pp. 195–204.
Lidbetter, H., *The Friends Meeting House,* 1961.
MacAndrew, D., 'The Sussex Cokelers: a curious sect', *Sussex County Magazine,* vol. 16 (1942), pp. 346–350.
Marsh, T. W., *Early Friends in Surrey and Sussex,* London, 1886.
Rector, K. W., 'Lewes Quakers in the Seventeenth and Eighteenth Centuries', *Sussex Archaeological Collections,* vol. CXVI (1978), pp. 31–40.
Reynolds, J. S., *Providence Chapel, Chichester,* Chichester, 1961.

CHURCHES AND CHURCH ARCHITECTURE, *c.* 1600–1900

Addleshaw, G. W. O., and Etchells, F ., *The Architectural Setting of Anglican Worship,* London, 1948.
Clarke, B. F. L., *The Building of the Eighteenth Century Church,* London, 1963.
Crook, J. M., *William Burges,* London, 1981.
Dale, A., *Brighton Churches,* London, 1989.
Dixon, R., and Muthesius, S., *Victorian Architecture,* London, 1978.
Elleray, D. R., *The Victorian Churches of Sussex,* Chichester, 1981.
Goodhart-Rendel, H. S., 'The Churches of Brighton and Hove', *Architectural Review,* vol. XLIV, 1918, pp. 23–29, 59–63, 75–79.
Hennock, E. P., 'The Anglo-Catholics and Church Extension in Victorian Brighton', *Studies in Sussex Church History,* ed. M. J. Kitch, London, 1981, pp. 173–188.
Howell, P., *Victorian Churches,* Feltham, Mx., 1968.
Pevsner, N., *Some Architectural Writers of the Nineteenth Century,* Oxford, 1972.
Saunders, M., *The Churches of S.S. Teulon,* Ecclesiological Society, London, 1982.
Steer, F. W., *The Church of St. John the Evangelist, Chichester, 1813–1963,* Chichester, 1963.
Whiffen, M., *Stuart and Georgian Churches,* London, 1948.
Yates, W. N., '"Bells and Smells": London, Brighton and South Coast Religion Reconsidered', *Southern History,* vol. 5, 1983, pp. 122–153.

NINETEENTH-CENTURY CHURCH RESTORATION IN SUSSEX

'Arlington Church Scrapbook', East Sussex Record Office, PAR/232/7/7.
'Arlington Church: Specification of work by C. E. Powell, A.R.I.B.A.', East Sussex Record Office, PAR/232/4/1.
Brandwood, G. K., 'Anglican Churches before the Restorers: A study from Leicestershire and Rutland', *Archaeological Journal,* 144 (1987), pp. 383–408.
Chatfield, M., *Churches the Victorians Forgot,* Derbyshire, 1979.
Clarke, B. F. L., 'Church Restoration in the Nineteenth Century', Typescript, *c.* 1976, in the library of the Council for the Care of Churches, London.
Ferriday, P., 'The Church Restorers', *Architecture Review,* CXXXVI (1964), pp. 87–95.
'Sir Stephen Glynn's Description of Sussex Churches', *Sussex Notes and Queries,* Nos. 8, 1940–41, pp. 118–121; 16, 1963–67, pp. 52–62; 17, 1968–71, p. 41.
Hare, J. C., *Charges to the Clergy of the Archdeaconry of Lewes, delivered at the Ordinary Visitations in the years 1840, 1843, 1845,* London, 1856.
Leeney, O. H., 'References to Ancient Sussex Churches in *The Ecclesiologist*', *Sussex Archaeological Collections,* vols. LXXXIII, 1943, pp. 137–150; LXXXIV, 1944–45, pp. 114–152; LXXXVI, 1947, pp. 155–184; LXXXVII, 1948, pp. 184–207; LXXXVIII, 1949, pp. 157–178, O. H. Leeney died before completing the work. The series only runs from Parishes A–E.
Nesbitt, A., 'Thoughts on Church "Restoration"', *Sussex Archaeological Collections,* vol. XXXIII, 1883, pp. 225–236.
Pevsner, N., 'The Cambridge Camden Society and the Ecclesiologists', in *Some Architectural Writers of the Nineteenth Century,* Oxford, 1972.
White, J. E., *The Cambridge Movement: The Ecclesiologists and the Gothic Revival,* Cambridge, 1962.

WALL-PAINTINGS AND STAINED GLASS

Cowen, P., *A Guide to Stained Glass in Britain,* London, 1985.
Croft-Murray, P., 'Lambert Barnard: An Early English Renaissance Painter', *Archaeology Journal,* vol. CXIII (1957), pp. 108–125.
Harrison, M., *Victorian Stained Glass,* London, 1980.
Johnston, P. M., 'Mural Paintings in Sussex Churches', in P. D. Mundy (ed.), *Memorials of Old Sussex,* London, 1909, pp. 242–282.
Johnston, P. M., 'A List of Mural Paintings in Sussex Churches', *Sussex Archaeological Collections,* vol. XLIII (1900).
Milner-Gullard, R. R., 'The Problem of the Early Sussex Frescoes', *Southern History,* vol. VII (1985), pp. 25–54.
Osborne, J., *Stained Glass in England,* London, 1981.
Park, D., 'The "Lewes Group" of Wall Paintings in Sussex', *Anglo-Norman Studies Proc. Battle Conference,'* vol. VI (1983), pp. 200–235.
Sewter, A. C., *The Stained Glass of William Morris and his Circle,* 2 vols., London, 1974–5.
Stavridi, M., *Master of Glass: Charles Eamer Kempe 1837–1907,* Kempe Society, 1988.

WOODWORK

Bond, F., *Screens and Galleries in English Churches,* London, 1908.
Cox, J. C., *Bench Ends in English Churches,* Oxford, 1916.
Cox, J. C., *Pulpits, Lecterns, and Organs in English Churches,* Oxford, 1915.
Eames, P., 'Furniture in England, France and the Netherlands from the Twelfth to the Fifteenth Century', *Furniture History,* vol. XIII (1977).
Remnant, G. L., *A Catalogue of Misericords in Great Britain,* Oxford, 1969.
Remnant, G. L., and Steer, F. W., *Misericords in Chichester Cathedral,* Chichester, 1961.

TOMBS, MONUMENTS AND CHURCHYARDS

Bertram, J., 'Incised Slabs in Sussex', *Transactions of the Monumental Brass Society,* vol. XIII (1984), pp. 387–396.
Burges, F., *English Churchyard Memorials,* Lutterworth, 1963.
David-Houston, C. E. D., 'Sussex Monumental Brasses', *Sussex Archaeological Collections,* vol. LXXVII (1936).
Esdaile, K. A., *English Church Monuments 1510–1840,* London, 1946.
Gunnis, R., 'Monuments by John Flaxman in Sussex', *Sussex Archaeological Collections,* vol. XCVII (1959).
Kelly, A., 'Coade Stone in Sussex', *Sussex Archaeological Collections,* vol. CXXVI (1988), pp. 179–193.
Kemp, B., *English Church Monuments,* London, 1980.
Macklin, H. W., 'Sussex Brasses', in P. D. Mundy (ed.), *Memorials of Old Sussex,* London, 1909, pp. 127–153.
Mosse, H. R., *The Monumental Effigies of Sussex,* 2nd ed., Hove, 1933.
Penny, N., *Church Monuments in Romantic England,* Yale, 1977.
Remnant, G. L., 'Jonathan Harmer's Terracottas', *Sussex Archaeological Collections,* vol. C (1962), pp. 142–148 and vol. CII (1964), pp. 48–54.
Sadler, A. C., *The Lost Monumental Brasses of Sussex,* 1988.
Tummers, H., 'The Medieval Effigial Tombs in Chichester Cathedral', *Journal of the Church Monuments Society,* vol. III (1988), p. 3–41.
Willatts, R. M., 'Iron Graveslabs: A Sideline of the Early Iron Industry', *Sussex Archaeological Collections,* vol. CXXV (1987), pp. 99–113.
Yoward, A. and M., 'Cast Iron Gravestones', *Bulletin of the Association for Industrial Archaeology,* vol. 15, no. 3 (1988).

CHURCH PLATE AND METALWORK

Copy or Creation: Victorian Treasures from English Churches, exhibition catalogue, Goldsmiths' Hall, London, 1967.
Couchman, J. E., 'Sussex Church Plate', *Sussex Archaeological Collections,* vols. LIII (1910), pp. 198–266; LIV (1911), pp. 183–258; LV (1912), pp. 126–219; LVI (1914), pp. 196–197.
Elphick, G. P., *Sussex Bells and Belfries,* London and Chichester, 1970.
Elphick, G. P., *The Craft of the Bellfounder,* Chichester, 1988.
Evans, Rev. A. A., 'The Altar Vessels of Sussex Churches', *Sussex County Magazine,* XIII, 1939, pp. 192–198.
Gilchrist, J., *Anglican Church Plate,* London, 1967.
Oman, C., *English Church Plate 597–1830,* Oxford, 1957.
Victorian Church Art, exhibition catalogue, Victoria and Albert Museum, 1971.

SUSSEX CHURCH MUSIC AFTER THE REFORMATION

Abraham, G. (ed.), *The New Oxford History of Music,* vol. IV, London, 1968.
Allen, G., *A Short History of Music in Sussex Churches,* Chichester, 1981.
Gammon, V., 'Babylonian Performances: The Rise and Suppression of Popular Church Music 1660–1870', in E. and S. Yeo (eds.), *Popular Culture and Class Conflict 1590–1914,* Sussex, 1981.
Gammon, V., 'Parochial Music in Sussex: A Study in Social and Cultural Conflict', unpublished Sussex University M.A. thesis, 1977.

Gammon, V., *James Nye: A Small Account of My Travels Through the Wilderness,* Brighton, n.d. *c.* 1981.
Macdermott, K. H., *Sussex Church Music in the Past,* Chichester, 1922.
Macdermott, K. H., *The Old Church Gallery Minstrels,* London, 1947.
Macdermott, K. H., 'Sussex Church Music in the Past', unpublished MS in library of the Sussex Archaeological Society.
Phillips, C. H., *The Singing Church,* London, 1946.
Temperley, N., *The Music of the English Parish Church,* Cambridge, 1979.
Wenlock, C., 'Old Barrel Organs in Sussex Churches', *Sussex County Magazine,* vol. XXIX (1955).

GLOSSARY

ANTIPHONER A book containing the sung portions of the office and mass.

AMBULATORY A semi-circular aisle behind the altar.

APSE Polygonal or semi-circular ending to a chapel or chancel.

BAR TRACERY Also known as Geometrical tracery. It consists of slender shafts branching out in the window-head to form a decorative mesh.

BEAKHEAD Norman motif consisting of a row of grotesque human or animal heads biting a roll moulding.

BILLET Norman ornament consisting of small blocks or billets placed at intervals in a hollow moulding.

BREVIARY A book containing the Holy Office for each day.

BROACH SPIRE An octagonal spire on a square tower. The four angles of the tower not covered by the base of the spire are filled with inclined masonry known as the broach.

CENSER A vessel with a perforated lid used for burning incense.

CHALICE AND PATEN The cup used to contain the wine at Mass or Holy Communion. The paten is a small plate to hold the consecrated bread or wafer.

CHANCEL East end of a church set apart for use of the clergy and choir.

CHASUBLE A circular or oval sleeveless vestment worn by the celebrant at Mass or Holy Communion.

CLERESTORY The upper storey of the nave above the roofs of the aisles, pierced with windows.

CLUNIAC STYLE Refers to developments in Romanesque architecture and sculpture influenced by the monastery church of the reformed Benedictine Order of the Cluniacs at Cluny in Burgundy. At the height of its influence the Cluniac Order controlled a network of some 1,450 houses.

CONVENTICLE Name given to a meeting of dissenters or non-conformists, especially the buildings used for such meetings.

CORBEL A projection on the face of a wall, often carved and moulded, used to support a beam or horizontal member.

COPE A long semi-circular sleeveless cloak held together at the front by a clasp or morse. Normally worn at non-Eucharistic ceremonies.

CROCKETS Hook-shaped carved leaves usually placed along the sloping edges of pinnacles, spires and canopies.

CUIUS REGIO EIUS RELIGIO The formula adopted in 1555 whereby princes of the Holy Roman Empire were allowed to decide whether to promote Roman Catholicism or Lutheranism. The words mean 'In a [prince's] land, the [prince's] religion'.

DECALOGUE The Ten Commandments.

DECORATED STYLE English Gothic architectural style of about 1290–1360.

GENEVAN GOWN A black preaching gown, originally adopted by Calvin in Geneva, worn by clergy of the reformed church.

FLAMBOYANT TRACERY A French tracery form occasionally found in England. It is a development of 14th-century flowing tracery and is characterised by sinuous flame-like forms.

JAMB The straight side of an arch, window or doorway.

LANCET WINDOW A tall slender pointed window characteristic of early 13th-century architecture.

LOLLARDS English 14th-century heretics who were followers of John Wycliffe (*c.* 1330–84). The name derives from the Middle Dutch *lollen* meaning a singer; this was construed to mean 'a mumbler at prayers'.

LONG-AND-SHORT-WORK A Saxon technique consisting of long stones set on end between flat ones; the stones are bonded into the wall to form quoins.

MISSAL The liturgical book containing the text for the Mass.

NAVE The main body of a church west of the chancel, often flanked by aisles. Traditionally the people's part of a church.
OCULI Round windows.
OFFERTORY Part of the Mass or Communion service at which offerings are made.
OGEE ARCH Pointed arch formed of two convex arcs and two concave arcs below. Especially popular in England in the early 14th-century.
PARCLOSE SCREEN A screen enclosing a chapel.
PAX A small metal plate, usually with a handle, which, after having been kissed by the priest, was then passed around the congregation to communicate the Kiss of Peace.
PERPENDICULAR Uniquely English style of Gothic architecture characterised by vertical tracery lines. It covers the period from about 1335–1530.
PIER A solid support, usually square sectioned, used to support the load from a beam or the thrust of an arch.
PILASTER STRIP A shallow rectangular pier without a base or capital. Often found on the exterior of Anglo-Saxon churches.
PISCINA A basin with a drain for washing Mass or Communion vessels. It is generally set in the wall to the south of the altar.
PLATE TRACERY A late 12th and early 13th-century form where simple round openings are punched through the stone windowhead.
PORTICUS A subsidiary cell opening from the main body of a church in pre-Conquest architecture.
PRECEPTORY Subordinate community of Knights Templars.
PYX A vessel, often chalice-shaped, in which the consecrated Host is reserved.
QUOINS Dressed stones at the corners of buildings.
RETROCHOIR The area behind the altar in a major church.
RIB VAULT The framework of arched ribs forming a support for the infilling of an arched roof or ceiling.
ROCHET A surplice like overgarment with narrow sleeves or no sleeves at all. Originally it served as a dustcoat and was in general use by the clergy, but it was later restricted to bishops.
ROGATIONTIDE The Monday, Tuesday and Wednesday preceding Ascension Day.
ROLL MOULDING Semi-circular moulding.
ROOD LOFT AND SCREEN A screen separating the chancel from the nave and supporting the loft on which the rood or crucifix was placed.
SACRING BELL A bell rung at the elevation of the Host.
SEDILIA A set of usually three seats for the clergy officiating at Mass. The seats are often recessed into the wall on the south side of the chancel and were used by the priest, deacon and sub-deacon.
SEVEN DEADLY SINS Pride, lechery, envy, anger, covetousness, gluttony, sloth.
SEVEN WORKS OF MERCY Feeding the hungry, giving drink to the thirsty, clothing the naked, harbouring the stranger, visiting the sick, ministering to prisoners, burying the dead.
SOFFIT The underside of an architectural element, in particular an arch.
SPANDREL A roughly triangular space between an arch and its containing rectangle, or between adjacent arches.
STIFF LEAF Lobe-shaped sculptured foliage found on late 12th and early 13th-century capitals.
SURPLICE A white gown with long flowing sleeves worn over the cassock by clergy and, later, by choristers.
TESTER OR SOUNDING BOARD A canopy serving as a sounding board above a pulpit.
TRACTARIAN Name given to supporters of the Oxford Movement, derived from a series of 'Tracts for the Times' written by Newman, Pusey, Keble and others between 1833–1841.
WATER-LEAF Tapering leaf shape used in later 12th-century capitals.

INDEX OF PLACES

numbers in italics refer to illustrations in the text